BREAKING
CRIME'S
VICIOUS
CYCLE

BREAKING CRIME'S VICIOUS CYCLE

DON DENNIS

with Shirley Stephens

BROADMAN PRESS

NASHVILLE, TENNESSEE

4251-14

ISBN: 0-8054-5114-5

Dewey Decimal Classification: B
Subject Headings: DENNIS, DON / EVANGELISTIC READINGS / WITNESSING
Library of Congress Card Catalog Number: 92-35227
Printed in the United States of America

Unless otherwise stated, all Scripture quotations are from the *New
American Standard Bible.* ©The Lockman Foundation, 1960, 1962, 1963,
1968, 1971, 1972, 1973, 1975, 1977. Used by permission.

Scripture quotations marked NIV are from the Holy Bible,
New International Version, copyright © 1973, 1978, 1984
by International Bible Society.

Some names in this book have been changed to preserve anonymity.
Names of family members, close friends, and co-workers have not been changed.

Library of Congress Cataloging-in-Publication Data

Dennis, Don, 1934-
    Breaking crime's vicious cycle / Don Dennis with Shirley Stephens.
        p.   cm.
    ISBN 0-8054-5114-5
    1. Dennis, Don, 1934-   2. Ex-convicts—United States—
Biography.   3. Ex-convicts—Rehabilitation—United States.   4. Ex-
convicts—United States—Religious life.   5. Prisoners—Pastoral
counseling of—United States.   I. Stephens, Shirley. II. Title.
HV9468.D46A3   1993
364.3'73'092—dc20
    [B]   92-35227
                                                                              CIP

To many *Masterlife* volunteers

all over the United States,

who unselfishly give of themselves,

week by week,

to teach inmates in state,

federal, and private prisons

how to live as followers

of our Lord Jesus Christ

CONTENTS

A Word from Charles *(Chuck)* Colson

Introduction

A Word from
Charles *(Chuck)* Colson

I first met Don Dennis in Walla Walla prison

fourteen years ago. He was a tough, hard

con who gave his heart to the Lord and

has been just as tough ever since—but

now as a warrior for Christ. A wonderful

example of God's grace: the One who can

save a Don Dennis or a Chuck Colson

can save *anyone*.

Introduction

It was 1977. Don Dennis stood at attention before a judge in a Seattle, Washington, courtroom.

"Mr. Dennis," the judge began, "you have been in and out of prison for more than twenty years. After reviewing your history of felonies, escapes, forgeries, and other crimes against society, I am sentencing you to life in prison.

"I am also going to write a letter to the Parole Board," the judge went on, "stating that I recommend and strongly suggest that you never be paroled. Because you have demonstrated that you cannot function in free society, you need to be kept locked up. You are a menace and dangerous to decent folks."

That was Don Dennis, the habitual criminal, almost fifteen years ago. Then, he looked at life this way: "It was me and my prison buddies at war against the police, guards, society. We were like blood brothers." Don was more comfortable behind prison walls than in free society. Each time he went back into prison, it was like "going home." That's where his friends were; that's where he had been more years than he had been free; that's where people understood him, or so he thought.

The Don Dennis who was sentenced to life without parole is no more. Fifteen years later, he is a man with a radically different kind of mission. He goes into prisons now, but not as an inmate. Rather than tearing down, he is building up by helping prisoners and ex-prisoners find a new way of looking at life. With a band of volunteers, he helps them rise above their mistakes and get going in the right direction. He does this through a discipleship program called MasterLife. Through this program, he points people to a better way to think and act. The name implies the emphasis—mastering life.

In August 1989 I spent a week with Don and Carol Dennis and their three dogs and three cats. It was a time of painful probing into the

11

Breaking Crime's Vicious Cycle

past. I saw a man sorry for the mistakes of the past. I saw a man who accepts personal responsibility for his attitudes and actions.

But there was more. Along with probing into the past, it was a time of looking to the future with expectant hope. I saw a man determined to help others overcome the same mistakes he made. I saw a man who wants to make a positive difference in this world by pointing prisoners to a better way of living—inside, as well as outside, prison. I saw a man determined to help ex-convicts make it in the free world.

This is the story of how Don Dennis got from there to here. It is nothing short of a miracle.

Shirley Stephens
Nashville, Tennessee

1

Paying My Respects

When the guard opened the door, I climbed awkwardly out of the front seat, handcuffed. Together, we climbed the steps to the funeral home for my dad's funeral.

A funeral home host was there to greet us just inside the door. His eyes were drawn immediately to the handcuffs. As I cringed at his response, I could feel the red warmth of embarrassment flood my face. I pulled the handcuffs close to my body, futilely trying to hide them.

The host nervously looked up. "Could I help you?" he asked with a faint quaver in his voice, glancing quickly at the armed officer and then at me. "What is the family name?" he continued, assuming the gentle tone of one trying to comfort the bereaved.

"Dennis," I replied firmly, standing up straight and looking him in the eye. "Clarence Dennis," I added.

A look of recognition spread across the middle-aged man's face. Word about me had gotten around to him, too. "Straight ahead," he said, moving his right arm to direct us down the hall, "third room on the left."

Just before we got to the room, the officer gently placed his hand on my arm to stop me. "Let me take those off," he offered, motioning to the handcuffs, "while you visit with your family."

A sense of relief raced through me. "I appreciate that, Officer," I said, holding my cuffed hands out to him.

The gesture was completely in character with everything I knew about Officer Benton. When Mac picked him to drive me to Fremont for the funeral, he did a good thing. Benton had been in the prison system for many years, but he hadn't allowed it to harden him. He still could relate to an inmate as an individual.

I breathed deeply to brace myself as I took the first step into the waiting room, then slowly moved on through the doorway to face the crowd of Dennis relatives and friends. Almost on signal, they all looked up. No one nudged anyone else; no one said anything, but everyone knew I was there. All eyes were on me.

In a split second, I saw a kaleidoscope of emotions written on their faces—surprise, embarrassment, curiosity, horror, panic, disgust, and, thankfully, even joy. My sister, Barbara—I always called her Barbie— looked tremendously happy to see me. She rushed over to greet me, jumping up to hug my neck as I leaned down to kiss her. She was still as pretty as ever, with her tiny figure and reddish-brown hair. Her pixie-like smile made me feel good.

I knew the spectacle of a felon would humiliate the Dennis clan, but I did want to pay my respects. "Don't worry about what they think," Barbie urged when she and Jim visited me the day before at Soledad. "You'll be sorry if you don't come. He made a lot of mistakes, but he was your dad."

In my heart I knew Barbie was right. She always had good common sense. I really didn't know why I wanted to go to the funeral, though. He was a pathetic excuse for a father. Barbie hit the nail on the head. My dad had made a lot of mistakes, more than anyone should be allowed.

Actually, the first thing I remembered after the lieutenant came to my cell to tell me my dad had died was the Christmas he walked out on us. He came home drunk, grabbed the tree me and Barbie and my mom had joyously decorated the night before, and threw it out the front door. I was eleven at the time; Barbie was eight. With ornaments scattered over the front lawn, my dad took off. He didn't even come back for Christmas dinner with the Dennis clan.

And I remembered a letter my dad wrote to me two months before he died. "Don," he pleaded, "I get down on my knees every night and pray that you will change." *What a disgusting farce*, I thought. *That man never prayed in his life!*

It was the only letter I received from my dad while I was in prison. As I recall, he was the first to give up on me—at least the first I cared anything about. "You're not going to see your twenty-first birthday," he warned, "if you don't straighten up." As usual, he was wrong.

If you had met Clarence Dennis, you would have thought he was some special person. He had the looks of a ladies' man—thick brown hair carefully combed in place, shiny white teeth, a captivating twin- kle in his baby-blue eyes, and a ready smile. "Your dad was popular with the girls in high school," Aunt Hazel told me. "All the girls wanted to go with him. They practically swooned when he looked at them with those pretty blue eyes." She obviously adored her brother.

My dad was kindhearted and fun-loving when he was sober. But, beneath his soft-spoken manner was a deep buried fury that booze unleashed. With a few drinks under his belt, he turned into a beastly tyrant. Those were the times that made an indelible impression on me.

Jim was right there with Barbie. He politely, but self-consciously, held out his hand to greet me. I didn't know how to put him at ease. He and Barbie got married after I left Longview. I was in prison so much that I really hadn't gotten to know him.

Uncle Roy, my dad's older, civic-minded brother, glared across the room at me. I winced at the look. Uncle Roy never knew it, but I always wished he was my father when I was growing up, especially when my dad came home drunk and slapped my mom around.

I remember Uncle Roy best in his three-piece, brown, pin-striped suit. When I was in grade school, he was the high school principal at Kelso, Washington, the county-seat town across the river from my hometown of Longview. He went up in the world of education to become superintendent of schools. It was no secret that I was an embarrassment to him.

Nudged on by Aunt Helen, Uncle Roy came over to greet me. He held out his hand like it was something his mama told him to do. I returned the gesture, standing eye to eye with him. He was about the same height as my dad.

In the manner of a probing school principal, Uncle Roy asked what I was going to do when I got out of prison. "I want to do something worthwhile with the rest of my life," I told him. "I've turned over a new leaf at Soledad."

A questioning look filled his face. He waited for a fuller explanation.

"They've really helped me," I continued. "I don't want to go to prison again. It's no fun," I added softly with a chuckle. He ignored the chuckle. He was not amused.

"Good," he said sternly, as if he were talking to a seven-year-old kid. "I hope you can stick with it this time."

"I mean it, Uncle Roy. I really do. I'm tired of looking over my shoulder."

"Good luck," he said with a skeptical look still firmly in place. He moved on to greet another relative.

I looked around for Aunt Aggie and Uncle Ray. Barbie explained that they didn't come because Aggie was sick. I was disappointed that I didn't get to see them. The youngest in my dad's family, Aggie was like a big sister to me.

Me and Aggie were in a church play together when I was five and she was fourteen. She played the piano; I played an angel. Halfway through the play, I got so nervous and excited that I wet my pants. I ran off the stage in tears. Aggie was so humiliated and mad that she bawled me out all the way to my house. "Donnie," she chided over and over, "you embarrassed me to death!"

"I couldn't help it, Aunt Aggie," I protested.

"Yes you could have! You could've told someone you needed to go to the bathroom." She teased me about that fiasco for a long time. Now, it was a distant and amusing memory.

My half sisters, Jeanne Kay and Patti, greeted me quickly, then moved on. My stepmother, Kathleen, finally got around to me just before time to go into the chapel. "Good to see you, Don," she said uneasily.

"Hi," I said softly but self-consciously. We had little more to say to each other.

My bitter feelings toward Kathleen lingered tenaciously. I deeply resented the fact that she took my dad away from my mom. It was a familiar scenario, the boss getting involved with the secretary. She was young and pretty then, with her curvy figure and shiny blond hair. One thing led to another, and they had an affair going on right under my mom's nose. All three worked at the same place.

Kathleen tried to put the past behind us, but I wouldn't let her. When I lived with them, I threw it up to her practically every time we got in a fight, which was often. And I refused to accept the idea of someone just nine years older than me being my mom.

Aunt Hazel and Uncle Cliff were missing from the clan. They helped raise me and Barbie when our parents left town after the divorce. They were the ones who went to my ball games and had heart-to-heart talks with me. Cliff was my idol. He and Hazel had died a year apart about ten years earlier. I went to Hazel's funeral, but missed Cliff's. I was doing time then, too.

MaMa and Granddad Dennis also were missing. In my growing-up years, they were the main stable influence in my life. They tried hard to make up for the failure of my parents, investing much time, love, and concern in trying to help me. I loved them dearly.

When MaMa and Granddad hassled me about how wild I was getting, I stubbornly ignored their pleas. "You don't understand," I told them. "You don't know what you're talking about." The older I got the more tiresome their advice became. I am still gripped with remorse when I picture the sad looks in their eyes as I angrily insisted that they leave me alone. Fortunately they died before my criminal career was going full steam.

My dad's Elks Club buddies were in charge of the funeral service.

Paying My Respects

You should have heard them brag about Clarence Dennis. It was amazing how many good things they remembered. I couldn't recall one. Two or three friends valiantly tried to pray him into heaven. I didn't recognize the man they presented to God. I felt sure God didn't either.

After the service, we went to Dad and Kathleen's home to eat. The torture of relating to skeptical relatives continued. "I've turned over a new leaf," I told one after another. The explanations got tiresome and monotonous. Minute by minute I became more nervous and fidgety.

"I'm ready to get out of here," I whispered to Benton the second we finished eating. I wanted to go back home. My friends were at Soledad. That's the crowd I felt most comfortable with. They knew how tough it was to make it in the world outside. They knew where I was coming from.

I awkwardly told relative after relative good-bye. "Be sure to call me when you get out," Barbie urged, as I walked out on the porch. "Jim will help you find a job."

Yeah, I thought. *What kind of job? Boring for sure.* The only real job I ever had in the Longview-Kelso area was running a machine in a lumber mill. I didn't want to do that for the rest of my life. Still, I said I would be in touch.

Benton slipped the handcuffs back on just before we got in the car. Standing on the porch, Barbie watched stoically, a deep, dark look forming in her eyes. She waved one last good-bye as we pulled away. I smiled faintly through the car window. *I'm not going to disappoint her again*, I vowed silently. *I've put her through enough.*

Riding down the highway in that cop car, I mused about the times when I had loved to swim at the Y, run through the woods, go fishing, and just be with my friends. How quickly the years had flown by. Now I was responsible for my actions but not able to control them. I was afraid of myself and what I might do. Yet I didn't want to give up the excitement or the challenge of making it in the fast lane of life. It was me and my prison buddies at war against the police, guards, and society. We were like blood brothers.

Luckily for my family, most of my prison career had centered in California. For almost fifteen years I had been moving in and out of California prisons. The Los Angeles County Jail was my first California joint. I spent nine months there for running bad checks. The money was good, but I passed one check too many. Barely out of jail, I got caught again on the same charge. They sent me to the county farm at Mira Loma. I was there two years.

The day they let me out of Mira Loma, I found out that my mother had died. I called Barbie to see how everyone was. "Why didn't you let me know she was that sick?" I asked. She mumbled some excuse about me knowing that Mom had an alcohol problem. "And, besides," she said. "I didn't know how to get in touch with you." Her indifference hurt. After the funeral, I called my dad and told him I held him personally responsible for my mom's death. "You're the one who beat her and drove her to drink," I told him. He was speechless.

I wasn't out of jail long when I got caught cashing forged checks again. This time it was payroll checks I stole from a construction company where I worked. A girl I met in a bar helped me pass them off as the real thing. This time I went to the state prison system. I was moving up.

They sent me to classification at Chino to receive my prison assignment. There, I renewed old acquaintances from the county farm and made some new friends, too, among them a member of the Mexican Mafia. I always made a special point of picking friends who were smart to prison life. By my standards, they were good men. They were loyal, no matter what. They didn't tell the cops anything. And they didn't cry about doing their time. Those guys are what seasoned convicts consider "regulars." The regulars have a saying—"If you're gonna play, you gotta pay." That became my philosophy, and it worked.

The classification people at Chino sent me to South C.C. a few blocks down the road. It was a minimum security prison with three dorms, about ninety men to a dorm. The superintendent— or "Supt" as we called him—was quite a character. He would bring his twelve-year-old son into the prison and let the boy tell the convicts what to do.

Generally, things were pretty peaceful at South C.C. It was a big thing to the Supt not to have any violence on his "yard." At Friday afternoon group meetings, he emphasized "no fighting, or you get sent to the hole at Chino." The hole was a solitary confinement cell that had a hole in the ground for a urinal. Most of the time the warning worked.

Sixty days before my release date, two black dudes got in a fight. The Supt called a group meeting of all three dorms to find out why the men who had witnessed the fight didn't try to stop them from fighting. Actually, he really didn't know who had witnessed the fight.

Sitting in folding chairs, we mumbled under our breath while the Supt went on and on about the fight. As the meeting progressed, it became clear that he was going to take privileges away from all of us because of the fight. We all thought that was stupid.

Paying My Respects

Chow time was close. *What the heck?* I thought. *I'm getting out soon. I'll rib the Supt and get this over with.* I stood up, lifted my chair over my head, and popped it together.

"Sit down," the Supt ordered.

"Group's over," I declared. "If anyone gets into a fight, let the guards break it up. That's not my job!"

"Sit down, Dennis," he ordered again. "or you're going to the hole at Chino."

"Supt," I said sarcastically. "You remind me of a movie I saw one time—*The Caine Mutiny.* You're like Captain Queeg. He was crazy, and so are you!"

A roar of laughter went up from the group. One man after another stood up and popped his chair together. "Group's over!" everyone yelled, erupting into a chant.

The Supt yelled for the guards to take me away. Two guards dragged me to the Supt's office and chained me to a chair. The Supt marched in a few minutes later.

Pacing back and forth in front of me, the Supt yelled, "Dennis, you're losing your date to go home! You're going to the hole!" The madder he got, the better I liked it. I laughed right in his face. He almost foamed at the mouth.

After three days in the hole at Chino, I went in front of a discipline board. They took away my date to go home and gave me ten more days in the hole. When they took me back to South C.C. I apologized to the Supt at the first group meeting to get back my date to get out. I told my friends it was the expedient thing to do. That stretch lasted three years.

San Quentin was unquestionably the big time. They sent me there on an armed robbery conviction. I pulled a job at a drive-in market in Long Beach. The clerk almost made a fatal mistake that time. When he started to open the cash drawer, I saw him reach for a button below it. I instinctively stretched over the counter to grab his arm.

"You lousy creep!" I threatened through clenched teeth, positioning my gun between his eyes. "I ought to waste you! Put the money in the bag, and forget about the buzzer."

"I didn't do anything," he protested, his hands trembling. "Honest! Honest!" he begged.

I pulled back the gun but kept it aimed at his head. He nervously put the money in the bag and handed it to me. I grabbed the bag, shaking the gun at him threateningly. "Hit the floor, you slimy creep," I ordered, "with your head face down." He quickly fell to the floor.

"Don't you dare get up until I'm gone," I snapped, still pointing the gun at him. "I'm warning you. I'll be back to get you if you cross me."

"Don't worry," he promised, his voice quavering, his body now trembling uncontrollably. "I won't tell anybody. I promise. I promise." His creepiness disgusted me.

I raced to my car, jumped in, and sped off down the road. Two blocks away siren-blaring cop cars descended on me from all directions. *I'll get that jerk,* I vowed silently. *I'll teach him a lesson.*

At the police station, the detectives tried to nail me for five other robberies in the Los Angeles area. I refused to admit to more than two. With my previous record, that was enough to send me up the river for five years.

My Mafia friends were what stood out most about San Quentin. I wasn't there a week when they picked me to help run the prison drug network. Word had spread that I was one tough dude and a smooth operator—a regular in the best sense of the word. The Mafia boys knew they could trust me. My friends enthusiastically verified that I would rather die than snitch on anybody. I was definitely in as far as criminals were concerned. I had paid my dues. Inside and outside prison I was into crime. And I loved every minute of it!

I was spending time in Soledad when I got the call that my dad had died. The judge sent me there for two years on an escape charge. I said good-bye to Chino without permission when I was on work release from San Quentin. I got fed up with the authorities taking a percentage from my paycheck for processing my work-release papers. What they did wasn't crooked. I just thought it was a stupid rule. I'll tell you about my three months on the run later.

In every prison, I spent a lot of time in the hole. I was always on some kind of crusade to make them treat prisoners better. I bugged the authorities all the time, often at the urging of friends. By the time I got to Soledad I didn't care what anyone in authority thought.

Soledad, the prison that gave the infamous Soledad Brothers their name, was hot with racial tension in the seventies. It didn't take long for me to realize that this prison was different from any I had been in before. So many of the inmates were hardened criminals, beyond anything I had ever seen, even at San Quentin. Killings were rampant in all parts of the Soledad complex. A disagreement over a minor debt often led to murder as one strong leader put out a contract on another inmate's head.

The situation at Soledad had a sobering effect on me, so sobering that I agreed to help cool the place down. Mac, the warden, asked me and two other guys to be a liaison team between inmates and the prison staff. It was because of this liaison work that I was able to go to my father's funeral. The normal requirement was that two guards accompany a convict outside the prison. Barbie and Jim paid for one guard. Mac waived the fee for the second guard.

Mac liked my liaison work so well that he arranged for me to take the written test to qualify for assistant parole officer. It was a program for ex-offenders. I took the written test about six months before my release date and passed with flying colors. Mac told me I made the highest score in California. Buoyed by that success, I planned to take the verbal test when I got out.

About three months after my dad's funeral, they let me out of Soledad. Mac made a special point of telling me good-bye. After I had completed all the necessary forms, he suddenly was standing beside me. I cheerfully welcomed his offer to walk me to the front gate.

"Don," Mac said as we moved across the yard. "I want to thank you for helping cool things down here. You did a lot of good. We sincerely appreciate your efforts."

"You know what, Mac, it made me feel good to do something right. I want to get on track this time. I really mean it."

"I know you do," he assured me. "You've demonstrated what you can do. You'll do fine if you use your leadership skills in positive ways. You have a way with people."

"I'll tell you for sure, Friend, I'm getting too old for this wild life," I said, chuckling. "I do want to find something worthwhile. Maybe I can make up for some of the bad I've done. I can't believe it's gone on this long."

"Is your sister picking you up?" he asked.

"No," I replied quickly. "I want to get settled in something before I get in touch with my family. I've put them through enough. I can't face them right now."

Mac looked surprised and uneasy.

"A lady friend I met on work release at Chino is picking me up," I explained. "She's had a bad marriage and wants to put her life back together. Maybe me and Maggie can help each other."

"Maybe so," he responded with little enthusiasm. "I guess you've been writing to her?" he questioned with the tone of his voice.

"Yes. She's been real good to me, sending me sweets and supplies for almost two years now. She's driven up here to see me several times. Even brought her kids with her."

"You're still planning to check into the assistant parole program, aren't you?" he asked.

"Sure, sure. I plan to. That sounds like something I can do. I think I would enjoy it, and maybe I can help dudes stay out of trouble, too. I understand them."

"I think you can help," he said confidently. "You still going to San Jose?"

"Yes, I like that area."

"When you get settled, contact Doug Stewart at the state probation office in San Francisco. Here's his telephone number," he added, handing me one of his business cards with Stewart's name and telephone number written on it.

"I'll do that," I said, putting the card in my shirt pocket. "I really appreciate your help."

"Be sure to give my name as a reference," Mac suggested. "I'll say something nice," he added with a chuckle.

Mac's confidence was exciting. He was an incurable optimist. It amazed me how anyone could be around losers all the time and stay so positive. I truly admired him.

Standing in front of the last door between me and the free world, Mac told me good-bye. "Don," he assured me, putting his left hand on my right shoulder and holding the other hand out to shake mine. "I want to wish you the best."

"Thanks," I said, holding his hand firmly. "I hope we meet again under different circumstances."

"I do, too," he replied, looking me in the eye with the tender, hopeful look I had seen so many times.

Mac raised his hand to signal the guard to open the gate. I walked slowly through the doorway, dreading to leave but hating worse to stay. The clanging of the door closing behind me was thunderous and decisive. I cringed at the sound.

Standing alone in front of the closed gate, the world outside looked ominous and threatening. A helpless, sinking feeling formed in the pit of my stomach. I felt totally, absolutely alone. *Can I make it this time?* I asked myself. *I'm forty-one, no long-term work experience, a lot of bad habits, and a mile-long criminal record. I am on my own again! How will I get anyone to give me a job?* The sinking feeling expanded to grip my whole body. I was leaving home! In the last twenty years I had been in prison more years than I had been free.

I stared straight ahead at the world that I knew would not welcome me. *I don't know how to live in the free world,* I sighed silently. *What am I going to do?* For an instant the terror paralyzed me. Then, almost like flipping a switch, defiance replaced the helpless feeling. *I'll show them,* I vowed. *I'll be somebody after all.*

"Don! Don!" Maggie called, interrupting my thoughts. She was across the parking lot, waving both arms wildly. "Here I am. I'll be right there."

Maggie drove up to the curb, smiling brightly, her dark brown eyes glistening. "Hi," I said softly while opening the car door. "This was good timing." I stuck my head inside to give her a quick kiss on the lips.

"Hi, girls," I said to Sandy and Susie in the backseat.

"Hi, Don," Sandy said, smiling bashfully, grudgingly revealing a recent tooth loss. "Hi," Susie chimed in.

"Can I put this duffel bag back there with you girls?"

"Yes," four-year-old Susie replied decisively. "You can put it right here by me."

"Is everybody ready to go to San Jose?" I asked gleefully, as I got in the front seat and pulled the door shut.

"I think so," Maggie replied excitedly. "We've been looking forward to this day for a long time."

"Then let's go!" I exclaimed joyfully. "I'm free!" Me and Maggie let out a big laugh together. Sandy and Susie joined in, not quite sure what they were laughing about.

"Sign your name and the date," the guard requested pleasantly at the exit gate. A thrill pulsed through my whole body as I looked at my signature.

"So long," I told the guard. "This is the last time I'm gonna come through this gate," I chuckled, smiling broadly.

"That's the attitude," he said, returning the smile.

Maggie headed for the main highway. Once there she turned north toward San Jose. I leaned back to enjoy the ride and take in the spacious California landscape.

It was one beautiful day!

2

Facing Life

Maggie stopped at a phone booth near San Jose for me to call Doug Stewart. In a friendly tone, he told me Mac had called him the day before. He said I could come in at one o'clock the next Thursday afternoon. I was elated.

By the next Thursday me and Maggie found a little furnished house, and she had landed a good job in an office not far away. We were settled in good.

I arrived for the appointment fifteen minutes early and quickly completed the form the receptionist gave me. When I gave it back to her, she said Mr. Stewart would be with me in a few minutes. Her friendly manner eased the tension I felt inside.

At one o'clock sharp, a tall, potbellied, balding man emerged from a hallway into the reception area. "Don Dennis," he said, looking from one side of the room to the other.

"Doug Stewart," he said with outstretched hand as I walked toward him. "Good to see you," he added pleasantly. Inside his office, he directed me to an empty chair in front of his desk, then sat down and opened a folder. With a hand planted palm down on each side of the folder, he slowly raised his head and glanced across the desk at me. "How are you doing?" he asked, smiling faintly.

"Fine. Feeling good," I replied enthusiastically. "I'm anxious to get to work. My girlfriend already has a job," I teased. "She doesn't want to support me."

Ignoring my remark, Stewart picked up a letter from the folder and leaned back in his chair. "Mac said you did real well on the written test," he said.

"Ninety-two," I replied proudly. "They told me it was the highest in California."

"Uh huh," he responded, moving forward in his chair to place the letter face down on the left side of the folder. He picked up the next

Facing Life

paper in the stack on the right and, once more, leaned back in his chair.

"Why do you want to do this kind of work?" he asked in a friendly but probing tone.

"Well, I've been around prisoners a lot," I began.

"'Uh huh," he acknowledged. "I see that," he added with a matter-of-fact expression, holding up the paper in his hand.

"I know how they think," I continued, passing over the observation. "Maybe I can help some of them realize what they're doing with their lives. In prison I did a lot of liaison work between prisoners and staff."

"They say you helped cool down Soledad a bit," he observed dryly. "You come highly recommended."

"Thanks," I replied politely, puzzled by the mixed signals he was sending. His remarks were stirring me up inside.

"Are you planning to stay in the San Jose area?" he asked, moving on to the next preplanned question.

"Yes. I've decided to settle down there. I'm determined to get my life on track."

His skeptical look made the juices churn in my stomach.

Stewart moved quickly through a number of routine questions. Was I married? Did I have children? Where was I originally from? Did I still have family living there? What kind of work experience did I have? As I responded to each question, he leaned forward on the desk and recorded my brief answers on a form. Then he posed a scenario.

"If you were assigned to help a parole officer," he began, leaning back in his chair as far as it would go, "and you discovered that a friend was violating parole? . . ."

Stewart paused, leaned forward, and placed both hands on the edge of his desk. He fixed his eyes squarely on mine and lowered his voice. "Would you report the offense?"

With our eyes locked in a stare, something clicked. "No," I said definitely and decisively.

His stare turned to a glare. "I don't think you're ready to be a parole officer," he snapped, sitting up straight in his chair and keeping his eyes fixed on mine. I stared back blankly. *This guy's already got his mind made up*, I decided. *Why bother defending myself?*

Stewart shuffled through the papers in the folder as if looking for a certain item. After what seemed like an eternity, he held up the form I had filled out earlier. "Is this your current address? Telephone number where you can be reached?" he asked. I nodded yes to both questions.

He stood up and held out his hand. "Thank you for coming in, Don," he said with business reserve. "You should get the results in the mail within a week."

I kicked myself in the seat of the pants all the way to the front entrance. *But he didn't give me a chance*, I protested in defense. No rationalizing could help, though.

Exactly one week later, the letter arrived. My heart skipped a beat when I found it mixed in with the junk mail. I got a beer from the refrigerator and sat down by the living room window. I took a couple of swigs of beer, then slowly opened the envelope and took out the letter. As I turned back the first fold, my ninety-two score for the written test was recorded in the first blank after my name, address, and telephone number. That made me smile.

In the next blank was the verbal test score—forty. The composite score was barely higher. Since the verbal score carried a higher percentage, the composite score fell well below the required minimum. I had flunked! I went limp.

"That jerk," I sighed. "Why didn't he give me a chance?"

I took one swig of beer after another, sitting in stony silence until the girls got home from school. I forced myself to greet them as if nothing had happened.

When Maggie got home from work, I gave the form to her without saying a word. "You'll find something else," she said, trying to be upbeat. "There's plenty of work here."

"Maybe," I said. "I probably wouldn't have liked it, anyway. But that guy didn't give me a chance. The good I did at Soledad meant nothing to him." Maggie sympathetically agreed.

I hit the street the next day to look for a job—and the next and the next. I got three job interviews through the state employment agency, but each time the people lost interest when they found out about my prison record. Oh, they didn't say that in so many words, but I could tell. Finally, after three weeks of hunting, a man at a corrugated box plant gave me a job running a machine. I had learned the skill from my dad when he was foreman at a plant in Oakland. Mentioning him had helped.

With my first paycheck I bought a 9 mm. gun, which I proudly showed to Maggie. She was visibly nervous about having a gun in the house and warned me that it was a violation of parole. "I don't care," I told her. "I need this gun."

"Why, are you going to rob somebody?" she asked, teasingly.

"No," I teased back. "It just helps me feel confident."

The next morning, I carefully secured my 9 mm. in the small of my back. That's where I always carried it. When I reported to my parole officer after work, I stashed the gun under the front seat of my car.

"How're you doing?" the parole officer asked routinely.

"Pretty good," I said softly. "I'm working every day."

"Good. That's good," he replied, making notes on a form.

"Any problems with drinking?" he continued, going from point to point on the form like a preoccupied doctor at a medical checkup.

"I'm keeping it in control, staying away from the bars." I had to say that. Going to bars was a violation of my parole.

"Keep up the good work," he replied. "You need to stay away from the booze."

"I will; I will," I assured him. "I've learned my lesson." He smiled approvingly. I loved the way I fooled people. My soft-spoken, low-key manner did the trick. It was one good thing I inherited from my dad.

I was back in touch with friends from prison in no time. We went to the same bars. Most days I stopped by a bar after work and came in late. I spent weekends with my buddies, drinking and smoking weed. Maggie got her fill right away. She packed up and took her kids back to El Monte.

With my second paycheck in my pocket, I left work with no intention of going back. The job bored me, and I was tired of living alone. I decided to go to Longview.

Around eleven o'clock Saturday morning, I was on Joycie and Danny's doorstep. "Don!" Joycie squealed, reaching up to hug me. "We've been wondering about you."

"I've been wondering about you guys, too," I said.

"Come on in the kitchen. I'll fix you a cup of coffee. Hey, kids," she called. "Uncle Don's here."

Michelle (I always called her Shelley), Monica, and Melody ran from their bedrooms screaming "Uncle Don! Uncle Don!" Melody got to me first, jumping up in my arms and hugging me tight. Monica and Shelley were close behind, hugging and kissing me. They were so cute.

"Did you get my last letter, Uncle Don?" Melody asked, with a big smile and a gleam in her eyes.

"I sure did," I replied. "It was very nice." In that letter Melody told me that I was her favorite uncle. I really wasn't her uncle, but I was so much older than her that she just couldn't think of me as a cousin.

"When did you get out?" Joycie asked.

"About two weeks ago," I lied.

She looked shocked. "You should have called us," she chided tenderly. "Danny and I have really been concerned."

"I know, but I wanted to get settled in a job before I got in touch. The job I had in mind didn't work out, though."

"I'm sorry. Maybe you can find work here. Danny will know about jobs. He had to work today, but he'll be home early."

I was almost fifteen years older than Joycie. An only child, she looked up to me as her big brother. Without a doubt, she was my prettiest cousin. She had coal black hair, fair skin, and the tenderest hazel eyes you ever saw. Her petite frame matched her sweet nature.

Melody was kind-hearted and trusting like her mother. She gladly gave up her room for me and moved in with Monica.

"Does Barbie know you're in town?" Joycie asked over our second cup of coffee.

"No. I haven't called her," I replied sheepishly. "I came here first."

"Don," she said firmly. "You know your sister wants to hear from you." Joycie got Barbie on the phone and teasingly asked her to guess who was there, then handed the phone to me. I made a feeble apology for not getting in touch with her sooner and invited her to come on over. She and Jim were there in ten minutes.

It was great to see everybody. Joycie made a delicious meal, and we talked for hours. They were all so glad to see me and told me they would help me in any way they could. "I think they're hiring at Longview Fibre," Danny told me. "Maybe you can get a job there."

"Yeah, maybe. I know how to run all the machines. I need to get settled in a job." I didn't tell them, but a regular job didn't interest me one bit. But to please everybody, I put in my application at Longview Fibre. Then I went to the state employment agency and put in an application.

While I waited for a job call, I passed the time sleeping late and knocking around town from bar to bar. I ran into old friends from high-school days. I had little in common with them, though. I met a few new women in the bars and went back and forth between their homes and Joycie's.

Two weeks passed without a job call. The little bit of money I had saved up was running low, and I was getting jittery staying around Joycie's house so much. I decided to do the thing I knew best—pull a robbery. But I didn't want to do it in Longview. On Friday afternoon, I used my last five dollars to put gas in my car and drove to Seattle to find someone to help me pull a robbery.

I met Regina in a bar. She reminded me of Barbie, with her reddish brown hair and tiny frame. Only twenty-one, she had been on her own since she was eighteen. Her parents got fed up with her wild ways. "You're in good company," I told her. "My family got fed up with me, too."

I qualified Regina out real good and then asked if she was interested in driving a getaway car. I promised her a percentage of the take and assured her that I would never tell on her if I got caught. She accepted my offer right away. Late that night she dropped me off at a drive-in market and parked down the street so no one could get the license plate number. That was her idea.

I casually walked into the market, pretending to be looking for something. I strolled from aisle to aisle to make sure there were no customers and just one clerk. Satisfied that it was clear, I walked over to the young man behind the counter, pulled out my gun, and leveled it at him. He turned white as a sheet. "I'll cooperate; I'll cooperate," he gasped, his lips quivering.

"Don't do nothin' stupid," I warned. "I know how to use this gun. Just give me the cash."

With trembling hands, the young man hurriedly emptied out the cash drawer into a bag and held it out to me. "Don't do nothin' stupid, if you know what's good for you," I warned as I grabbed the bag.

"I won't. I won't," he promised nervously.

"You should have seen that guy," I chuckled, jumping into the car. "He was petrified. It was funny. I would have blown him away, and he knew it." I let out a big laugh, patted my gun, and returned it to the small of my back. Regina joined in the laughter as she sped out to the highway. I could tell she had been through this before. She knew exactly what to do. And she made sure she got her cut right away.

To celebrate, we bought a fifth of whiskey at an all-night liquor store and went to Regina's place. I spent the night with her and drove back to Longview the next day. She offered to help me again if I wanted her to. She liked the easy money. I didn't tell her my right name, but I promised to look her up the next time I came to Seattle.

With the free rent at Joycie's and gifts from women friends, the take from the robbery kept money in my pockets for several weeks. Joycie and Danny suspected that something wasn't quite right, but they didn't confront me. Barbie and Jim were not so quiet. They probed about my activities virtually every time they saw me. Barbie hinted that people in town were wondering what I was doing for a living. I started avoiding her and Jim and everybody else in the family. If they were going to bug me all the time, I really didn't care what they thought.

Breaking Crime's Vicious Cycle

What became monthly robbery trips to Seattle continued until I met a pretty black woman named Lorraine. A friend introduced me to her in a bar in Longview one afternoon. She was fun to talk to and had a lot of class. In a short time, we became a number.

Going with Lorraine was a unique experience. I got special pleasure from the way people reacted to our relationship. I loved to see the looks go from surprise to shock to disgust. I even got up the nerve to take Lorraine over to see Joycie. She wasn't shocked about our relationship. After all, Joycie had learned to expect absolutely anything from me.

Lorraine didn't tell me how she made a living, but I knew it had to be a good source. She had a nice house and plenty of money. I figured she was living off insurance money she got from her husband, who had been killed in a family feud.

Lorraine's money source came to light when she took me to Seattle to meet her brother, Leroy. Crippled by a shot in the spine, he stayed in circulation selling cocaine and weed. He lined up his pushers by throwing wild parties. Usually, I was the only white dude there.

Lorraine must have told Leroy that I would be open to pushing drugs, because Leroy approached me about selling them the first time I met him. I accepted his offer on the spot. In no time, I was not only dealing drugs, I was dipping deeper and deeper into them myself. I liked the money. I liked the high. And I liked the steady work.

At one of Leroy's parties, I smoked weed with a skinny, light-skinned black dude named Dewayne. With both of us high as a kite, he made a proposal. "Hey, Don," he slurred, "I know a place that's real easy to rob."

"Is that so, Dee-wayne?" I slurred back, with the accent on the "Dee." "What kind of business is it?"

"A fancy restaurant down on State Street. They take in big money."

"Oh, man," I laughed. "I'm doing OK pushing for Leroy."

"Think about it. It's easy money in ten minutes tops."

"OK. I'll think about it."

Dewayne had caught me at a good time. I was itching to pull another robbery.

On the way back to Longview the next day, I asked Lorraine about Dewayne. "I used to go with him," she told me. "And he still makes moves to get back with me. But, to tell you the truth, Don, he gives me the creeps. I don't trust him."

"Why?"

"You can't depend on him. Nobody I know will work with him anymore. I guess the drugs have fried his brain."

Facing Life

"If he's so bad, why does Leroy let him hang around?"

"Leroy thinks he owes him for past favors. I'm warning you, Don. Stay away from the jerk."

"I know he acts a little strange at times. But maybe you're being a little hard on him," I protested.

"You know what I think, Don? I think he's jealous of you for going with me."

"He's never said a word about it. He acts like you're just a good friend."

"He's a good actor. I know these black dudes, and he's not a good one. He can't be trusted."

"We'll see. I have ways of checking dudes out."

"Do you?" she teased.

Dewayne was waiting for me when we went back to Leroy's the next weekend. I was barely through the front door when he grabbed me by the arm, staring up at me glassy-eyed. "Come on, Don," he said, guiding me into a side room. "I wanna talk to ya. Ya got your piece?"

"Sure, Dewayne. I'm never without it. Right here," I said, putting my hand on the 9 mm. in the small of my back.

"So, what are we waiting for? Let's hit the restaurant tomorrow night," he said excitedly. "I hear they're having a special singing group. More money than usual."

"You don't say?" I questioned.

"Yeah."

"Come on, Dewayne, are you sure it's good for an easy hit? They'll probably have cops all over the place."

"No, they won't. I've got sources. Anyway, we can check it out tonight."

"OK, we'll check it out."

Me and Dewayne dressed in our suits and cased the place. We hung around long enough to know when the cops came by. Dewayne was right. It looked like an easy hit.

"You want to go in and get the dough, Dewayne?" I asked on the way back to Leroy's. "Or do you want me to go in?"

"Either way, Man. You tell me. You're the boss." That's all I needed to know. I could trust Dewayne.

"I'll go in," I said decisively. "And you drive the car."

"OK. Right on! I'll be by to pick you up at eight-thirty."

At eight-thirty sharp Dewayne pulled up in front of Leroy's place. His older but fancy black Cadillac sported a fresh wash. The extra wide white sidewalls glowed in the dark. He glided into the house, nearly out of his mind with excitement about pulling the job.

"Let's drive by a couple of times," I suggested, "to make sure no cops are around, just in case they change their schedule from one day to the next."

"Sure," Dewayne replied. "Whatever you say, Don."

After two sweeps, I told Dewayne to let me out at the corner, two doors from the restaurant. "Park across the street in the dark spot just behind the fire hydrant. You be there to pick me up," I said firmly. "Right?"

"Right on!" he exclaimed with his big smile. "I'll be Johnny-on-the-spot. You have nothing to worry about, Don. You get the money, and I'll move us out."

I buttoned my suit coat as I walked in the front door of the restaurant, making sure everything was neatly in place. The hostess greeted me the minute I walked in. "Ma'am, is the manager in?" I asked in a pleasant tone.

"Yes, he is," she replied, with a questioning look.

"I'd like to talk to him," I requested softly.

"Just one minute," she replied. "I'll get him."

When the manager came out, I took him aside. "Don't look surprised," I began, almost in a whisper, "and don't change your expression," I warned him, "when I tell you what I want." I paused, then said decisively, "This is a holdup.

"I have a gun in my pocket," I continued. "I want you to take me to the office first and get the money out of the safe. Then we'll get the money from the cash register. Don't make any signals, or I'll waste you. I mean it."

"No problem," he replied nervously, the muscles in his neck tightening. "I'll do what you ask. This way," he said, turning to go to the office. I followed at his heels.

The man got the money out of the safe and put it in the plastic bag I handed him. Carrying the bag, he led the way to the cashier, careful not to make any false moves.

"Sharon," the manager said, his voice developing a nervous quiver, "I need to get some money from the cash register." She looked puzzled but quickly stepped aside to let him empty the drawer. When he handed the money bag to me, I glared threateningly at him. His eyes began to twitch.

I turned around and walked briskly to the front door and out to the street. I glanced at my watch. It had taken exactly six minutes to pull the job. I was proud.

Facing Life

I tucked the bag under my arm inside my suit coat and hurried across the street to meet Dewayne. I was almost to the meeting place when I realized that another car was in the designated parking place. I frantically looked up and down the street. Dewayne was nowhere in sight. *Maybe he circled the block,* I concluded, *when that guy took his parking place.* I stood next to the fire hydrant, expecting Dewayne to show up any second.

Two men ran out of the restaurant. They spotted me right away and started moving in my direction. "Get back, or I'll shoot!" I shrieked. They kept coming toward me. I fired a shot into the air. They froze in place.

I raised my gun chest high, aiming it at one and then the other. "Get back," I yelled. "I mean it." I was ready to pull the trigger when they hurried back inside.

Suddenly, sirens wailed in the distance. Holding my gun close to my body, I raced down the street, ducked into an alley, and came out on a side street. Two doors down, the lights from a blood bank illuminated the dark street. I ran inside, hoping to cut through to the next street. Two nurses gasped in terror when I bounded through the door, pointing my gun in their direction. "The back door, the back door!" I exclaimed, waving the gun toward one nurse and then the other.

"Over there; over there," one shouted frantically, pointing to the door in the far corner.

I ran out the door into a paved area that was bordered by buildings on three sides with a high wall on the end. In the pitch dark, I couldn't see an opening. I moved down the building nearest to me, desperately searching for a way out.

Sirens blared louder and louder, closer and closer. Cop cars screeched to a stop nearby. I kept moving, searching. A bullet bounced off the brick just above my head, narrowly missing me. Then another and another. *They're trying to kill me!* I gasped silently. I kept moving.

As I turned the corner where two buildings met, a ray of light broke through the narrow opening. I frantically moved toward the light, hugging the building. A barrage of shots flew around me. I turned around and leaned back against the building, my heart pounding furiously. By now I had the money bag draped over my left arm.

"You are surrounded," a voice thundered across the paved area. "Throw your gun out, and put your hands up."

"OK, OK," I yelled nervously, throwing my gun on the pavement, well away from me. I stepped out from the building and raised both hands high.

One cop lunged at me, throwing me against the wall and grabbing the money bag. A second cop kneed me in the side. "Hey, Man!" I yelled. "Easy. I'm not resisting."

"Whata you expect, Big Boy?" the other cop snarled, clamping on the handcuffs.

Each cop grabbed an arm and hurriedly marched me down a narrow walkway to a squad car. With sirens wailing, the driver sped through the city toward King County Jail.

I glanced from one gloating cop to the other. The smirks on their faces were disgusting. "I do not care!" I murmured under my breath. "You dirty pigs, I do not care!"

At the jail I was immediately fingerprinted and booked for armed robbery. A cop then escorted me to a holding cell. The only other person in there was a young kid, slobbering all over himself in self-pity. "I know they're going to throw me in jail for a long time," he whined.

"What're you in here for?" I asked impatiently.

"Drinking and driving," he whined again. "But I just had a few beers."

"Yeah, that's what they all say. How many times you been in?" I snapped.

"It's the first time, but . . ."

"The first time!" I exclaimed, interrupting him.

"I know they're going to throw the book at me," he moaned. "I've been in here since two this morning, and my mother hasn't come to get me yet." He choked back tears.

"Oh, I don't want to hear about it!" I snapped. "The most you can get is a few days. I'm going to the joint for a long time." I stretched out the word *long*.

"What'd you do?" he asked.

"Armed robbery," I replied sharply.

His eyes widened. "With a gun?" he questioned.

"Yeah, Bud," I said sarcastically. "That's how you get the money." The color drained from his face.

"So, don't cry the blues to me. You did it. Pay for it. And don't whine. That's what big boys do."

The kid sulked in a corner until lights out. The next morning his mother was there to bail him out. I grudgingly wished him good luck.

I called Joycie just before I went to court. She acted worried but didn't say anything about coming to Seattle. I couldn't blame her.

At ten-thirty I stood at attention before the judge. "Mr. Dennis," he said, lifting his head up to take a quick glance at me over his reading

Facing Life

glasses, "the charge against you is armed robbery. Do you have funds for counsel, or do you want to be assigned a public defender?"

"I don't have no funds. I need a public defender."

"You will be assigned a public defender," he said dryly. "The public defender will contact you shortly."

After the court appearance, a cop took me to the barracks. I started making friends right away.

The following day the public defender called me to the attorneys' room. "Hello, Don," he said pleasantly. "I'm Albert Smithson."

"Hello, Sir," I replied dryly, looking him over good. Right away I saw that he was too slick, with his fancy suit and styled hair. His kind couldn't relate to dudes like me.

Smithson pointed to a seat across the table. "Sit down," he said. "How are things?"

"OK, I guess."

"Is Washington State your home?"

"I lived in California for a long time, but I'm originally from Longview."

"You grew up in this area then. Do you have friends who could witness for you?"

"Not really," I replied. "Most of my friends aren't very reliable. No one would take much stock in them."

"Can you make bail?",

"No, I don't have no money. And my family is pretty disgusted with me. I don't want to ask them for nothin'."

"It sure would help to have somebody speak for you. There's a good chance they'll try to stick you with the habitual criminal charge."

"Habitual criminal!" I exclaimed. "I thought that was discarded."

"No. It's still around. It goes in two directions. The major charge carries a life sentence. The lesser one is twenty years." He was disgustingly precise and proper.

"Yeah, yeah. I know," I snapped impatiently. "Big Bitch and Little Bitch. I've been around. Which one do you think they'll try to put on me?"

"I don't know. They may go for the big one."

"How can they do that? On what charge?"

"You've got a record a mile long. I don't have to tell you that."

"I know," I admitted. "But can't you do something?"

"What I can do is limited. I'll do the best I can."

Smithson paused, then looked me straight in the eye. "It will help if you cooperate," he advised.

"Whata ya mean?"

"The detectives want to ask you about your accomplice."

Breaking Crime's Vicious Cycle

"Is that a fact?" I quipped. "What's in it for me?"

"I can't say, but you might get a lighter sentence."

"Send 'em in," I chuckled. "Let's see what they can do."

"Remember, it will pay you to cooperate," Smithson warned as he asked the guard to get the detectives.

"Hello, Don," one detective said pleasantly, reaching across the table to shake my hand. "I'm detective Martin; this is Roberts." They both sat down to face me.

"Will you help us?" Martin asked.

"Maybe. Depends on what you want me to do."

"Would you like a cigarette?" Roberts asked, holding a pack of cigarettes out to me and pushing one up. I took out the cigarette and slowly put it in my mouth.

"There's a good chance you will spend the rest of your life in prison," Martin warned, holding a lighter to the cigarette.

"Is that so?" I said with a smirk, taking a deep drag, then blowing the smoke up to the ceiling.

"If you'll tell us who was driving the car," he continued, "we possibly could make it easier on you."

"How's that?"

"We could just charge you with armed robbery and ask the DA to forget about the habitual criminal charge."

"Forget about it?" I questioned in a skeptical tone. "Could you really do that?"

"Possibly," Roberts offered. "We can't guarantee anything, though; it's up to the DA and the judge. But I think they will carefully consider our recommendation."

"Yeah, yeah," I snapped. "I've heard that before."

"Face it, Don," Martin replied. "What have you got to lose? The guy couldn't be much of a friend, leaving you stranded like that."

I took several deep drags on the cigarette, pondering the situation. *Dewayne's not worth shooting*, I thought. *He's slime. He deserves to go to prison.* It was clear now. He wanted me out of the way, so he could have Lorraine to himself.

"Well, Don," Roberts urged. "What do you say?"

I glanced from one detective to the other. Their smug looks disgusted me. *What will all my friends think about me if I snitch?* I asked myself. *A snitch is worse than slime.*

"What do you say, Don?" Martin urged.

I've gotten this far without being a snitch, I decided. *Anyway, I'm not convicted yet.*

I glanced from one detective to the other, looking each one in the eye. They raised their eyebrows expectantly. *They're scum, too,* I concluded. *Just like Dewayne.*

"What driver?" I asked, with a smirk.

"Well, the one that drove you to the robbery," Roberts said impatiently.

"I took a bus," I snapped.

"You mean you took a bus to the restaurant and were going to catch another bus back home?" Martin asked.

"I was going to call a cab, but I couldn't find a phone booth," I quipped back sarcastically.

"Well, Don," Roberts stated firmly. "if you want to bury yourself in Walla Walla, that's your prerogative."

"I'm not there yet," I said decisively. "They haven't convicted me. I just don't have any information."

"Well, that's it," Martin said just as decisively. "Let them throw the book at you."

Martin turned to Roberts. "I don't think we need to waste any more time with this guy, do you?" he asked, pushing his chair back and standing up. Roberts nodded in agreement and stood up. The two detectives moved toward the door, both shrugging their shoulders. Martin tapped on the door to signal to the guard to let them out.

The public defender said he would see me later, then told the guard he could take me back to the barracks. I could tell he agreed with the detectives. *I've got no chance at all with this jerk,* I decided. *I've got to get someone else.*

After lunch I called the public defender's office. "This Smithson's no good," I told them. "You've got to get me another public defender," I demanded.

A new PD called me to the attorneys' room around ten the next morning. "Mike Braswell," he said, holding out his hand to greet me. "How're you doing?" he asked pleasantly.

"Not too bad," I replied, sitting down across the table from him.

"What's been going on?"

"Nothin' much."

Braswell told me that he had reviewed my case and planned to talk to the district attorney soon. "Are you willing to plead guilty to the robbery charge if he won't file the habitual criminal charge?" he asked.

"Yeah, I'll do that. I'm guilty. I pulled the robbery."

"Then we'll try that first. The DA may be glad to get you out of the way."

Braswell was back the next day. "I've talked to the DA," he began. "He said 'No deal.' He's going for the max."

Breaking Crime's Vicious Cycle

"The Big Bitch!" I exclaimed, hitting the table with my fist. "I can't believe it! I haven't killed anyone."

"I'm going to tell you the truth, Don," Braswell explained. "Right now, there's a run on filing the habitual criminal charge. The DA is building a name for himself. With your record, you're wide open."

"But the Big Bitch means life."

"At this point, I don't know which one he has in mind. I may be able to present enough information to get the lesser charge. I'll keep talking, but I can't promise anything."

"I sure hope you can. I can't spend the rest of my life in prison. I've learned my lesson. Tell the judge I want to change. Would you do that?"

"I'll do what I can," he promised. "I'll do my best."

I slept fitfully that night. I thought about my dad and how he had let me down. I thought about MaMa and Granddad and how good they were to me. I thought about Joycie and how she always stuck by me. I thought about times when Barbie tried to help me see how I was ruining my life. I had let so many people down. And here I was, facing life in prison.

At the preliminary hearing, I entered a guilty plea to the armed robbery charge. At the next hearing the judge informed me that he was adding the habitual criminal charge but did not specify which one. I waived my right to a jury trial. Braswell said I would be better off letting the judge decide. Sentencing date was set for October 1.

Just before the sentencing date, Braswell called me to the attorneys' room to go over my criminal record, point by point. He asked if it was all correct. I agreed that it was.

"That's some record, isn't it?" I asked nervously.

"Pretty long," Braswell replied.

"But, I promise you, Mr. Braswell, I'm going to do better when I get out this time. I really mean it. Have you told the judge I want to do better?"

"Yes," Braswell assured me, then paused and took a deep breath. "I need to tell you, Don," he warned. "You can't avoid the habitual criminal charge completely. What I'm working for now is to get you a limited sentence instead of life. That's the best we can hope for."

"If that's the best you can do," I said. "I'll have to settle for that. I just can't face life."

"I've presented evidence to show that you aren't violent and that you are determined to get your life straightened out. I think it will help. But whatever happens, we'll appeal the habitual criminal charge." I trusted Braswell.

Facing Life

On October 1 Braswell was with me when I stood at attention before the same judge for the third time.

"Mr. Dennis," the judge began in his usual monotonous, rote style. "You have entered a plea of guilty to the charge of armed robbery. Is that correct?"

"Yes, Your Honor, " I acknowledged.

"I am sentencing you to three years on the charge of armed robbery." That was the expected sentence.

"Mr. Dennis," he continued, peering down at me over his reading glasses, giving me a long, hard gaze. "You have been in and out of prison for more than twenty years."

Twenty years! Twenty years! The words thundered inside my head. It didn't seem possible.

"After reviewing your history of felonies, escapes, forgeries, and other crimes against society," the judge droned on in rote fashion, "I am sentencing you to life in prison."

My stomach tightened into a knot. *Life in prison!* I couldn't believe it. I stood expressionless, staring blankly at the judge.

It really won't be forever, I quickly reasoned. *I'll get out in a few years. That's how it's always been.*

I turned to go to my seat, expecting the court clerk to call another name. Braswell grabbed my arm, holding me in place. The judge was not through.

"Mr. Dennis," he began again. "I am also going to write a letter to the Parole Board, stating that I recommend and strongly suggest that you never be paroled."

My mouth flew open. *Never* pounded inside my head like a migraine. For the first time, I detected strong emotion in the judge's voice. This part wasn't spoken by rote. Every word was carefully chosen. He had given this sentence a great deal of thought.

"I feel that you are unable to adjust to society," the judge stated firmly. "You are a menace and dangerous to decent folks. Because you have demonstrated that you cannot function in free society, you need to be kept locked up."

I reeled at the finality of the decree. I could feel the blood drain from my face. My knees turned to rubber. My palms grew clammy. I broke out in a cold sweat. My heart pounded violently in my chest. Braswell gently placed his hand under my arm to brace me, then guided me to my seat as the court clerk called the name of the next defendant.

"I thought you gave him some information," I frantically whispered to Braswell.

"I did," he replied. "He didn't buy it, though."

"I'm going to spend the rest of my life behind bars! Do you know what that means?"

"I'll file an appeal right away," he assured me.

"How long will that take?" I asked.

"It varies."

"What chance do I have?"

"I can't say. Another PD will contact you." He hurriedly shook my hand and wished me good luck.

Bitterness set in as I watched Braswell walk down the aisle and out of the courtroom. I wondered if he really had done all he could.

"Hey, Don," a friend called to me the minute the guard let me into the barracks. "How'd it go?" he asked with a big smile on his face.

"I can't believe I got life," I moaned, collapsing on a bed.

"Oh, that ain't nothin' for a stepper like you," a tall, black dude joked, dancing around with a weed in his mouth. "I got that, too."

"You can do that," a pock-marked dude chimed in. "All you have to do is walk slow and drink lots of water." They all broke out in a chorus of laughter. I grinned without meaning to. In that company it was hard to feel sorry for myself.

"Give me a hit," I said.

The black dude took a quick drag and passed the joint to me. I took a long drag while staring up at the ceiling. I felt better right away. The weed and the friends helped me put the judge out of my mind. I played cards and joked with the guys until lights out.

Lying in my bunk that night, I thought about what I was facing. *I'm forty-three years old, and I'm going to spend the rest of my life in the pen. What the judge said is true. I cannot deal with life. I cannot function in the free world. Every time I get out, I just get worse. Anyway, I do not care! Let 'em keep me behind bars for the rest of my life. I do not care!* Tears trickled down my cheeks to the pillow.

By breakfast the next morning, I was well into preparing myself for prison life. Defiance had replaced despair. I wasn't going to let a heartless judge break me. I would get with my old Mafia friends and funnel dope into the prison. If I got a job in the kitchen, I could make pruno, the beer of prison. With dope and pruno and friends who understood me, I knew I could make it.

Three weeks later I was bound for Walla Walla, Washington State's infamous prison. On a cloudy, dreary Friday afternoon the guards chained us in pairs and herded us onto the Gray Goose, the ugly, depressing bus reserved for transporting convicts to prison.

As the bus pulled onto the highway that went south to Yakima,

Facing Life

everybody was laughing and telling jokes about prison life. Most were veterans of some pen. A few were newcomers. The kid chained to me was a Huckleberry Finn look alike, with buck teeth, scraggly hair, baggy pants, and stupid jabbering. He was in prison for helping a buddy slit a woman's throat. He had big plans for his time in prison.

"I'll run dope, and I'll escape right away," Huckleberry bragged, loud enough for everyone to hear.

I cringed at his ignorance. He was so naive to prison life. No one with power would trust a big-mouthed murderer like that. *I've ended up with the scum of the earth*, I sighed to myself. *The hardest part of doing time is living with a bunch of stupid jerks!*

Late in the afternoon the Gray Goose rumbled down the road leading to the grounds of Walla Walla. As the driver eased toward the gigantic front gates, I could see the main building of the prison rising ominously above the massive wall, reaching for the gray sky. It looked like an old, ugly castle. The structure matched the gray day and the gray bus and the gray mountains of remote southeastern Washington.

That's my home for the rest of my life, I groaned silently. *I'm going to die here in the middle of nowhere. What a disgrace I am. What an outcast I have become.*

3

A Dennis Christmas

I never knew Granddad Dennis without snow-white hair. Short, chubby, and jolly, he reminded me of Santa Claus. I thought he was the kindest man in the whole world. I cannot remember one time that he raised his voice to me.

Granddad loved to sit in his rocking chair, smoking a pipe, and tell me stories about the trip from Tennessee to Washington. For some reason I always called him "Dad." I guess that's what he wanted to be called. My friends thought it was kind of weird, though. They never knew for sure whether I was talking about my dad or my granddad.

MaMa—as I called my grandmother—had, by nature, a calming tenderness. She always had a special welcome for me at her house. When we lived in the little rent house behind her, she had a bed reserved for me on the back porch. I slept there more than at my own house. A big attraction was the indoor plumbing. We had the bathroom outside.

Every Christmas MaMa gave me five dollars to go Christmas shopping. It was enough to buy presents for everyone. I usually got aftershave for the men, perfume and costume jewelry for the women, and a toy for Barbie. MaMa went shopping with me and gave me advice about the gifts when I asked her. I didn't realize it then, but she carefully guided me in my selections. She would say things like "Aunt Aggie will like this," or "Uncle Roy would enjoy this." The hints always convinced me.

On Christmas Eve morning I watched in horror as Granddad killed the turkey. Seeing him chop its head off was bad enough; but then the poor headless creature jumped wildly around the yard, slinging blood all over the place. I ran for cover. Still, even though it scared me to death, I made Granddad promise not to kill the bird without me there. It was exciting. It was part of Christmas. I liked to help MaMa stuff it, too.

For the Christmas celebration, all the Dennis clan gathered at MaMa

A Dennis Christmas

and Granddad's home on Nineteenth Street. MaMa made sure all the relatives knew they were supposed to come to her house. It was a tradition, whether you were born a Dennis or married into the family. She expected it, and everybody wanted to see all the clan. The out-of-town relatives came in on Christmas Eve afternoon. Every bed was taken; some slept on the floor. MaMa loved all the company.

By the time I was six the Christmas crowd had grown to twenty or more. On Christmas morning, those of us who lived in Longview took our presents to MaMa's. Aunt Hazel and Aunt Aggie were at MaMa's door to grab the presents out of our hands and put them under the tree. Aunt Hazel wanted them arranged in a certain way. I never figured out exactly what she had in mind, but she made a big fuss about it.

Aunt Hazel and Uncle Cliff were two of my favorite people. Hazel looked a lot like MaMa. She was tall like MaMa and had brown hair and pretty hazel eyes. It didn't take much to make her laugh. She was fun to be with.

Uncle Cliff was a full-blooded Indian. Tall, handsome, and outgoing, he had a terrific sense of humor. He delighted in talking to me about life. "Donnie," he told me, "you've got to work hard in school so you can get a good job. And you've got to learn how to get along with people. Be nice to your sister." Coming from anyone else that would have been nagging. From Cliff, it was like advice from a big brother.

Uncle Cliff talked to me about prejudice, too. "Donnie," he said, "don't be prejudiced against a person just because of his race. That's not fair. Judge people by who they are, not by the color of their skin or where they grew up." In that one-horse town of Longview he personally felt the sting of prejudice. People looked down on him because he was an Indian. He had to deal with prejudice all of his life. I took his advice. With all the bad habits I developed over the years, prejudice was not one of them.

Aunt Hazel was clearly in charge of the gift-opening ritual. I don't know whether it was by common consent or pure power that she became the leader; but, somewhere along the way, she had taken over that responsibility. Not one person dared to move toward the gifts until she said it was time. In some ways, she was like a top sergeant. As manager of Longview Cleaners, she had a lot of practice. She told people what to do all week. Over the years she had built the cleaners into a thriving business.

"OK," Aunt Hazel announced in a lighthearted tone, going from room to room, "gather 'round. It's time to open the gifts." At that signal, all of us kids raced to the Christmas tree in the living room. Aunt Hazel took her place next to the tree, and Uncle Cliff sat beside her. Granddad came next. He made a place for MaMa, but she didn't stay there much. She was always jumping up and down checking on the food or getting something for the grandkids.

Uncle Roy and Aunt Helen were always there, too. Uncle Roy was five years older than my dad. He and Aunt Helen had three children, Nancy, Susan, and Paul. I never knew Nancy. She died shortly before her third birthday. MaMa told me it just about killed them. "They're still not over it," I heard her tell Aunt Hazel. "Nancy was such a precious child."

Aunt Aggie and Uncle Ray usually sat next to Roy and Helen. Of all the aunts and uncles, I knew Aggie best. Ray was part-time song leader at the church where MaMa took me every Sunday.

Uncle Joe and Aunt Roetta, two of my favorite people, were sometimes at our Christmas celebration. They had their own family, so they couldn't come every year. Uncle Joe was Granddad's brother. Like Granddad, he had a kind, gentle, and quiet nature. He looked a lot like Granddad, too, with his chubby frame and receding hairline.

Aunt Roetta was small and thin and had snow-white, fluffy hair. She was a bundle of energy and loved to tease. Every summer, MaMa and Granddad took me and Barbie on the train to Seattle to see them. Aunt Roetta's good-byes are what I remember best. She liked to get the last tag when she told somebody good-bye. I challenged her position as champion of the tag. When the train departure was announced over the loud speaker and we all started saying good-bye, I would hug her and Uncle Joe first. Then when she was hugging everybody else, I would tag her real fast and run for the train. She went ahead and hugged everybody, acting like she didn't care a bit. Then, when the last call was made and I was safely in my seat, I felt a tap on my shoulder.

"Bye, bye, Donnie," she giggled and ran for the door, barely getting out before it shut.

When I jumped up and started to run after her, MaMa grabbed my arm and held me firmly in place. "Donnie, Honey, that's enough; it's time to go," she told me. "I'm sorry," she added with her sympathetic smile.

"Oh, MaMa," I pleaded, "let me get her."

"No, you'll be left behind," she said firmly. "Sit down, now. You can get her next time."

I sat back down to hear a tap at the window. Barely able to get her

A Dennis Christmas

head up to the window, Roetta was there, grinning widely. I stuck my tongue out at her. Her grin got bigger.

"I'll get her next time," I vowed. "It's not fair." I leaned back in my chair, sulking, and plotting how I would get the last tag on Aunt Roetta the next time.

Great-uncle John Price, MaMa's bachelor brother, was the last of the adults. He was the first Price that MaMa talked into coming to Washington. He was a deputy sheriff in Cowlitz County and looked the part in every way. His broad, firm chin and the no nonsense look in his eyes warned me not to mess with him. His heavy eyebrows completed his serious look. And he walked with a certain amount of authority. He always came to the Christmas celebration in his broad-brimmed hat. When everyone teased him about wearing it, he flashed a great big smile. That's when I knew he was human, after all.

Aunt Hazel told everyone when and how to open the presents. But she made it fun and different, at least my friends told me it was different from what they did. She had a ritual for each present. She would slowly pick up a present, look at it thoughtfully, and tease about it.

"This one's marked for Barbie."

"Give it to me, then, Aunt Hazel," Barbie implored.

"I know what's in it. You don't want it. It's no good."

"Come on," she begged.

"Well, OK, but don't forget that I warned you."

One by one she passed out the gifts with a similar routine. If anyone looked like they were going to open a present, she would say, "Don't open it yet. Wait 'till everyone gets one; then we'll all open one together."

I sat there impatiently feeling and shaking my first gift. When Aunt Hazel said it was OK, we all tore in. We laughed and teased and thanked everybody for what they gave us. Every kid got a gift from every adult, and the kids all gave little gifts to the big folks.

Granddad joked about having a real Tennessee Christmas in Washington. The roots of the Dennis clan were deep in East Tennessee. Uncle Joe, a railroad man, was the first to migrate west to Seattle, Washington. His job gave him the opportunity to go all over Washington state and beyond. The more he traveled around the area the more he liked his new home. "It's a beautiful state," he wrote to Granddad and MaMa. "You ought to come on out here. You'll love it."

Eventually, Uncle Joe's persuasion worked. In the early part of the summer of 1921 Granddad took the train to Seattle to visit Joe and Roetta. Even before he got off the train, he was captivated by the lush, green valleys, fresh, clear streams, cascading waterfalls, and thick forests.

While in Seattle, Uncle Joe and Aunt Roetta drove Granddad down to Longview. Situated about seventy miles from the Pacific Ocean at the meeting place of the Cowlitz and Columbia Rivers, this beautiful town of tree-lined streets was bordered by famous Lake Sacajawea, with its scenic trails for summer fun and ice-skating in the winter. Adding to this beauty was a flourishing lumber industry. Granddad was promised a job at Longbell Lumber if he came to Longview.

Granddad's decision was firm. Longview was beautiful. The weather was great. And the jobs were there. He went back to Tennessee to convince MaMa, armed with two rolls of film to develop and a contagious enthusiasm. The next summer Granddad and MaMa were on their way to Longview, Washington, with their four kids—Roy, my dad, Hazel, and Agnes.

All the Dennis kids went to R. A. Long High in Longview. Over the years an intense football rivalry had developed between this school and Kelso High across the river. Every Thanksgiving morning the two teams squared off against each other. After one of these games, a friend introduced Clarence Dennis to Ruth Parker. Clarence, nineteen, had just graduated from high school and was working at Longview Fibre. Ruth Parker was seventeen and a senior at Kelso High.

"Your mom was a real looker when we got married," my dad told me more than once. "She was the prettiest girl around here." He told me he fell for her the minute he met her.

I thought my mom was the prettiest mom in town, too. Her willowy dark brown hair framed her dark eyes, small nose, and bright red lips. The baby in the family, she had three pretty sisters. They all attracted the boys, with their carefully made-up faces, curvy figures, and fancy clothes. Like her sisters, my mom had a buxom figure, and she knew how to dress to the greatest advantage. Added to this was a tremendous sense of humor. She loved to tell jokes.

MaMa and Granddad Dennis were against the match from the beginning. The Dennis clan couldn't boast of money, but they did have rich traditions. MaMa grew up on a plantation and was from a family that held to high moral principles. Granddad, too, was from an upstanding, respectable family. The Parker family was another story. For starters, they weren't "our kind of folk," as MaMa put it. In a day when women who smoked were considered to have loose morals, Ruth Parker had picked up the habit from her older sisters. And, like her sisters, Ruth had a foul mouth, although she did control it around MaMa and Granddad. Still, they learned all they needed to know from the small-town grapevine. "She just isn't good for Clarence," MaMa told Granddad. He agreed.

MaMa and Granddad tried to talk some sense into Clarence, but he wouldn't listen. Before year's end he married Ruth Parker. On a Friday afternoon in May they went down to the justice of the peace in Kelso and tied the knot. They told MaMa and Granddad about it two days later. MaMa and Granddad tried to make the best of the situation, offering to let them move into the little rent house in back.

Me and Barbie were both born in the little rent house. I came along about two years after my parents married; Barbie followed three years later. Soon after Barbie was born, my mom went to work at Longview Fibre where Daddy worked.

MaMa kept care of me and Barbie. She and Granddad didn't have much money, but they had lots of love. Almost every day MaMa gave me a dollar and sent me to the grocery store to buy a half pound of hamburger, a loaf of bread, and a quart of milk. With fruit and vegetables added from their garden, that was our evening meal. Every Sunday we had chicken.

Granddad took a second job as a night watchman at Longview Laundry. He took me to work with him a lot of time. It was fun to follow him on his rounds and watch him click a clock as he walked from one building to the next. Inside the buildings and outside, he clicked the clock. "Granddad, why do you click that clock?" I asked. He explained that it was to keep track of his rounds and to make sure he checked every location. When we got back to the main building, he would make a bed for me in one of the huge laundry carts.

MaMa made clothes for me and Barbie. I will never forget the Halloween outfit she created for me when I was in the third grade. The outfit began with a shiny white silk shirt. I loved the feel of it. Added to this flashy piece were slick, shiny black pants and a red cummerbund. To complete the outfit, MaMa bought me a black hat with tassels and a Zorro mask. "You're going to be the slickest bullfighter anyone ever saw," she teased, giggling like Aunt Roetta.

"Can I go show Mrs. Slottin?" I asked. Mrs. Slottin was a kind widowed lady who lived across the street.

"No," she said firmly. "Don't show anyone until we go to have it judged. Then you can show everyone. Turn around and let me make sure no strings are hanging."

MaMa turned me around slowly, checking every detail. "I know you're going to win," she declared confidently. "What a handsome young man you are!" I was so excited and proud.

MaMa and Granddad took us down to the YMCA for the costume

competition. It seemed like every kid in town was there. We had to walk across a stage in front of everyone. My parents weren't there. They said they had to work.

When they announced me as the winner, MaMa and Granddad led in the cheering. I could hear Aunt Aggie and Barbie, too. I walked timidly to the front to claim the prize—a $25.00 war bond. I was ecstatic. Afterward, all the kids teased me about how snazzy I looked. Mrs. Slottin nearly went out of her mind about the outfit. "Oh, Donnie," she screeched in her high-pitched voice, "You are one handsome fella." She hugged me and kissed me and told me what a good boy I was.

During the summer I worked in the garden with my granddad. The big money-making project was picking raspberries. We sold them to the grocery stores and to people who came by. We made enough from this project to buy train tickets for all four of us to go to Seattle to visit Uncle Joe and Aunt Roetta. This trip was the highlight of the year and the last fun event of the summer. While we were there, Joe and Roetta took us to picnics on the lake and to the Woodland Zoo in Seattle. It was great fun to see all the animals.

Joe and Roetta's kids were around the age of my parents. One cousin, Kermit, was a merchant marine. He sent salt and pepper shakers to Aunt Roetta from all over the world. She always made a special point of showing us the additions to her collection. Kermit also took lots of pictures during his travels. He kept them in the old-fashioned slide holders that clicked when turned from frame to frame. I loved to look at the pictures and see sights from all over the world.

Cousin Zelfa's husband worked near Puget Sound on an oiler as a cook. He took me out on the boat with him and let me stay overnight. I cherished those visits. It was fun to talk to the crew and run all over the boat. I was always disappointed when it was time to go back to Longview.

MaMa went to church every Sunday, and took Barbie and me with her. "It's really your mom and dad's responsibility," she told me. She just couldn't understand why Clarence never went to church. "He wasn't raised that way," she told me. She blamed his behavior on the girl he married. "If Ruth would just encourage Clarence a little," I heard her tell Aunt Agnes, "he would go." Aunt Agnes agreed.

Why Granddad didn't go to church was a completely different matter. "He's really a good man," MaMa told me and then made all kinds of excuses for him, like he had a bad heart, or he was tired.

A Dennis Christmas

Every Sunday morning MaMa, Aunt Agnes, and me and Barbie walked the block to church, rain or shine.

The summer after first grade I went to Vacation Bible School at a church camp north of Longview. The camp pastor really knew how to communicate with kids. His talks each morning touched my heart. Soon after Bible school I told MaMa that I wanted to give my heart to Jesus. She talked to me about what that meant, then took me to the pastor of our church. In his study he explained to me what it meant to follow Jesus. He said I needed to do what Jesus wanted me to do every day. I told him that I understood what it meant to let Jesus come into my heart. I knew I was supposed to be a better boy now. I admitted that I had done lots of things I shouldn't do, but I thought Jesus could help me to do better.

The next Sunday after the sermon I walked to the front of the church to tell all the people about my decision. MaMa said that was what I was supposed to do. While I stood there by the pastor he asked me again if I knew what I was doing. "Donnie," he began, with all the people staring at us, "do you understand what it means to give your heart to Jesus?"

"It means I'm going to live for Jesus," I replied, almost in a whisper. From the time I wet my pants in the play, I was terrified of getting up in front of people.

"Donnie," the pastor explained, "we want you to stand here in front so everybody can tell you how happy they are that you have made this decision. After Brother Jim prays, all these people will come up here to shake your hand." He paused, then looked toward MaMa and Granddad. "I'm going to ask your grandparents to come up here and stand with you." I was relieved. I didn't want to stand there alone.

Mrs. Slottin rushed up to the front as soon as Brother Jim said "amen." "Donnie," she sobbed, tears running down her cheeks. "I am so happy for you! I just love you. You are such a good boy." She hugged me so hard I thought I was going to lose my breath. And she kissed me all over my face. "I'll be praying for you," she promised. I smiled weakly.

As soon as we got to MaMa's house, I ran to tell my dad and mom what had happened. "Good," my mom said matter-of-factly. My dad just grunted.

"You're invited to my baptism," I said excitedly. "Will you come?"

"We'll try," my mom told me. My dad responded with a dry, "Sure." The next Sunday evening I was baptized. They were too tired to come. They had gone to a party the night before and got in late.

Every day I prayed that I would be a good boy. I vowed to quit using the bad words I had picked up from friends at school and from my mom and dad when they had one of their fights. I was determined to go on the straight and narrow, as the preacher called living a good life. I wanted to be a good Christian.

My first test came the next week at a meeting of my Cub Scout group. Me and Bryan Price, a second cousin, both had made a statue out of soap. I got in a fight with him about which one looked best and threw his statue across his front yard. His mother made me leave and told me I couldn't come back. MaMa was mad about it, but she didn't say anything to Bryan's mom. "Just don't go back over there," she said. I wasn't sorry I got kicked out. I decided the only reason I went to the meetings, anyway, was to wear the blue uniform.

My second test came when I tried to help Barbie. We were staying with MaMa on a Saturday, and she told me about a place where I could make money picking beans. Barbie talked me into letting her tag along. Then I talked the crew chief into letting her pick. But she couldn't keep up with me.

"Donnie," Barbie whined, "I can't pick as fast as you. I won't get any money."

"Yes, you will," I assured her. "I'll make your bag heavier," I said, picking up a handful of dirt clods. I filled Barbie's bag a quarter full with the clods and told her to make sure she picked enough beans to cover them good.

When we went through the line to have our bags weighed, the crew chief gave Barbie a funny look. "Little girl," he said, "you've picked a bunch of beans for someone your size. How did you do that?" Barbie shrugged her shoulders, smiling sheepishly.

"Let's check this out," he snapped, turning Barbie's sack upside down. Tears formed in Barbie's eyes as the clods fell out on top of the beans. The man turned straight to me.

"That's cheating," he said, his eyes red with rage. "Don't you know better than that?"

"She whined about me doing better than her," I explained, trying to excuse myself. "So I tried to help her out."

"That's not the way to help your little sister," he assured me, his voice still filled with anger. "You kids are fired. And you can't pick here anymore."

With our heads hanging down, we headed for MaMa's. "Don't you tell MaMa," I warned Barbie. "It was your fault, too."

"I won't, Donnie. I won't," she promised. But we were hardly

A Dennis Christmas

through the front door when Barbie blurted out to MaMa, "Donnie cheated. Donnie cheated! And we got fired."

MaMa bawled me out good. But it didn't seem fair that Barbie should get off scot-free. And I made sure she didn't. She was scared of the dark; so, when she went to bed that night, I made eerie sounds until MaMa made me stop.

My third test came when I decided I would rather have a coke than go to Sunday School. When MaMa wasn't looking I took Barbie to the drugstore. Since we got back in time for worship, I figured MaMa would never know the difference. But somebody came up to MaMa right after church and told her what we did. She chewed me out good on the way home.

"You're the oldest," she told me. "You should set a good example for your sister."

A few months after my baptism we moved from the rent house behind MaMa and Granddad to our new house on Twenty-fifth Street, about six blocks away. I didn't realize how bad the rent house was until we moved. The new house was like a palace in comparison. Me and Barbie had a bigger bedroom, and we had indoor plumbing. I still went to MaMa's almost every day. On Sunday me and Barbie walked over there to go to church with her.

The Christmas after we moved into our new house, Mom and Dad got me a bicycle. I started delivering newspapers and the *Saturday Evening Post*. Before I got the job, me and Barbie picked up coke and beer bottles in the street to make sure we had enough money for the movie. We didn't have to do that anymore. I had enough money to pay for both of us every Saturday. Roy Rogers was my favorite. Barbie was gaga over Gene Autry.

A new house and money in my pockets—life was pretty good. And I was trying hard to be a good boy.

4

Cheating

Clarence Dennis reached for the bottle of beer on the nightstand. Sitting halfway up in bed, he took a swig, letting out a faint groan. The drink made him feel a little better, but the headache would not go away. He had really tied one on the night before.

Moving down the hall with the beer bottle in his hand, he stopped to lean against the wall. With his back to the wall, he pressed his head against it, touching certain pressure points. He claimed that eased the headache a bit.

I was about seven when I realized my dad drank a lot. But I didn't notice what the excessive drinking did to him until we moved to our new house on Twenty-fifth Street. Daddy got mean as a snake with a few drinks under his belt. When he came home late, he would start knocking my mom around if she said one word of complaint to him.

One night my dad knocked my mom against a cupboard door. Blood went everywhere—down her face, in her eyes, on her dress, on the floor. I heard the noise and ran in. The scene sickened me. My mom looked so sad, so beat up. My dad ordered me back to my bedroom.

The next morning, things were quiet. Nobody talked about the night before. Mom and Dad acted like nothing was wrong. After every fight I was very unhappy with my dad. I hated him so much when he hurt my mom. At the same time, I loved him, worshiped him when he was sober. I always dreamed that he would start loving me again and be nice to my mom. I wanted so badly to feel love in the house again. But it was an empty dream. The fights got more frequent and more intense.

Maybe it was because I stayed at MaMa's so much when we lived on Nineteenth Street that I had never noticed how much my mom and dad fought. Or maybe the intense fights began when we moved to our new house. I really don't know. But it took so little for an argument to get going. They fought about everything. Most of the

Cheating

time they made it through supper before getting into a fight. Then a little spark would ignite it.

Since Mom and Dad worked at the same place, they saw each other off and on during the day. Many times, that conversation was what started the first fight of the evening. One typical fight began with my mom confronting my dad about his flirty ways.

"I saw you flirting with Sandra today," Mom said, her voice cracking. "Everybody was talking about it."

"I was just being friendly," he protested strongly. "It was only small talk. I can't believe everybody was talking about that. You're lying."

"I'm not either. You've got a problem," she insisted.

"You're crazy," he shrieked, then jumped up out of his chair like a madman, pointing his finger threateningly at her. "You always find something to fight about. I'm not going to stay here and listen to this crap. I'm going down to the Elks Club where they'll leave me alone. I want some peace and quiet."

"I hope you don't gamble again," she said, refusing to be cowed.

"I'll gamble if I want to."

"Yeah, you will. And you'll drink a ton of beer, too. Then we won't have money to pay the bills. All you ever think about is yourself and what you want."

"Yeah," Dad countered. "And who do you think about? You're getting where you hardly ever fix a decent meal."

"What was wrong with the meal tonight?" Mom protested.

"It was OK, but you didn't fix one last night."

On and on it went from one gripe to another. The volume got louder and louder. Finally, Daddy called it to a halt.

"Shut up! Shut up! I don't want to hear any more." He moved toward Mom, gesturing wildly with his arms, threatening to hit her. She dodged instinctively.

"I don't have to shut up. You've got some responsibility for these kids. You go down to that Elks Club practically every night. You always find an excuse to leave."

"If you weren't such a nag, I might stay around."

"If you'd at least try to be a decent husband, it would help."

"That does it," Daddy yelled. He flew out the door, jumped in the car, and sped off down the street.

Mom told me and Barbie to do our homework. She got a book to read and sat in a corner of the living room, listening to the radio. Sometimes she cried for a while after he left. With Daddy gone, it was peaceful. But I knew the peace would end when he came in drunk a few hours later, ranting and raving and pushing Mom around.

Me and Barbie developed a technique to shut out the noise. We each put a pillow over our head and sang songs to each other, like "Don't sit under the apple tree with anyone else but me" or "Mares eat oats" or "Jesus loves me, this I know, for the Bible tells me so." The louder the argument got, the louder we sang. In a strange way, the singing helped us forget what was happening.

Often on Saturday night, my mom would go to the club with my dad. They always seemed happy when they let us out at MaMa's on the way. But, at MaMa's I had to listen to her bemoan the fact that my mom and dad were such bad parents. "They just don't have enough time for you kids," she would say. "That's not right. They have plenty of time to be with their wild friends."

MaMa was right about that. They didn't seem to be interested in anything I did, especially Daddy. I liked all kinds of sports—basketball, baseball, football, and tennis. My first team competition was in basketball. I was excited about getting to play and asked my mom and dad to come to the Thursday night game. "We'll try," Daddy told me. He didn't make it to the game, but he did make it to a bar. After I was in bed, he came home drunk.

The next year I played second base on the American Legion baseball team. I asked my dad again and again to come see me play. Each time he said, "I'll try." I looked for my mom and dad where MaMa and Granddad sat. They never showed up. Mom usually said she was too tired or had to work. Daddy always told me he was sorry he didn't make it to the game and made all kinds of excuses. Sometimes, he said he got busy at work. I knew that wasn't true, but I still forgave him.

Clarence and Ruth were the talk of the Dennis clan. MaMa, Aunt Hazel, and Aunt Aggie talked about them every time they got together. One Saturday, sitting around the kitchen table drinking coffee, they freely expressed their opinions about the situation. I was working a puzzle in the living room, too engrossed, they thought, to hear them.

"I'm afraid they're going to break up," Hazel told MaMa.

"It looks pretty bad," MaMa agreed sadly.

"I know Clarence drinks too much," Hazel admitted, "But it's a lot her fault, too. She nags him all the time."

"It's a bad situation," MaMa said. "I knew from the very beginning that the match was no good."

"He hits her all the time," I chimed in from the living room.

Cheating

A hushed silence fell over the women.

"She antagonizes him," Hazel assured me to break the silence. "I've seen her do it over and over again."

She moved to the doorway to face me. "Donnie," she said, "We go to the Elks Club with them. You don't know everything that goes on."

"Aunt Hazel," I pleaded, "you just don't understand. My mom's good to us. Daddy comes in drunk almost every night and screams at Mom and hits her. He even keeps a bottle of beer by his bed for hangovers."

"But does he ever hit you kids?"

"No, but he scares us to death," I said, opening my eyes wide to emphasize my point. "Me and Barbie are afraid he will hit us sometime. If you were there, you'd understand."

"He's had to put up with a lot, Donnie," Aunt Hazel explained. "Maybe he wouldn't drink so much if your mom didn't nag him so much."

"Yeah," Aunt Aggie agreed, getting up from the table to stand by Hazel. "She just wasn't raised right. Those sisters of hers are nothing but trash. I heard they were prostitutes up in Alaska during the war."

"Aggie," MaMa cautioned. "You don't know that for a fact, do you?"

"We've all heard it, Mother. You know that."

"Your mother isn't much better," Hazel said. "A friend of mine saw her stepping out on Clarence."

"You liars! You liars!" I screamed. "He's the one that cheats. They're always fighting about the women he flirts with at work. You just don't know what's going on. I don't want to hear this garbage. You're not fair," I yelled, covering my ears. The tears flowed down my cheeks.

Aunt Aggie slowly moved to the couch and sat down beside me. "Oh, Donnie," she said tenderly, putting her arm around my shoulder. "You're going to have to face up to the truth. Your dad may lose his temper and yell at your mom, but she's always looking for a fight. I've heard her accuse him of things he doesn't do. She's got a terrible temper herself, and you know she cusses like a sailor. If she would just keep her mouth shut and leave him alone, he wouldn't drink so much. He's a good person. I know he is, Donnie."

"Aunt Aggie, you just don't understand," I sobbed. "He's mean. All he does is gripe at me and beat up my mom. I'm afraid he's going to kill her. I really am."

"Oh, Donnie," she said softly, "your dad wouldn't do anything like that. He just isn't that kind of person. We do understand, but there's two sides to this situation."

"Two sides?" I questioned. "I've seen him hit her so hard she bled all over the place."

Aunt Aggie looked surprised and skeptical.

The Dennis clan's narrow-minded, one-sided view of the situation drove me crazy. No matter what I told them, they refused to admit what was happening. Even with all my dad's faults, they always took his side. Always! Ma Parker would come over to MaMa's and tell her that her son was doing wrong. The complaint fell on deaf ears. A Dennis could do no wrong. A Parker could do no right.

Mom got the word that one of my dad's flirtations had turned into the real thing. She asked me to help her check out the rumor. "Sure, Mom," I agreed.

"Here's what I want you to do," Mom explained. "After supper, you slip out and hide in the backseat of the car. If he asks about where you are, I'll tell him I sent you on an errand. I want to know if he goes to see Kathleen."

"Kathleen? Who's Kathleen?"

"It's one of the secretaries at work," she said nervously.

"OK, OK," I agreed. That sounded like an exciting thing to do, like being a real detective.

"What's she look like?" I asked. I wanted to know if I saw the right person.

"She's got blond hair, about my height, slim, a lot younger than me."

"OK. I think I can recognize her."

Mom got a bemused look on her face. "Now, make sure he doesn't see you," she warned. "After he meets Kathleen, you get out of the car and call me."

I was barely in the backseat of the car when my dad got in. He drove straight to the parking lot of a grocery store, way in the back. Almost at the same time, another car parked right beside him.

"Hi, Honey," he said, "where are we going tonight?"

"Better not go to the Elks," the lady warned. "Ruth will find out." She giggled as she talked.

"I really don't care if she knows," Daddy bragged. "What can she do?"

"Divorce you," she teased.

"Yeah," Daddy agreed.

I jumped up, grabbing the back of the front seat. "I caught you! I caught you! That's Kathleen!" I exclaimed, pointing to her. "She looks just like Mom said."

Kathleen's mouth flew open.

Cheating

"What're you doing here?" Daddy demanded angrily.

"Mom wanted to find out," I said nervously. "She wanted to know what you were really doing. This isn't right, Daddy." I cried, tears welling up in my eyes.

"That's not for you to decide, young man," he snapped, untouched by my tears. "You don't know what I go through."

"Kathleen, Honey," he called to her. "Don't worry about anything. I'll be back in a minute. Wait here for me."

"OK," she said quietly, self-consciously making sure she didn't look in my direction.

Daddy ordered me to get in the front seat. He bawled me out all the way home. "You better never do this again, young man," he warned. "You should know better. Next time, you tell your mom to do her own dirty work." On and on it went. The more he bawled me out, the harder I cried.

I hate you! I hate you! I exclaimed to myself.

When we got home, Daddy angrily pushed me up the steps to the front door. He opened the door and stuck his head in. "Ruth," he yelled demandingly. "Come here."

My mom stepped into the living room, standing back from the door. A look of terror flooded her face when she saw me.

"I thought you had better sense than to do something like this," he snapped. "I'm gonna whip you both when I get home."

As Daddy pushed me toward my mom, she stood there silent and stunned. He marched down the steps and drove off. My heart pounded furiously in my chest.

Mom listened stoically as I related what had happened. She didn't cry; she didn't criticize me for letting my dad know I was there. She just quietly thanked me for helping her out and told me to finish my homework and get in bed. She got a book and sat in a corner of the room and read.

The fight that night was bigger than ever. When my dad took a break to go to the bathroom, I heard my mom on the telephone. "Uncle John," she sobbed. "You've got to get over here. Clarence is beating up on me." She hurriedly hung up the phone when my dad came out of the bathroom.

"What're you doing?" he yelled.

"I called Uncle John," she said defiantly. "He's coming over here."

"Now you've done it," he moaned angrily.

It was deathly quiet until the knock on the door. Uncle John got right to the point. "What's the problem?" he asked in his no-nonsense, authoritative tone.

Breaking Crime's Vicious Cycle

"We just got into a fight," my dad replied sheepishly.

"You got carried away with your muscle a little bit, didn't you, Clarence?" Uncle John asked dryly.

"Guess so," he admitted quietly.

"Do you realize what you've done?"

My dad grunted an "Uh huh."

"Look at Ruth," Uncle John said sternly. "Look at her. I ought to haul you off to jail. A man shouldn't treat his wife like this."

"Please, Uncle John," Daddy begged. "Don't embarrass me. I didn't mean to hurt her. We just got in a big fight, and I lost my temper."

"Not the first time, is it, Clarence?" Uncle John questioned with a trace of sarcasm. He opened his eyes wide and looked my dad straight in the eye.

"I won't do it again, Uncle John. I promise. I'll stop drinking so much and be a better husband and father. I really mean it."

"Do you think you can quit that drinking?"

"I really do."

"You know that's what starts it all, don't you?"

"Yeah, I do."

"You're going to have to stay away from the Club and be home more. You've got to be a better father to these kids."

"I will. I will," my dad promised again.

That was the only time I ever saw anyone from the Dennis side of the family take up for my mom. Uncle John was so stern that I was sure Daddy would change.

Uncle John's talk scared Daddy good. He stayed home more and didn't hit my mom. They still didn't come to my ball games, but things were happier around the house.

The peace lasted until the Christmas-party season. About three weeks before Christmas, Daddy was back to his old habit of going out every night and coming in drunk and beating up on my mom. Me and Barbie started covering our heads with pillows and singing again. I was eleven by now. Barbie was eight.

At seven o'clock on Christmas Eve, Daddy was still out. He had promised to be in no later than five to help us decorate the Christmas tree. At ten he still wasn't home.

"We better go ahead," Mom said, "so you kids can go to bed."

The three of us had a lot of fun decorating the tree. We put on some ornaments that me and Barbie had made in Vacation Bible School and some new ones. We were proud when we got through. It looked really pretty. But we were disappointed that Daddy wasn't there before we went to bed.

Cheating

I lay awake in bed—excited and afraid. I was excited about Christmas and scared to death about what my dad would do when he came home. Around twelve I heard him stagger through the front door. Mom was sitting on the couch waiting for him. "Where have you been?" she snapped impatiently the minute he came through the door. "These kids waited for you to come home all evening."

"What's it to you, anyway, you nag."

"After all, you are their father. Remember what you told Uncle John."

"I'm sick of you throwing that up to me. I've got to have some fun."

"Fun? Here you are, drunk on Christmas Eve. You ought to be ashamed of yourself."

"Shut up!" he yelled. "Shut up! I don't want to hear it. It doesn't matter what I do, you always find something to gripe about. There's no pleasing you. Shut up."

"I don't have to!" she shouted back defiantly. "You owe us something."

"Why? All you ever do is gripe at me. And all those kids do is spy on me."

"If you didn't have something to be ashamed of, you wouldn't need to worry about them seeing you."

"I'm not ashamed. I'm just sick of you—sick to death of you. Get out of here!"

"I don't have to. It's my house, too. You're a no good, drunken, two-timing slob."

"Don't you talk to me like that. I don't have to take it."

"I'll say what I want."

"No you won't," he yelled through clenched teeth.

The first slap echoed through the house. I heard my mom hit the wall and fall to the floor with a big thud.

I got up the courage to run out of my bedroom. Barbie was close behind me, crying, "Mom, Mom."

Mom was on the floor, cringing in fear and crying uncontrollably. Blood was spewing from her mouth. Daddy straddled her limp body, with one hand holding the telephone cord around her neck. In the other hand, he held a lighted cigarette to her face.

"Don't do it! Don't do it!" she screamed.

"Stop it, Daddy! Stop it!" I screamed, rushing to my mom's side.

"No, Daddy. No, Daddy," Barbie screamed.

Leaning on one arm, my dad looked up at me with the meanest look I had ever seen on his face.

Breaking Crime's Vicious Cycle

"You stay out of it, Donnie," he ordered angrily. "This is none of your business."

"I don't want you to hurt my mom," I sobbed, trembling all over.

He let go of the telephone cord, stood up, and glared down at me. It was as if he had suddenly sobered up. He reached down and grabbed me by the collar of my pajamas, practically picking me up off the floor.

"If you love her so much," he sneered, "get on top of her." With all the force of his weight, he shoved me to the floor beside my bleeding mom. Then, like a crazed maniac, he moved to the Christmas tree and pulled it up out of the bucket of sand. Moving toward the front door, he yanked the plug for the lights out of the socket, knocking over the bucket of sand at the same time. Sand and tree ornaments flew all over the room. I watched in stunned silence as he opened the front door and threw the once-beautiful tree into the front yard. Me and Barbie cried harder and harder.

Daddy ran back in the house, stepped over my mom, and grabbed his coat off the couch. He pulled his car keys out of his pants pocket, ran out the door to the car, and jumped in. He didn't look back.

With Christmas tree lights shining from every house on the block but ours, I sadly watched my dad speed down the street, the view clouded by the tears streaming down my face. I stood in the doorway until his car lights were out of sight. When I turned around, my mom had already gone to her bedroom.

I shut the door and slowly and silently walked to my bedroom. I was relieved and desperately lonely at the same time. I wanted my dad back, but I was glad the violence was over. I was sick of being afraid.

My dad didn't come to the Christmas celebration at MaMa's. Mom didn't go either. She helped me and Barbie carry the gifts over and then went back home. No one questioned why they weren't there. I guess they all figured that Clarence and Ruth had another one of their big fights.

Christmas 1945 is dramatically etched in my memory. My mom, dad, me and Barbie were never together again as a family. I cannot remember a sadder day in my life.

5

Abandoned

Three days went by. We hadn't seen Daddy since the big fight. That night he called Mom on the phone. It didn't sound pleasant. The next day Mom talked to me and Barbie about the situation at the supper table.

"Things are pretty bad between me and your dad," she began. "And I don't think it will get any better if he comes back. Do you want me to divorce your dad?"

"Yes, I do," I said quickly. "I'm scared of him."

"Me, too," Barbie chimed in. "He's mean."

"I don't want to listen to the fighting anymore," I told her. "He's gonna kill you. I know he is."

"I've never been accepted in this family," Mom sighed. "I just don't fit in. Maybe things will be better now."

The next day I went over to MaMa's to tell her what Mom was going to do. She was disappointed but not surprised. "It's just not right," she said. "It's against the Bible."

I didn't say anything to MaMa, but I wondered if she thought beating your wife was against the Bible.

In no time, the whole town knew that my folks were getting a divorce. John Bell, my next-door neighbor, was the first to say anything to me. "How come your folks are getting divorced?" he asked me when we were playing outside.

"They just can't get along," I replied.

"Where you gonna live?"

"With my mom," I replied definitely. "We're gonna stay in our house."

"Does your dad have a girlfriend?"

"Yeah," I said, cringing inside with embarrassment. "He's had one for a long time."

My church friends didn't understand either. I didn't feel comfortable with them anymore. They didn't mean to shut me out; they just didn't know how to deal with my problem. Decent people simply didn't get a divorce.

Almost every day I stopped by MaMa's on my way home from school. I had to talk to somebody. When Aunt Hazel and Aunt Aggie came around, it was always "If Ruth had made a better home" or "If Ruth didn't nag so much." As far as they were concerned, my mother didn't have one redeeming quality. In fact, the whole Dennis clan sided with my dad, except maybe Uncle John. Their attitude was disillusioning. I saw with my own eyes what was happening. *Where is love?* I wondered.

I lost interest in everything. At school, I just sat at my desk and stared into space. "What's wrong?" my teacher asked. "Don't you feel good?"

"I feel awful," I replied, choking back the tears.

"You better go to the nurse's office then."

"What's the matter?" the nurse asked.

I started crying. "I don't want to go to school no more."

"Why?" she asked.

"Just 'cause."

She called MaMa on the telephone and sent me to her house. MaMa had a long talk with me. "Donnie, you need to do your schoolwork, so you can get a good job someday," she pleaded.

"I don't care," I told MaMa. "I do not care."

MaMa's talk made me feel a little better.

Me and John Bell played together after school almost every day. He understood what it was like not to have a dad, because his dad died when he was four. His mom was my teacher in school, and she understood, too. I talked to her a lot about my situation. "It's not fair," I told her. "All the other kids have a mom and dad."

"John doesn't have a dad, and he's doing OK," she said.

"But his dad didn't leave him. He died."

"I know, but its been hard on him."

"But this is worse," I protested. "That woman took him away from me and my mom. She's ruined my life."

"You have to go on with your life, Donnie," Mrs. Bell urged. "You can't let this destroy you."

All through my conversations with Mrs. Bell, I cried and cried. But, when I went back home, I usually felt better. She really cared what happened to me.

One Saturday Mom left Barbie at MaMa's and took me to get a hamburger. "Donnie," she urged, "you've got to deal with the fact that your dad and I aren't together anymore and never will be again. You've got to get happy again."

"But everybody thinks it's terrible that you're getting a divorce."

"Don't worry about it. They don't hold it against you."

"Yes they do," I said, as the tears began to flow.

"Donnie," she pleaded. "They wouldn't hold it against a kid."

She got real quiet, then looked me in the eye. "Donnie, I need you," she said tenderly. "I really do. I need you to help me with the house and to look out for Barbara. You can be the man of the house." I felt better after our talk.

Being the man of the house sounded exciting. I took my new responsibilities seriously. Every day I made sure I was home when Barbie got there. Mom usually came in from work around six and fixed supper for us. The three of us were getting along good. I enjoyed the peaceful evenings. I was doing better in school, too. *Everything is going to be OK*, I decided. I began to feel happy again.

On a Monday in April, Mom went to work as usual. She kissed me and Barbie good-bye and wished us a happy day. It was a normal Monday. Nothing seemed different. Me and Barbie walked home from school with John Bell. I played outside with him until his mom called him in for supper.

Six-thirty came, and Mom wasn't home yet. Me and Barbie started looking out the window for her. "Maybe she had to work late," I concluded. Barbie agreed.

Seven-thirty came and no mom. I found us something to eat.

"Shouldn't we go to MaMa's?" Barbie asked. "I'm scared to stay here without Mom."

"Don't worry," I assured her. "If Mom wanted us to go to MaMa's, she would have told us. Don't worry. I won't let anyone hurt you. Anyway, Mrs. Bell is next door. She'll help us if we need her." I figured Mom must really trust me to leave me in charge like that and not make us go to MaMa's.

I didn't want to go to MaMa's house. I didn't want to hear her talk about the no-good mother we had.

I set the alarm for seven o'clock and went to bed. I slept fitfully all night, hoping to hear my mom come in. The next morning, the first thing I did was look in Mom's room. Nothing was changed. Nobody had slept in the bed.

I fixed me and Barbie some toast, and we went on to school. I told Barbie not to tell anyone. "I'm sure Mom will be back when we get home," I told her, "so there's no point in telling anyone." Everybody thought my mom was no-good because she was getting a divorce. I didn't want them to think worse of her. And I was ashamed for myself, too.

All day I wondered where my mom was. I rushed home so I would be there if she came home early. Six-thirty came and no mom. Around seven me and Barbie went next door to tell Mrs. Bell. I knew she wouldn't make me feel bad.

"Has she left like this before?" she asked.

"No. Never," I told her.

"Well, maybe she'll be back tomorrow," she said hopefully. She said she and John would come over and stay with us.

When me and Barbie got home from school the next day, I checked the closet in Mom's room. My heart sank when I saw that it was almost empty.

"Maybe she went to visit Aunt Dorothy," I told Barbie. She was Mom's older sister. They were close.

Mrs. Bell invited us over for supper. After supper she told us we would have to go to MaMa's. She helped us put some clothes together and drove us there.

"These kids don't have anyone at their house anymore," she told MaMa and Granddad, as we sat in their living room.

"Well, I'll swanee," MaMa sighed, leaning back in her rocking chair. Tears welled up in her eyes.

Granddad took his pipe out of his mouth and shook his head in dismay. "What's wrong with that woman?" he said.

Mrs. Bell gave me and Barbie a hug before she went back home and told me she would see me at school. MaMa thanked her over and over again for helping us kids.

"How can Mom do this?" Barbie cried as MaMa shut the door.

"They don't love us," I sobbed.

"They don't, do they, MaMa?" Barbie questioned through the tears. "They're mean."

"I hate them both," I snapped.

MaMa pulled us close to her, hugging us real tight. "Don't you kids worry. Everything is going to be OK. Granddad and I will see to that."

That night, as I slept in my old bed on the porch, I looked up at the stars through the windows. *Why was I born to people like this?* I wondered. *What's the point of two little kids going through all this? Why is God letting this happen? I've tried to be a good boy. I wish Uncle Roy was my father. Things would be different then.*

On my back in MaMa's yard or out by the lake, I asked God why all this was going on. I never heard Him reply. I got no answers at all. God was strangely quiet.

I asked MaMa why all the bad things were happening to me and Barbie. Most of the time she would blame it on the wild life of my mom and dad. She hinted that my dad might be different now, since he wasn't with my mom anymore.

"You kids have gone through more than your share," she told me. "But God will see you through this."

I was skeptical, but I didn't argue. I couldn't see the reason for all the suffering, and I couldn't see where God had the strength to overcome. If He did, I couldn't understand why He didn't do something to make it all stop.

A few months later Mom came to see us at MaMa's. She had a boyfriend with her named Kelly. She said she had met him at the grocery store in Kelso where she went to work after the divorce. Funny thing, I didn't know she was just across the river in Kelso all that time.

Mom told me and Barbie that she couldn't take being near Longview anymore, that she was getting married and moving to Spokane. She promised to come back soon and get us. The visit was so short that I didn't get to tell her how mad and hurt I was about her leaving without telling us.

Not long after Mom's visit, my dad got married to Kathleen and moved into the rent house behind MaMa. Soon they moved to a larger place where Jeanne Kay was born. A few months after her birth, my dad talked with MaMa and Granddad about us. They all decided we should go live with him and Kathleen. MaMa said I needed his strong discipline.

Barbie was happy about the move, but I couldn't help resenting Kathleen. I knew she didn't like me for spying on them, and it just didn't seem right for somebody that young to tell me what to do. She was more like a bossy older sister. I found ways to spend most of the time at MaMa's.

I felt lucky when my dad told me and Barbie that Longview Fibre was transferring him to Oakland. He said we would stay with MaMa until he got settled there. That was the last he said about living with him. I really didn't care, because I was more comfortable at MaMa's.

Soon after Daddy and Kathleen moved to Oakland, Barbie went to live across the river in Kelso with Aunt Hazel and Uncle Cliff. They told me she was going to live with them to baby-sit Joyce, their new baby, but I knew it was because Barbie wanted to live better. MaMa and Granddad were poor, and Barbie wanted to have nice clothes. I was jealous and hurt that they didn't offer to have me live with them.

I felt abandoned all over again when Barbie left. She was the last link with my real family. Oh, Hazel and Cliff brought her over on Sunday morning to go to church with me and MaMa. And I saw her around town with her good clothes, and we went to movies together; but it wasn't the same. We were drifting apart.

When I turned twelve, my grandparents suddenly seemed so old-fashioned. They didn't want me to do anything that was fun. I had to sneak out to go to the school dances. They nagged me when I talked to a girl on the phone. "You're too young for that," MaMa told me.

I knew Hazel and Cliff were more up-to-date than MaMa and Granddad. How I wanted to live with them, but I didn't dare ask. I knew they didn't have room for me, and it would have been disloyal to MaMa and Granddad.

The months went by, and I never heard from my mom. I asked MaMa what had happened to her. All she knew was that my mom was still in Spokane. She never wrote. She never called. Two years went by without any contact with her. Then one day, out of the blue, she showed up at my junior high. I couldn't believe it when my teacher told me she was out in the hall.

As I walked out to see Mom, I was mad and happy at the same time. She grabbed me the minute I came through the door. "Hi, Donnie," she said, hugging me real tight.

I let my arms hang straight. She looked puzzled, hurt. I moved away from her. "How could you do that to us?" I sulked.

"What do you mean?"

"Leaving me and Barbie."

"Honey, I am sorry," she pleaded. "I hated to do it that way. But there were so many bad memories in that house."

"Why didn't you at least tell us you were leaving?"

"I'm sorry. I really am. But that's in the past now. The principal said you could have the day off. We'll get Barbie and go to that hamburger place you like so much."

"OK," I said, still trying to sulk but too excited to be convincing. "I'm hungry."

Barbie was so excited when her teacher told her Mom was there. She ran out in the hall and hugged her before she could say a word. In an instant she forgave all. I thought it was pretty hypocritical after all the bad things she said about Mom for leaving us.

Abandoned

We went to the same hamburger place where my mom had asked me to be the man of the house. Then we went out to the lake. It was fun to be with Mom again. She was smiling and joking and hugging us and telling us how much she had missed us.

Walking by the lake, I told her I didn't want to live with MaMa and Granddad anymore. "They're too old-fashioned," I said. "I want to come live with you."

A look of panic froze on her face. "You can't right now," she replied nervously. Then she told us the good news. "Kelly and I will be moving to Kelso to work in the Safeway store. He's going to be the manager," she added proudly. "And he'll be head of the union there, too." She seemed happier than I had ever seen her.

"What about me?" I asked. "Barbie's got it good at Aunt Hazel's. But I don't have any decent clothes. And MaMa's house is so ugly and rundown."

"When we get back to Kelso, I'll see if you can come live with me."

"Promise?"

"I promise," she said firmly. I believed her.

Mom and Kelly stopped by MaMa's to see me when they first came to live in Kelso. Kelly was a big man, towering over me. Mom thought he was well built, but he looked fat to me, with his flabby beer belly. I didn't think he was particularly good-looking, although Mom did. His medium blond hair was already thinning and receding a bit.

Kelly had a big, broad smile and bright white teeth. He was really friendly, asking me how I was doing in school and what my favorite sports were. I thought he liked me. But he and Mom left without saying one word about me living with them. I was so disappointed I cried myself to sleep.

A few weeks later Mom and Kelly came by again. It was on a Sunday afternoon and Barbie was there for the day. MaMa invited them in to have a cup of coffee.

"We can't stay long," Kelly said, as they sat around the kitchen table. "We just came by to get a radio."

"What radio?" Granddad asked, looking him in the eye.

"The one the kids took from Ruth's house," Kelly replied.

"I think you've done enough harm to these children," Granddad snapped.

"This is not fair," MaMa exclaimed. "At least leave the radio for them to listen to. They don't have anything else."

"It belongs to Ruth, and I think she should have it," Kelly insisted.

Breaking Crime's Vicious Cycle

Mom stood up. "Kelly," she said. "Let's just leave. I'll manage."

Kelly stood up beside her. "That's your radio, Ruth," he insisted, "and you're going to get it."

"Donnie," Granddad told me slowly and quietly, his voice quivering. "I want you to go in that bedroom and get my gun and the bullets." I had never seen him that upset.

With great excitement, I went to get Granddad's .32 silver-plated pistol. Facing Kelly, he slowly and deliberately put the bullets in the gun chamber. "I want you to get out of here," he said, pointing the gun at Kelly's fat belly.

The color drained from Kelly's face. His big lips turned blue. "OK, OK," he said nervously, turning toward the door. Mom followed close behind with her head down.

"No," Granddad called to them. "Wait a minute."

Kelly and Mom turned around, their eyes wide with fright.

"You take the radio with you," he said, unplugging the cord from the wall socket, "and don't ever come back here."

"No, that's all right," Kelly said. "We'll manage."

"I insist," Granddad said, still holding the gun.

I watched sadly as Mom and Kelly left with the radio.

As long as I was at MaMa's Kelly never came there again. And, for a long time, he held it against me because I so enthusiastically got the gun.

Since Barbie lived in Kelso, she saw Mom and Kelly all the time. When we went to movies together she talked about seeing them, going over to their house to eat, and Mom buying her clothes. She told me Kelly was pretty nice. Hazel and Cliff and Mom and Kelly got together for drinks at the Moose Club. Everybody was getting together in Kelso, and I was stuck in Longview. I didn't even know where Mom and Kelly lived. I felt left out.

One Saturday afternoon, me and a friend went to the movies in Kelso. After the movie, we went to the Safeway store to buy a coke and a candy bar. While my friend waited at the front of the store, I went back to the meat department where Mom was behind the counter wrapping meat.

"Hi, Mom. How you doing?" I said, smiling.

"Hi, Donnie," she said with a surprised look on her face."What're you doing here?"

"Me and Andy came over here to go to the movies."

"Oh," she said.

"I want to come and see you."

"Come on over," she said pleasantly. "I'll fix you supper."

Abandoned

"I don't know where you live."

She wrote down the address on a piece of paper and handed it to me. "It's on the bus route," she explained.

"I'm coming real soon."

"I'll look for you," she replied, smiling broadly.

The next Tuesday evening I took the bus to Kelso. MaMa said it was too late to go, but I told her I would be OK. It was beginning to rain when I got off the bus across the street from my mom's house. As I walked up the sidewalk in front of the house, I started feeling nervous about how Kelly would act toward me. So, before I knocked, I found a big stick and put it beside the front door. I kind of hoped he would act bad. That way I would have an excuse to hit him. I was relieved when Mom answered the door. She looked shocked, though. I opened the screen door to go in, but she didn't move.

"What are you doing over here in the rain?" she asked impatiently.

"You told me to come see you."

"I didn't mean this late."

"What's the matter?" Kelly asked, pulling the door open wider. When he saw me, he got a mean look on his face.

"What are you doing here?" he asked sternly.

"None of your business," I sneered.

"If you're going to act like this, come to see your mom when I'm not here."

I reached over and picked up the big stick and held it by my side. "If you get smart with me, I'll hit you," I threatened, raising the stick.

"Go on," he said, holding his fist in front of my face. "Get out of here! Don't come back until you can act decent."

I stood in place, defiantly staring up at Kelly.

"You better go on," he warned, then shut the door in my face.

I dropped the stick and began pounding furiously on the door with both hands. I almost fell inside when Mom opened the door. "Go on, Donnie," she said, her voice cracking. "I'll see you later."

"No," I insisted angrily. "I'm not leaving 'til you fix me a peanut butter and jelly sandwich." I have no idea why I said that. It wasn't my favorite kind of sandwich.

Mom didn't say anything. She just gave me a blank stare, shut the door, and turned off the living room light.

I jumped to the ground and walked to the big tree in the front yard, so I wouldn't get wet. I sat there sulking, fighting back the tears. In a few minutes, the light came back on. Mom opened the door.

"Donnie," she called.

I walked slowly to the door.

"Here's the sandwich. I'll give it to you, but I want you to promise to go to MaMa's and Granddad's right now."

"Yeah, I'll leave," I said with a smirk. I took the sandwich, put it in my jacket pocket, and dejectedly walked down the steps. The rain had let up to a fine mist as I crossed the street to the bus stop. I didn't have to choke back the tears anymore. I was too hurt to cry. *I'm not going back to see her no more*, I vowed.

Gradually, I began to draw away from the entire Dennis clan, even MaMa and Granddad. Somewhere between twelve and fourteen I made a conscious decision that I was through with MaMa's brand of religion. I didn't like reading the Bible or memorizing Scripture anymore. My church friends suddenly bored me. I went to church less and less. When I started running around with some of the fast kids at school, my friends at church quit calling me on the phone. They didn't come over to MaMa's, either. We didn't have much in common.

My new friends were more interested in girls than sports, so I dropped the sports. Most of them were older than me and had cars. Andy Reed became my best friend. He had a reputation for being a ladies' man. He was good-looking and could really sing. The kids at school thought he sang like Frank Sinatra. His parents went to church, but he didn't go much.

Andy took me to the first party where drinks were served. I had sneaked sips of beer from my dad's supply and at Uncle Cliff's house, but I had never drunk hard liquor. Four of us—Andy, Henry, Jack, and Lonnie—decided to leave the main party and have our own separate party. We got a bottle of vodka and went next door to a house under construction. We sat on the rafters and downed the vodka straight from the bottle, chasing it with grapefruit juice. I got happier and happier. We laughed and laughed. I was having a great time.

All of a sudden, I started crying. The other guys laughed and asked me why I was crying. "I don't know," I cried, tears flowing down my cheeks.

I guess I was crying because I never dreamed I would do that. I thought of myself as good person. All my friends went to church. I played in the church leagues. I loved to memorize Scripture. In fact, I got a prize in Vacation Bible School for memorizing the most verses. At that moment, all the good was passing away. I felt dirty. I didn't respect myself. I knew my old friends didn't want to be a part of what I was becoming. I felt abandoned once more.

The sadness and shame passed as quickly as it began. I liked the new life of parties and good-looking girls. I knew girls were attracted

Abandoned

to me. I saw my good looks as a tool to gain acceptance. I went to parties with jocks and cheerleaders—the most popular kids in school.

The more I went to parties the more old-fashioned MaMa and Granddad became and the more I withdrew from my family. I still saw Barbie most weekends, but she didn't understand me too well either. I had started seeing Kelly and Mom some, but they really just tolerated me. My dad was in California, and I never saw him. The kids at church were afraid to be around me because of my wild ways. The parties were the one place I fit in, and it was a great place to fit in!

One school night I stayed out after MaMa and Granddad's ten o'clock curfew. I had been drinking beer with my buddies. When MaMa met me at the door, I knew she could smell the beer. "I guess you've been with Andy Reed."

"Sure," I admitted proudly. "He's a cool guy."

"You better quit running around with him. He's not a good boy."

"How do you know that?" I asked.

"His parents can't do anything with him. He never goes to church. And he's taking you away from church."

Me and Andy compared notes. His parents said the same thing to him about me. We had a good laugh about that.

Together, me and Andy developed a lot of the same interests. Both of us liked to skip school and drink beer. On one of our excursions from school, we decided to go to Portland. We met two girls at a basketball game and went home with them. When the girl's parents told us it was time for us to go home, we stayed in a park nearby. The next day we stood on a street corner downtown asking people for money. We got enough to buy gas to drive back home.

Andy's parents were out of their minds with worry. MaMa and Granddad were all distraught, too.

"Where have you been?" MaMa implored when I came strolling through the door with a big smile on my face.

"We just went to Portland," I replied lightheartedly.

"Without telling anybody?"

"Yeah, without telling anybody," I chuckled. "What's the matter with that? Me and Andy are in high school now."

"You're not as big as you think," Granddad snapped. "You're worrying MaMa and me to death. I'm going to call your dad. You don't care how much you hurt anybody."

"Go ahead and call him," I sneered.

Granddad called Daddy the next day. He told Granddad that I

could come and live with him and Kathleen. The next day Kathleen came to Longview on the bus to get me. She acted real nice to me and told me she thought I would like Oakland. She seemed sincere. I thought we might get along OK.

I wasn't sad as I waved good-bye to MaMa and Granddad. I hated that they looked so sad and that I was leaving my friends. But I was excited about going to live in California. All my friends in Longview thought California was the place where really cool kids lived.

I looked forward to a fresh start.

6

A Fresh Start

As I remember, it was late summer when I went to live with Dad and Kathleen in Oakland. They rented an apartment in the Ninety-eighth Street projects. With both of them working at good jobs I was surprised they didn't live in a better place.

Living with Dad, Kathleen, Jeanne Kay, and Patti was more like being a family. There was a lot of love between Dad and Kathleen. I felt good about that. *Maybe this will work out OK,* I thought. *I can get a fresh start here, get back to studying, and try to slow down my wild pace of living.*

Soon after I arrived in Oakland, I enrolled as a sophomore at Castlemont High. I should have been a junior; but I had skipped school so much, I didn't have enough credits.

Castlemont was a jungle compared to R. A. Long. The tough guys—black and white—taunted me, saying things like "Pretty boy, are you tough or what?" Everywhere I looked, guys had intense, hateful looks plastered on their faces. It was like nothing I had ever experienced. The school scared me to death.

I made it OK through the first class. But when I came out, a bunch of black dudes were standing in the hall and wouldn't let me by. I walked the other way. I didn't want to get in trouble. I was determined to do good in school.

At lunch two Mexicans asked me my name and where I was from. "Don Dennis. Longview, Washington," I told them

"Longview?" one questioned. "Where the h— is that?" I couldn't believe the whole world didn't know about Longview.

Coming from a school where I knew everybody to a school of strangers was overwhelming. Everybody talked different, looked different, dressed different. At R. A. Long High, I had seen one black guy. He was the hero of the football, track, and baseball teams. In Oakland it was fifty-fifty—half black and half everything else—Italians, Portuguese, Mexicans, Anglos.

The girls were the same, though. There were many gorgeous ones, and they liked me! After a few days, Annie, a beautiful Portuguese girl with big brown eyes, came up to me after class. "Don," she said. "Margie Lopez likes you."

"Who's Margie Lopez?" I asked.

"She's the girl standing over by the lockers."

The girl she pointed out had to be the best looking fifteen-year-old in the whole school. She was as pretty as a Hawaiian hula dancer, which was my idea of a really gorgeous girl. I could not believe I was so lucky. At that moment, I couldn't get up the courage to go talk to her, but it was enough to know that I appealed to her.

On Monday of the second week, a guy named Jimmy Di Matteo came up to me at an eating place across the street from school. I was flattered that he would talk to a newcomer like me, because everyone looked up to him.

Jimmy introduced me to a table full of friends. They were all smoking and asked me if I wanted to join them. I didn't know how to smoke then, but I knew that everybody who was anybody smoked. So I learned how. Before we went back to class, they asked me if I'd like to go to the movies with them on Saturday. I jumped at the chance.

Man, I felt like a million bucks! I mean, it was too good to be true. These guys were exciting. Jimmy even had a car. They all dressed in real slick, pegged pants, leather jackets, stomper shoes. Their hair was longer than mine and looked real cool to me. They combed it into a ducktail in the back and spent a lot of time making sure it was perfect. I swore I'd have my hair just like that. I desperately wanted a leather jacket, too.

During the week, our family was fairly normal. But, when the weekend came, a drinking spree started, along with the Friday-night fights. My dad was still vicious when he got drunk. There was one big difference, though. Kathleen stood up to him. She was pretty, but she was one tough lady. She could hold her own. Too, she was young, and she let him know she would go out with other men if he didn't treat her right. Sometimes, she would get mad at him and take off. He would go looking for her and eventually bring her back home. I got a certain satisfaction out of seeing him squirm, since he had put my mom through so much agony.

The fights didn't bother me like they did before. I didn't really care what my dad and Kathleen did to each other as long as I could come and go with my friends as I pleased.

On weekends I started staying over at Jimmy's a lot. His mom and dad were like parents to me. Mrs. D. always invited me for supper when I went over there. She introduced me to delicious, homemade Italian food—ravioli, spaghetti, pastries. Mr. D. made me feel right at home, too. I told them Dad and Kathleen didn't make much of a home. Even when I exaggerated things, they believed me.

The Di Matteos yelled at each other, and it scared me at first. I thought they would end up fighting like my mom and dad did. But they yelled a while and then kissed and made up. Jimmy laughed about them and said it was the only way they could communicate.

Jimmy was my contact for making cool friends. In a time when marijuana wasn't plentiful, he and his friend, Kenny, knew where to get it. We prepared the weed for smoking in Jimmy's basement. One time Mrs. D. caught us with a lid spread out on a card table. She was horrified.

"How can you do this?" Mrs. D. screamed at Jimmy, flipping over the card table and pushing him around. "That stuff will kill you." She threw the weed in the garbage. Jimmy told me not to worry, that his mom would get over it. Sure enough, they were hugging and kissing in ten minutes.

After school and on weekends when I wasn't baby-sitting, I hung out with Jimmy and Kenny at a pool hall on Seventy-third Avenue. The manager let us drink beer, even though we were under age. We went into the alley behind the pool hall to smoke marijuana. I liked how it made me feel. After a couple of drags, my troubles faded away.

Fighting for your friends was a way to be admired and respected. Jimmy taught me some street-fighting moves. "The first thing you do," he told me "is to cop the first Sunday." That meant you hit the dude before he hit you.

"When you see you're going to get in a fight," Jimmy explained, "you give the dude the evil eye. Then you say, 'What are you hocking me for?' and invite him outside. You let him go through the door first, then you hit him before he gets out the door."

That was the fighting strategy for the Circle Gang me and Jimmy organized. The idea for the gang came from *Amboy Dukes*, a book about street gangs. I admired the hero of that book and wanted a gang just like his. There were eight in our gang—Jimmy, Chuck, James, Artie, Johnny, Kenny, Tommy, and me. Half of us were Anglo; the other half were Mexican, Italian, or Portuguese.

The standard way to "plan" a fight was to "choose" someone or be chosen. Choosing meant a kid would stick his finger in your chest and say, "Man, I choose you. Meet me at Elmhurst Park after school." The first time it happened I didn't know what the guy meant. I had to ask someone.

Before that first fight, I was torn up inside with fear. For sure, I was afraid of being hurt, but, more than that, I was afraid of looking bad in front of new friends. I couldn't let anyone think I was chicken; so I looked the guy up during the afternoon and told him I would definitely meet him at Elmhurst Park. It was on Ninety-eighth Street, a ghetto area.

Jimmy and a few other friends went with me to the fight. In all, about fifty kids showed up. With the crowd circling us, the big guy moved toward me. Using our gang's strategy, I hit him before he could hit me. He went down. I waited until he got about halfway up and hit him again. He grabbed me and tried to wrestle me down. I was about halfway down when this guy named Joe threw a coat over my head. While I frantically tried to get the coat off, the guy kept hitting me. Somehow I fell on him and held him down. I started hitting him as hard as I could. I liked the feeling of pounding him.

When we had just about beat each other to a pulp, some guys jumped in and broke up the fight. All the guys in my gang said I was the best. I was on top of the world! After that, I got in one fight after another. I had a "rep" all over Oakland for being a fighter. That was a special delight to me and my friends.

The Circle Gang got together almost every day. If we felt like going to school, we went. If we felt like skipping school, we found some fun thing to do. We smoked weed and played chicken in cars. Going at high speed, one guy climbed out the car window, got on the hood, slid across the roof to the trunk, and climbed in the other window. It was scary, especially when the driver turned a corner at high speed when you were on top of the car.

Plenty of girls were on the streets. They ran in gangs and met us at the pool hall on Seventy-third. Like us, they went to school when they felt like it. A girl named Eleanor was a member of the girls' gang we teamed up with. She was a real knockout, with sparkling, dark brown eyes and hair, a terrific figure, and a happy, carefree disposition. Her beauty came from her racial mix. Born in Hawaii, she was part Portuguese, part Spanish, part Indian, part Chinese, part everything. She was like no girl I had ever known in the little town of Longview. She knew how to dress and how to make herself look beautiful. It was instant attraction. She became my steady girlfriend right away.

A Fresh Start

When prom time came, Mrs. D. told Jimmy she would buy him a suit if he wanted to go. He jumped at the chance and got the suit made at a tailor shop on Ninety-eighth Avenue. I went with him when he told the tailor what he wanted. The suit he chose was a one-button roll, baby blue sharkskin. The tailor had one on display that was a little different from Jimmy's but was made out of the same material. I loved it.

"How much is that?" I asked the tailor.

"Sixty bucks; same as Jimmy's," he replied.

"I'm gonna see if I can get it. Don't sell it."

"Don't worry," he told me. "If I sell it, I can make another one."

That night at the supper table, I got up the nerve to ask my dad if he would buy me a suit.

"What do you want a suit for?" he asked.

"To go to the prom."

"The prom?" he questioned. "You're just a sophomore."

"I know, but Jimmy will help me get in."

"Who are you going with?"

"Eleanor."

"Eleanor? Who's she?"

"She's a pretty girl I met at school."

He smiled, then asked, "How much will the suit cost?"

"Just sixty bucks. I've got enough to buy the shoes."

"Just sixty bucks!" he exclaimed, stretching out the *just*. "I don't have that kind of money."

"Sixty dollars is way too much," Kathleen chimed in angrily. "That's extravagant. Don, you don't go to school that much, anyway. So, why do you want to go to the dance?"

"Forget it!" I snapped and stormed to my bedroom. I stayed in there all evening, sulking. *They spend all that money for booze*, I thought. *But they don't have any for me.*

I told Jimmy what happened. He sympathized with me but didn't know what I could do about it. I brooded about the situation, trying to figure out a way to get the money. Saturday night Dad and Kathleen came in drunk. I saw an opportunity. *Let them pass out*, I thought. *Then I'll pick my old man's wallet.*

I waited at least an hour. Then I quietly moved down the hallway to their bedroom and put my ear to the door. I could hear my dad snoring and Kathleen breathing hard. I eased the door open a bit and spotted my dad's pants on the back of a chair. I crawled to the chair, reached up to the pocket of the pants, and took out the wallet. I crawled back out into the hall to the bathroom. I carefully closed the door and turned on the light, then opened the wallet. He had four twenty dollar bills and two ones. I put three of the twenties in my pocket, crawled to the bedroom, and put the wallet back in my dad's pants. He was still snoring; Kathleen was still breathing hard.

Back in the bedroom that I shared with my stepsister, Jeanne Kay, I hid the three bills way down in my pillow case. Excitement raced through my body. I fell asleep with a smile on my face.

I was jolted awake the next morning by Kathleen standing over my bed. "You no good, lazy—" she screamed, loud enough to hear downtown. "Give us back that money!"

"What money?" I asked, nonchalantly, with a big yawn. "I don't know what you're talking about!"

"Yes, you do," she yelled back, reaching down to shake me by the shoulders. I threw up my hands to push her away.

"You slut!" I yelled. "Keep your hands off of me. You don't have any right to accuse me of taking money."

"Your father doesn't have the guts to whip you or stand up to you anymore. But I'm not afraid of you."

"He doesn't have the guts to stand up to a pig like you, let alone me. You're both pigs and drunks."

"Get out!" she shrieked. "And don't come back."

"Go to hell!" I yelled, jumping to the floor. "I'll stay here until I get tired of it," I sneered. "You don't have no right to tell me to leave. You're the reason my dad was so mean to my mom. You're the one that broke up our home."

Kathleen's mouth flew open. "I am not," she protested, her voice lowering to a strained whisper. "That marriage was over before I came into the picture."

By now my dad was standing in the bedroom door. "That's enough," he said firmly, directing his words to me. "Donnie, I don't want to hear any more of that kind of talk," he warned with a nervous shakiness in his voice.

"Forget about the money, Honey," he said, trying to be calm. "It's not worth all this fuss." He looked so helpless, like a man who couldn't do anything about a big mistake. I loved him and hated him at the same time.

The scene confirmed what I had gradually come to suspect. My dad blamed himself for my behavior. I had him right where I wanted him. If he was too ashamed to whip me for stealing from him, I was free to do as I pleased. From that point on, I knew I had the advantage.

Monday morning I put the money inside my sock. After school, Jimmy went with me to order the suit. "Where'd you get the money?" he asked on the way to the tailor shop.

"I took it out of my dad's wallet," I bragged.

"Really! Does he know you took it?"

"Sure, but he can't do anything about it."

"I wouldn't dare do that," Jimmy said, obviously shocked. "But my dad's not like yours," he added quickly. "They never get you any clothes. They deserve to get ripped off."

Mrs. D. agreed with Jimmy that my folks deserved what I did. She even let me bring the suit over there when I picked it up from the tailor. And, to complete my outfit for the prom, she bought me a white shirt and a tie.

On prom night I changed my clothes at Jimmy's. His mom and dad teased me about how handsome I was. Then we went to pick up Angie and Eleanor in the white Caddy that Jimmy's boss let him use. Eleanor wore a baby blue formal that almost matched my suit. She was beautiful! I was so proud.

Life was really great. I was going steady with the most beautiful girl in town. I had a reputation for being a good fighter. I had lots of cool friends. I could come and go as I pleased. What more could anyone ask for?

In the summer my dad got me a job at the Oakland branch of Longview Fibre. I bought some clothes, spent plenty on marijuana and beer at the pool hall, and took Eleanor to the movies and other places.

Several nights a week, some of us in the Circle Gang roamed around town looking for excitement. One hot August night, me and Tommy and Chuck went to the T & D Theater in downtown Oakland. We picked up some girls inside the theater, then went walking down the street, laughing and cutting up. A carload of older dudes, between nineteen and twenty-one, came cruising by. When they saw us, they slowed down and gave us long, hard looks. We glared back defiantly.

"_____ you," one of the dudes yelled, throwing a bird at the same time. All the other dudes followed his lead, throwing birds from every window. We did the same thing to them.

"You punks," they yelled.

"You sissies," we sneered back.

Breaking Crime's Vicious Cycle

After exchanging more foul remarks, they took off. "I guess we look too tough," Tommy laughed.

"Yeah," me and Chuck agreed.

The girls said we better get out of there. As we assured them we could match anybody, the car suddenly came by again.

"Stop the car," I yelled, waving my arms wildly.

"Yeah!" Kenny exclaimed. "Stop the car!"

The driver slowed down. The girls moved back. "I'll get on the driver's side," I told Tommy and Chuck. "You guys go to the other side. Don't let them get out of the car."

We bounded toward the car and took our positions as the driver squealed to a stop. I punched the driver through the opened window, grabbed his hair, and hit his head against the door. Tommy and Chuck pounced on two other guys as they pushed their way out of the car. The driver got loose of me and pushed the door open. We scuffled and fell to the ground. I landed on top, but his friend pulled me off.

A dude in the backseat flew out of the car with a knife aimed at me. He cut me on the hand, then went for my body, cutting me first under the right arm and next under the left armpit. I felt the warm blood gushing out.

"I'm cut! I'm cut!" I screamed, staggering to the curb.

"Let's get out of here," the knife-wielding dude yelled. The six of them piled in the car and took off.

Chuck and Tommy frantically rushed over to me. "Oh, my God," Chuck yelled. "You're hurt bad."

"Call me an ambulance," I moaned. "I'm bleeding to death."

Tommy tried to flag down a car, but nobody would stop. "____ you," he defiantly yelled at each car that drove by.

"The substation's two blocks down," Chuck suggested nervously. "Let's go down there to get help."

With Tommy and Chuck supporting me, I walked the two blocks, barely able to stand up. My pants were soaked with blood by the time they got me to the station.

"We need to get him to the hospital," Chuck yelled frantically to the cop on duty.

A police officer calmly guided me to a chair and told me he would call an ambulance. I nervously rocked back and forth in the chair, getting weaker and weaker by the moment. Blood dripped to the floor around the chair.

"Why don't you take him in the cop car?" Chuck questioned. "You're going to let him die."

A Fresh Start

"It'll be here in a minute," the officer assured us. "Don't worry. He'll be OK."

When the ambulance got there, Tommy and Chuck got in after me. They kept telling the driver to hurry up. "You don't give a ＿＿＿ about him," Tommy yelled. "Hurry up!"

I reached up to squeeze Tommy's mouth to make him stop cussing. I couldn't close my hand. "I'm gonna die," I moaned. "I know I'm gonna die."

All of a sudden I felt like I was going down into a subway, a really dark tunnel. At the end of the tunnel was a bright light. The light surrounded and covered me completely. That made me feel real good. I wanted to go through the light to see what was on the other side. The next thing I knew I was on the operating table in the emergency room at the county hospital. I had tubes coming from all parts of my body. Needles were in both of my arms. A nurse was shaving my chest. She said I had been there for four hours. I fell asleep again while she was still talking to me.

"Good morning," someone called to me.

I turned my head to see a skinny little black man sitting on the bed next to me, flashing a broad smile. He looked about fifty.

"Good morning," I said weakly.

"You've been sleeping a long time," the man said cheerily. "How do you feel?"

"I feel all right, I guess. I'm just a little sleepy."

I looked down at my body. My arm was in a sling. I was taped all around my stomach.

"Brother, you just about bought the farm," he chuckled.

"Whata you mean?" I questioned.

"You almost died. They didn't think you were going to make it. You had a fourteen-inch cut. That guy cut the muscle under your arm, through the rib cage, and all the way to your lung. You lost a passel of blood."

A Chinese nurse came in with a bedpan. "I don't need no bed pan," I protested. "I feel good enough to get up and go to the bathroom." I was embarrassed to use it.

"I can close the curtains around you," she offered.

"No," I said definitely. "I can go to the bathroom."

"You're weaker than you think," she warned. "They gave you twelve minutes to live when you came in here. They called your folks, but they weren't at home."

"They're never at home," I quipped sarcastically.

"Some little lady was here. Black hair."

"Probably Mrs. D. Where was I at? How did it happen?"

"They said you were in a street fight."

"Oh, yeah, I remember. But I feel OK now. Would you help me up to go to the bathroom?"

Reluctantly, she untied the band holding me in place, eased me out of bed, and helped me into the bathroom. When I came out, she eased me back in bed and tied me down. "You've got to be still now," she said tenderly. "Remember, you almost died."

"OK, I'll be still. I promise," I added, raising my hand like a Boy Scout.

When the nurse went out the door, I turned to the black guy. "Hey, Man, I need a cigarette."

"I'd be happy to give you one, Son; but you can't smoke it here. And you're too weak to go to the lounge."

"How far is it?"

"About halfway down the hall."

"I can make it that far," I said, untying the band with my free hand, then slowly sitting up in bed and hanging my legs down the side. "I'm dying for a smoke."

"No, you can't make it alone," he said in a brotherly tone. "I'll go with you."

I leaned on the black man all the way to the lounge. He was strong for such a little dude. He carefully eased me into a padded chair and then lit the cigarette for me. After I took a couple of drags, everything suddenly went black. The next thing I knew, the little black dude was helping me get back in bed. I didn't try to get up again that day.

Jimmy, Eleanor, Mrs. D., and all my friends came to see me the next day. Mrs. D. brought me some of her delicious homemade minestrone soup. I downed it while Jimmy and Tommy talked about what they were going to do to the dudes who cut me up. I made them promise to wait until I got out.

I was in the hospital two weeks. Mrs. D. came to see me almost every day. Dad and Kathleen came once, acting distraught and worried about me. My dad told Mrs. D. that they had been working long hours.

The hospital called Dad and Kathleen when I was ready to be released. Dad started in on me right away. "You're really lucky," he said. "You could've been killed."

"I know it," I agreed impatiently.

"If you keep going the way you are, you won't see your twenty-first birthday."

A Fresh Start

"I know it, Daddy," I said impatiently. "I'm going to slow down." I didn't mean a word I said.

It was Friday. My folks had planned to go out if I didn't mind. "Sure," I said. "But, since you're not gonna be here, could I have some friends over?" They said that would be OK.

All the gang came over—Jimmy, Eleanor, Tommy, Adrienne, and everybody in the Circle Gang. They brought wine, beer, potato chips, sandwich meat, and some marijuana. Over and over, I opened my shirt to let everybody see the bandaged wound. They all made me feel like a hero. I was wounded, but I had fought and survived! I was a knife fighter now.

Annie, a cute girl with big brown eyes and a curvy figure, went into the kitchen to fix sandwiches. I followed her in there just to shoot the breeze and to help her find the stuff to fix the sandwiches. We were laughing and talking when, suddenly, Eleanor was staring me in the face. "I stuck by you in the hospital," she shouted, "and here you are trying to make out with Annie."

"Eleanor, you're crazy," I protested. "I'm just helping her find stuff to make sandwiches."

"I am not crazy, you two-timer," Eleanor yelled.

"He wasn't doing anything, Eleanor," Annie insisted.

"Yeah," Eleanor sneered, impulsively grabbing the tape on my stomach and pulling it back. Blood started oozing out of the open wound.

"Oh, I'm sorry,"she gasped, moving back from me.

I angrily reached down with my free hand and pulled the oven door open. I then grabbed Eleanor's long hair, pulled her to the stove, and pushed her face down on the oven door. "Turn the gas on, Annie!" I yelled. "Turn the gas on!"

Annie didn't hesitate. She was mad at Eleanor, too. With Eleanor screaming at the top of her lungs, I pushed her head on in. Jimmy and Chuck rushed into the kitchen. "Don, you're crazy; stop that, Man," Jimmy yelled, pulling me away from Eleanor.

"You were going to kill me," Eleanor sobbed uncontrollably.

"I wouldn't have done it," I chuckled. "I was just mad."

I moved toward the cabinet, reaching out to hug her.

"Yeah," she said, shoving me away.

Eleanor was so shaken by the experience that she asked Jimmy to take her home. We never went together again.

I didn't admit it to anyone, but I, too, was shocked by what I did to Eleanor. Dropping off to sleep that night I resolved to slow down. I was going to work at controlling my temper. I wasn't going to get in fights so much.

When school started, Jimmy landed an after-school job where he had worked during the summer. He got serious about doing good in school. He said it was his last year, and he wanted to go out with a better record. It was different for me. I wasn't in the mood to break the vacation pattern. Right away, I was getting straight F's, except for history.

James of the Circle Gang lived near me in the Ninety-eighth Street projects. His parents were never home, so he came over to my house a lot. One Saturday night he came over while I was baby-sitting. Barbie was there, too. She had come to stay with us for the Christmas vacation. James told me he was hungry; so we looked for some food in the house. There was one egg in the refrigerator, no milk, nothing but one egg. "They just don't think about getting food for us kids," I sneered. "They never forget to get themselves beer, though. You'd think they'd be better in the Christmas season, wouldn't you, James?"

"Yeah, you sure would," he agreed.

"I tell you what, let's go get some pies out of that bakery we go by on the way home from school," I suggested.

"Yeah," James agreed enthusiastically. "Let's get 'em."

After prying off the lock with a crowbar from Jimmy's house, we slipped into the pitch-dark building. Once we found the light, we headed for the front showcase. I bagged three mincemeat and a couple of pumpkin pies. James headed for the milk case and took out a quart of chocolate and two quarts of white milk. On our way out I stopped at a desk. I put my sack down and started going through the drawers.

"Come on, Don," James whispered frantically. "Let's get out of here. They'll catch us."

"Hang on for a minute, James. We need some money."

In the bottom drawer, I felt a bag way in the back. I pulled it out and opened it up. It was full of dimes! I quickly shoved the bag in my coat pocket, picked up my sack, and headed for the back door. James followed close behind.

"Where have you been?" Barbie asked nervously when we came through the front door, laughing. "I was scared to death. Don't you leave me here alone again, Don!" she exclaimed.

"We just got something to eat, Barbie. You'd like something to eat, wouldn't you?"

"I suppose," she replied angrily, refusing to be teased out of her feelings. "I'm not going to come to see you at Christmas again, if you treat me like this."

Me and James cut two pieces of the pie apiece, got a big glass of milk, and went to my bedroom. "We'll be out in a minute," I called to Barbie. "Don't come back here. Get you a piece of pie, if you want to."

We started counting the dimes, arranging them in stacks of ten. We ended up with forty full stacks.

"Why don't I go down to the grocery store and find a wino to buy us some wine," James suggested.

"Good idea!" I exclaimed. "I'd love to have some."

When James got back with three bottles of wine, we drank some more milk and shared two pies. Then we started in on the wine. We downed it all. By the time we were through, I was deathly sick. I threw up at least four times.

In bed that night, still sick as a dog, I heard a train whistle. I thought about MaMa and Granddad, and my friends, and the Thanksgiving and Christmas get-togethers with all the Dennis clan. Compared to Oakland, life in Longview was simple and peaceful and happy. *Why stay in Oakland?* I wondered. *Me and Eleanor are broken up. I don't go to school half the time. Dad and Kathleen drink all the time. It's one fight after another with Kathleen.*

Life was one big zero. For the first time in five years, I prayed. "Lord Jesus," I whispered, "please let me go back to Longview to my MaMa and Granddad." Over and over, I begged God. I didn't hear Him answer one way or the other.

In the spring, MaMa and Granddad went on a trip to Tennessee. They came by Oakland on the way back to Longview. When I showed them the scars from the knife fight, they were shocked beyond description.

During the visit MaMa and Granddad asked how things were going in school. "I'm not going to school much," I told them. "I'm flunking everything. I just don't like it here."

I begged them to take me back to Longview. "It's no good for me here," I said. "I can't get along with Kathleen. They're drinking all the time. They don't have any time for me. They won't buy me any clothes."

"If we take you to live with us, will you get back in school?" MaMa asked.

"Sure," I promised.

"You've go to quit drinking," Granddad told me.

"And you've go to get back in church," MaMa added.

Breaking Crime's Vicious Cycle

"Yeah, I've got to quit drinking; I've got to get back in church," I agreed.

The three of us talked with Daddy about me going back to Longview. "It's up to Don," he told MaMa and Granddad. Then he turned to me. "You can go with them if you want to, Don. I'll buy the ticket."

"I think I'd be happier in Longview," I said confidently.

We were on the bus to Longview the next day. I daydreamed all the way. I thought about seeing Barbie more. I thought about R. A. Long High, beautiful Lake Sacajawea, old friends. In my mind, Longview was a symbol of the period in my life when I was a good boy. I longed for a fresh start, a chance to reclaim my early innocence.

7

Dropping Out

The driver turned off the highway toward Kelso. A surge of anticipation raced through my body as the bus crossed the Cowlitz River
and quickly reached the outskirts of Longview.

The town was beautiful. Flowers were in bloom. Blossoms covered
tree after tree. Lake Sacajawea was breathtaking, with its sky-blue
water. As we passed by, memories flooded in—picnics by the lake,
ball games in the park, walks down the hiking trails with Granddad
as he told stories about the trip from Tennessee. I smiled, then quickly
turned serious when MaMa looked my way.

Moving slowly toward the bus station, I spotted the YMCA building where I spent hour after hour swimming; playing basketball,
tennis, and Ping-Pong; and drinking cokes with friends. I had lots of
good, decent friends then.

Seeing the theater where I took Barbie reminded me of the time I
lost track of her when I went to sit with my girlfriend, Ruby. Barbie
tattled on me, and my Dad bawled me out good. The post office
hadn't moved, and the flower shop and the bakery and the drugstore
were still there, too. It felt great to be home!

Uncle John was at the station to drive us home. He greeted me as
warmly as he could, given his stern, authoritative nature. He said he
was glad I was back.

The minute we got to MaMa's, I jumped out of the car and rushed
into the house to call up my old buddies. I dialed Andy Reed's
number first. I still knew it by heart.

"You're back!" Andy exclaimed.

"Yeah, I'm back for good."

"Great."

"Can you come over?" I asked.

"I would," he explained, "but I've got a date with Linda Hoskins.
Are you coming to school tomorrow?"

"Yeah. I need to get started back in school right away."

Breaking Crime's Vicious Cycle

"I'll see you then. OK?"

"Sure."

I made four more calls. Everybody acted excited that I was back home, but no one offered to come over.

I was already awake when MaMa called to me the next morning. I woke up thinking about my bad grades at Oakland. And I kept thinking about them while I was getting dressed.

"You need to get started back in school right away," MaMa told me at breakfast.

"Yeah, I do," I agreed quickly.

"Do you want me to go with you to enroll?" she asked.

"No," I replied quickly. "I know what to do, MaMa. Remember? I transferred to Oakland."

"Yes. Donnie," she said impatiently. MaMa had changed, too. I wasn't the little kid who slept on the porch anymore.

I left the house at the right time, but I had no intention of going to school. I wasn't ready to tell the principal about my bad grades in Oakland. I wandered around town all morning, stopping to talk with people I knew. In the afternoon, I stayed out by the lake until time for school to let out. I was at the snack bar across the street from school when the dismissal bell echoed across the neighborhood. Andy and John and a bunch of old friends were there right away.

"Don," John yelled, slapping me on the back. "You're really back. Andy said you were here."

"Yeah, Man, it's really me," I quipped.

Anxious to get a firsthand report on California, they all pounced on me with one question after another.

"What are the California girls like?" Andy asked.

"Really slick," I told him.

"Did you see any movie stars?" Tim asked.

"Not really," I replied. "We lived too far north."

"What did you do for excitement?" John questioned.

"Oh, movies and parties. And I learned how to fight really good," I said, flexing my muscles in my right arm. I told them about the gang fights and how I stomped dudes good and sent them to the hospital. They all forced polite grins. I could almost hear them say, "This guy's a low-life creep." One by one the guys found reasons to be on their way. Only Andy lingered. We went way back as best friends.

By the time I got to MaMa's, I had decided I couldn't go back to that school. Seeing my friends made everything come into focus. While they were all looking forward to graduation, my grades from Oakland were so bad I would have to be a junior all over again. That meant I would have to go to class with younger boys. I couldn't bear the thought.

Still, I wanted to be with my friends. Almost every day I went to school to see them. When I kept talking about drugs and fights, the decent ones started avoiding me. The guys I had played football and basketball with acted like they didn't know me. The nice girls wouldn't look my way.

Like everyone else, my church friends related to me in a different way. *What the hell*, I reasoned. *These people are so square, compared to the super-fast crowd in California. Longview is a jerk town of rednecks and dummies. The big deal here is to land a job at some boring place like Longview Fibre and make paper boxes for thirty years like my dad, get drunk on the weekends, and die in this stupid town. I have bigger plans. I'm good-looking; I'll find me a rich girl and not worry about nothin'.*

When I definitely decided not to go back to school, I looked up Rick, one of my former drinking buddies. He had dropped out of school and was working with his dad building houses. Tall and good-looking, with bright red hair and a contagious smile, Rick had developed the rugged build of one in that line of work.

I borrowed money from Granddad and sneaked a dollar or two from MaMa's purse to go to the movies with Rick and his friends and to buy beer. Rick put me in touch with some swinging girls, and he loaned me money when I couldn't get any from MaMa or Granddad.

MaMa gave up on getting me to church, but she kept trying to get me back in school. "I just don't fit in anywhere," I told her and Granddad. "I don't have any decent clothes. All my friends are graduating, and I'll have to start my junior year over. I can't go to school with young kids."

"If you're not going to school, you need to work," MaMa finally suggested. "You can't sit around here all day."

"How about me getting you a job at Longbell Lumber?" Granddad offered.

"I would like that," I told him. "Find me a job, and I'll go to work." I desperately wanted some money of my own.

Granddad retired from Longbell Lumber early because of a heart condition, but he had kept in touch with work friends. He called the plant foreman and set up an interview for me on Friday. They told me to report for work on Monday. I was out of my mind with excitement. I envisioned all kinds of good things that would happen because of

Breaking Crime's Vicious Cycle

my job—a car, nice clothes, money to party. Life would be great again.

One of Granddad's friends offered to give me a ride to and from work. Everything was in place. Five-thirty Monday morning, I dragged out of bed, sleepy but full of anticipation.

Riding to work that first day was a nostalgic experience. *I grew up on this street,* I mused. *And now I'm growing into a full-fledged man, going to work from this street. This is my first full-time job. It could turn into a job for life. Lots of guys work in those mills all their lives. They have homes and families. Maybe that's my future, too.*

I was kind of nervous inside, as I walked into Longbell. Naturally, I was relieved when the foreman met me just inside the door, extending his hand to greet me. "We're looking forward to you working with us, Don," he said, smiling. "Your granddad says you're a hard worker."

"Thanks," I replied. "I'll try to do my best."

The foreman spent a few minutes telling me about my job, then took me to my work station. As he led me to an oversized band saw in a far corner, there was a flurry of activity. The other workers were hurrying to their work stations to start on the dot of seven. The more zealous ones already had their equipment warming up.

The old man at the band saw had already started working. He didn't move his eyes from the piece of wood he was cutting when me and the foreman walked up. Finally, when the piece of wood dropped into a big box, he shut down the saw, turned around, and greeted the foreman.

"John, this is Don Dennis."

"Hello, Don," the man said pleasantly, extending his hand to greet me. "Glad to have you aboard."

The two of them talked for a few minutes about my responsibilities; then the foreman left. John proceeded to coach me on my job. "Grab a piece of wood from the stack," he said, straining to make himself heard over the piercing sounds of the saws, "and place it on the conveyer belt. Make sure you always have a piece ready for me to cut. When the boxes fill up, call a forklift operator to pick them up."

Man, this is easy! I thought. I just needed to hand John the piece of wood about eighteen inches long and ten inches wide. It was no sweat keeping up with him.

While John operated the saw, he never looked up, and he never said a word. He kept his eyes glued to the saw and to the piece of

Dropping Out

wood I handed him. I kept feeding the pieces of wood to him. He seemed pleased with my efforts.

When I thought several hours had gone by, I yelled to John. He quickly stopped the saw. "What's the problem?" he asked, a trace of impatience evident in his voice.

"Could I go to the restroom?"

"Make it fast," he replied sharply. "We've got a lot of work to do."

"OK. I will. I'll just take a minute," I assured him.

Once inside the restroom, I decided to sneak a quick smoke. Just as I lit up, some old guy walked in. "You better not get caught smoking," he warned. "You're supposed to wait for break time for that."

"When's the break?" I asked.

"Nine," he replied. "They'll blow a whistle."

"What time is it now?"

He took a pocket watch and held it away from his body as far as his arm would reach. "Eight-thirty," he replied.

"Thanks," I said, trying not to reveal my alarm. *Eight-thirty!* I exclaimed silently. I couldn't believe it. Only an hour and a half had gone by.

At nine o'clock sharp the shrill whistle blew. Saws came to a screeching halt all over the plant. Without a word, John turned off the saw and moved toward the lunchroom at a fast pace. I followed close behind.

The lunchroom quickly filled with smoke, as one worker after another lit up. Everyone was yelling and laughing, as they shared stories about the weekend. By the time I got my coffee, the big clock on the wall was 9:05. We were supposed to be back at our stations by 9:10! Just a quick smoke, down the hot coffee, then back to the screaming saws. I kept feeding the pieces of wood to John, one after another. I never got behind. John had no complaints. After what seemed like an eternity, the whistle shrieked again. Lunchtime had arrived. At the sound of the whistle, John immediately switched off the saw and reached for his sack lunch on the shelf behind him. Following his lead, I grabbed the lunch MaMa had made me and headed for the lunchroom. I figured now was the time to get acquainted.

I got a cup of coffee, sat down in a vacant seat, and set my lunch sack on the table in front of me. Before I had time to open the sack, a fifty-year-old man was standing beside me. "Son," he said in a raspy voice.

Breaking Crime's Vicious Cycle

I looked up to greet him. The serious look on his face told me something was wrong.

"You got my chair," he explained with a half smile.

"Sorry," I said quietly, picking up my lunch sack. I walked over to a bench positioned along the outside wall, and selected a place under a window.

That was my first lesson in defining territory. The men offered a friendly greeting to the new kid on the block. None offered his seat. Every workday, each man sat at a certain table in a certain chair to eat his lunch. That was the way it was; no arguments. Those who had no seniority sat along the wall.

The jovial atmosphere helped me adjust to my newcomer status. The men all seemed happy with life. They laughed, cussed, smoked, shared stories. Some played dominoes while they ate. They gladly let me look on and listen. They talked about the union, women, cars, women, sex, and more sex.

At twelve-thirty the shrill whistle blew again. Once more, we all scurried back to our work stations. The afternoon was more of the same, tedious and boring. I thought four o'clock would never come. It helped to daydream about what I was going to do with my first paycheck. I figured I would save most of it and just keep enough to get by on. That way I'd have enough for a car in two or three months.

Picking up my paycheck was like a new beginning. I cashed the eighty-dollar check before I left the plant. It was exhilarating to have money in my pocket. MaMa and Granddad reminded me that I should open a savings account and start saving money. They didn't know I had already decided that it was a smart thing to do.

I called up Rick to brag about the money. He drove right over to pick me up. We were ready to party! I only took twenty dollars with me. I didn't even plan to spend all of that. But I did want to buy some beer for my friends and maybe find a girl to take to the drive-in restaurant. I did a lot of drinking that weekend and had lots of fun.

Early Monday morning it was back to what I considered the most boring job in the world. Curious, I asked John how long he had been working there. "Well," he said proudly, "I guess this makes the twenty-seventh year!"

Twenty-seven years on this job, I thought. *He's got to be kidding me.* "You mean you've been working at Longbell on this same saw for twenty-seven years?" I asked.

"Yep, that's right," he said, chuckling. "Started in 1925. I've been

Dropping Out

driving down the same street to work, sitting in the same spot for nigh on twenty-seven years."

"How do you like the work, John?" I asked.

"Never have really thought about it. It's my job. I guess I don't like it all that much, but it's the only thing I know. The pay isn't big, but the work is steady. It feeds my family and puts a roof over our heads."

Hell, I said to myself. *I'm not going to do that! No way! I'm not staying here to dry up from boredom. I'd rather be dead. I can't take it. The time creeps by; it seems like fifty-hour days, instead of eight.* The conversation tore me up inside. I wanted to quit right then. But, if I quit, I didn't know what else there was to do. I hated wandering around Longview with no money.

At the beginning of my third month on the job, I couldn't stand it any longer. I quit. I didn't give formal notice. I just stopped getting up in the morning.

I could tell MaMa was overcome with worry. Most of the time Granddad just sat in a rocking chair smoking his pipe, looked sad and bewildered. I really cared about my grandparents, but they were so old and so old-fashioned. I knew too much about the fast life to stop. I wanted the parties, the girls, my wild friends. I didn't want to vegetate in the lumber mill.

With no work responsibility, it was drinking every night. When my money ran out, I borrowed from girlfriends and a few bucks from Granddad. I sneaked a little from MaMa's purse.

Just by chance I found a new money source. The winter after I returned to Longview, Aunt Hazel and Uncle Cliff moved back to one of MaMa and Granddad's little run-down rental houses. They rented the house for $18.00 a month, practically nothing, even in 1952. The reason Cliff and Hazel were living in such a little house was because Uncle Cliff was an adventurer. He would move to Alaska to make a lot of money or down to California, even though he had a good job where he was. He was a carpenter, steel worker, and businessman. The guy was able to get a good-paying job wherever he went, but he spent it as fast as he made it. This time he was a manager at the Moose Club.

One night, soon after Hazel and Cliff came back to Longview, I went over to visit with them and Joycie, who was four. While I was there, I snooped around in the bathroom just for something to do. On the bottom shelf of the linen closet I saw bottle after bottle of whiskey lined up. The sight was overwhelming and exciting, but I didn't dare say anything to anyone. MaMa would have been shocked.

94

Breaking Crime's Vicious Cycle

At breakfast my eyes were drawn to the extra set of house keys on a nail by the kitchen window. MaMa kept them for emergencies. The keys triggered an idea. *Why not get some whiskey? They wouldn't miss a bottle or two.*

When MaMa and Granddad went to the grocery store, I carried out my quickly-developed plan. I slipped the key ring off the nail, walked down the alley to Cliff and Hazel's, and opened the back door. I knew they were both at work.

As I reached for a bottle of whiskey on the bottom shelf in the closet, I saw that there was even more whiskey than I had seen the night before. Bottles were lined up on the upper shelf as well. I proceeded to search the whole closet to see what else I could find. Away in the back were more bottles—whiskey, scotch, vodka, gin— all kinds of booze.

Then I hit pay dirt! In the farthest corner of the closet were two clear glass, quart-size bottles filled with shiny objects. I held one of the bottles up to the light. It was filled to the brim with shiny silver dollars.

Where did he get all that money? I wondered. I figured Cliff was either skimming money from the Moose Club, or it was his way of keeping money safe. I really didn't care which. All I cared about was getting my share. I hurriedly stashed about fifteen silver dollars into my pockets. I then took two bottles of whiskey from the top shelf, carefully rearranging the others to take up the space.

I locked the back door and moved at a brisk pace down the alley to MaMa's. I hid the whiskey in the woodshed behind MaMa's and returned the key ring to the nail. "Now I can go out and have some fun," I whispered to myself. I felt great!

Gradually, I fell into a regular weekly routine of dipping into Cliff's money and booze. Between my raids on the cache, the level in the silver-dollar bottle would go down some more. Each week the bottle would be full again and sometimes another bottle started. I noted the rise and fall on my frequent visits to their house. I made my move at the high tide. My conscience didn't bother me. I figured Cliff was skimming from the Moose Club, and I was skimming from him. No one was hurt, except the Moose, and they could afford it.

Not long after I left Oakland, Dad and Kathleen moved back to Longview to the house on Ohio Street. In a short time, my dad was transferred to Yakima, Washington. I used some of the silver dollars to buy a bus ticket to visit them there. Absence had made the heart grow fonder. They seemed happy to see me. I stayed with them for a

Dropping Out

couple of days, and we all got along fine. It was fun to see Jeanne Kay and Patti.

With my money and liquor source so steady, I was drinking more and more. I had long since forgotten about marijuana, because there was none to be found in Longview. When I finished what I brought back from Oakland, that was it. Anyway I liked booze a whole lot better than weed.

One Friday night Rick called me when he was baby-sitting with a girlfriend. "Hey, Don, I'm over here at the Sherricks helping Marsha baby-sit. Why don't you come over and drink some beer with us? I've got a couple of six packs."

"Just you and Marsha?" I asked.

"Marsha's got a friend coming over. We can have a party!"

"Sure thing. Where's she live?" I asked.

"It's the house that's hooked on to the grocery store we pass by all the time. You know?"

"Yeah, I know. It's close enough to walk. I'll be right over, Man. I'm ready for a party!"

Marsha's friend was OK. We got acquainted fast. We talked, listened to records, danced, drank beer, and made out.

Rick asked Marsha if she had some more beer. "No, it's all gone," she replied with a giddy laugh.

"Think we could get a couple of six packs from the grocery store?" he asked.

Marsha sobered up fast. "I guess so," she replied, with a tentative tone in her voice. "But what if they miss it?"

"Oh, they won't miss two little six packs," he teased.

"Guess not," she agreed reluctantly.

A door from the house led into the grocery store. The shelves in the beer section were packed full for Saturday business, with cartons lined up on the floor. The overabundance gave me an idea. "Hey, Rick," I suggested. "Let's slip some beer out without the girls knowing. These people have got so much beer in here, they'll never miss it. We can hide it in the field out back and get it later."

"Sure, Man!" he whispered excitedly.

We each got two cases of beer, went out the back door, and hid them under some bushes. We went back into the grocery store and grabbed two six packs to take into the house.

"What took you so long?" Marsha asked impatiently. "We started to come in there to see what was wrong."

"We had to rearrange the cases so they wouldn't notice any was missing," Rick explained. The explanation satisfied her.

Just as soon as we finished off the six packs, me and Rick made an excuse to leave. We then drove down the alley to retrieve the beer. Outside town, we found a quiet spot to guzzle it down. Rick took the extra beer home with him.

Around noon the next day two cops were at MaMa's doorstep. Their knock woke me up. "We need to see Don Dennis," one of the cops told her. "Is he here?"

"Yes, he is," she said nervously.

MaMa stuck her head into the bedroom. She looked worried and angry at the same time. "Don," she said, "some policemen are here to see you."

"Really?" I questioned. "Whata they want?"

"I don't know. They just said they wanted to see you."

"OK. I'll be right there."

When I came into the living room, the cops were sitting on the couch. MaMa was sitting in her chair, sadly staring into space.

The cops stood up. "What's the problem?" I asked calmly.

"We need to ask you a few questions. You'll have to go to the station in Kelso with us."

"OK," I agreed quickly. I didn't want to discuss anything in front of MaMa and Granddad.

"See you later," I said, looking first at MaMa and then Granddad. They mumbled a faint "OK."

"What's this all about?" I asked on the way to the car.

"We want to question you about a robbery," one officer explained.

"What robbery?" I asked. "I don't know nothin' about a robbery."

"We'll discuss it at the station," the driver replied.

Rick was sitting beside a desk talking with a detective when we walked into the station. He looked glum. The two officers ushered me right by him into an office and shut the door. Two detectives were waiting there for me.

"Where were you last night?" one asked after I sat down.

"I was over at a friend's house in Longview."

"What were you doing."

"Just having some fun with friends."

"Did you drink a little beer?"

"A little."

"Where'd you get it?"

"From friends."

Dropping Out

"Did you and your friends get the beer from the Sherrick's grocery store?" the other detective asked.

"No. I didn't take no beer. My friends already had it when I got there."

"You might as well save us all some time and tell the truth," the detective suggested. "The baby-sitter told us what happened."

A piercing pain hit me in the pit of my stomach. My mouth went dry. My hands grew clammy. "OK. OK," I admitted. "But it wasn't very much."

"That's not what they say. They're missing several cases."

"That's not true. We couldn't drink that much."

"You might as well admit it," the detective suggested. "Rick's admitted everything, too."

I went ahead and confessed to everything. Within an hour, me and Rick were sitting in court together. MaMa and Uncle John were there. He came because Granddad didn't feel good. Dressed in his deputy sheriff's uniform, Uncle John looked somber and stern, as usual.

Me and Rick pleaded guilty. The judge gave us forty-five days in the Cowlitz County Jail. They put us in a cell together. In a few minutes Uncle John and MaMa came to see me. MaMa looked so worried. Uncle John looked mad. For a few long seconds, they stood outside the cell, silent.

"I told the judge to give you some time," Uncle John blurted out barely above a whisper.

"That's stupid," I snapped. "Time isn't what I need."

"Well, what do you need?" he asked impatiently.

"Some help besides jail."

"We've all been trying to help you, Don. You won't listen. You've been on a terror for five years. If this doesn't wake you up, the next step is the state penitentiary."

I stared at Uncle John blankly. The mere mention of the word *penitentiary* terrified me, but I didn't let them know.

The visit was short. They were both too disgusted to say much.

Right away me and Rick were made trusties. They told us it was because we were so young. I got a job serving meals. Rick worked in the laundry. Every day they let us go up on the roof. Sometimes my mother came by, and I would wave at her and grin. I could tell she was embarrassed. That amused me. MaMa came to visit and brought cookies and pies. Rick's mom brought goodies, too. We shared the take.

After forty-five boring days, I was paroled to MaMa. Rick was paroled to his parents. The next day we both were back with our old friends.

On the second visit to my parole officer, he suggested that I go to live with my dad and Kathleen. He said I needed to get away from my Longview friends. I knew he was right, and I was ready for a change. So, that night I called my dad and asked if I could come live with them.

"If you'll work and not come in drunk, it will be OK," he told me. Kathleen agreed on those conditions.

"I'll do better this time," I promised. "I mean it."

I looked forward to a fresh start.

8

Jail or Army

My dad got me a job running a press machine at the box company where he worked. A year later I was still working at the same place, some kind of record for me. I bought some nice clothes and a neat car, and had plenty of money for fun and booze. Life was good again.

At the pool hall where I hung out, I met a guy named Eddie. His girlfriend fixed me up with a pretty girl named Nancy. I was still on probation at the time. When I jokingly told her, she didn't seem to mind.

Nancy had a sweet innocence about her—different from the girls I usually picked. She was tiny, with bright hazel eyes and natural blond hair that was bleached from the California sun. Her sweet disposition and ready smile made me feel good. We hit it off good from the start. And her parents liked me, too. In less than two weeks we were going steady; and, by the time we had been going together for a month, we were talking about getting married. We were both nineteen.

One Friday night when Nancy was in Seattle visiting relatives, me and Eddie went out on the town. In one bar, a burly hunk of a man was yelling all over the place, generally harassing the customers. Sloppily dressed, he wore a red, short-sleeved sport shirt unbuttoned to the waist, exposing a chest covered with a thick growth of hair. He looked like a grizzly bear.

Everybody tried to ignore the bear. When he looked my way, though, I threw a sneer at him. That was all the encouragement he needed. When I went to the restroom, he was right behind me. He stood over in one corner glaring at me. As I turned toward the door to go back into the bar, he stepped in front of me, planting his feet firmly in place. He then stuck his head in my face, his bloodshot eyes glued to mine. "What's a punk kid like you doing in this joint?" he snarled, barely opening his mouth. "You're not even dry behind the ears."

I matched his sneer; then, without saying a word, I stepped around him and moved toward the door. He quickly wheeled around to catch the door before it closed behind me. "I'm gonna turn you in, Punk," he shouted as I walked on, "if you don't get outta here."

"Go ahead, Big Man," I snapped, as the door closed.

I positioned myself against the opposite wall to wait for the bear. When he lumbered out, I landed two quick punches, using the moves Jimmy D. taught me. He lunged back at me, yelling and punching wildly with both arms. People in the bar frantically moved back to give us room. Eddie jumped off the bar stool and ran over to help. Together, we wrestled the bear to the floor. With Eddie holding him in place, I reared back and took aim, hitting him in the head with the full force of my weight. He was out cold.

"Let's get out of here, Eddie," I mumbled nervously. We raced out the front door and took off in Eddie's pickup.

"Think he's hurt bad?" Eddie questioned.

"He'll live," I quipped sarcastically. "I doubt that he'll get much sympathy in there."

"Yeah," Eddie laughed. "They probably think that bully got what he deserved."

Three days later, two cops were at my dad's door asking for me. "You've got company," my dad said impatiently, as he stuck his head in the bedroom door.

"Who is it?" I asked calmly.

"Two policemen," he snapped.

"Oh?" I questioned, trying to look surprised.

"What have you done now?" he asked in a strained whisper.

"Nothin'," I insisted. "Tell 'em I'll be right there."

My dad relayed the message, then went to the back of the house.

The two men quickly stood up to introduce themselves when I walked into the living room. "I'm Officer Holcomb," the tall one said matter-of-factly. "This is Officer Larson."

Officer Larson got right to the point. "Were you in a fight at Hank's bar on Tuesday night?"

"Yeah," I admitted nonchalantly. "I exchanged a few blows with a big bully."

"Did you know they had to take him to the hospital?"

"No. I didn't know that," I said softly. "He looked OK when I left."

"Bad head injury," Holcomb added. "The doctors say he almost died."

"He's filing assault charges against you." Larson explained curtly. "We'll have to take you in." He pulled out a set of handcuffs and told me to put my hands behind me, then clamped them on.

By now Jeanne Kay and Patti were standing in the hall doorway. With them looking on curiously, the two policemen proceeded to escort me to the squad car. I light-heartedly told them good-bye.

"What's the guy's name?" I asked in the squad car.

"Thomas Edwards," Larson said, referring to a form.

"Well, Big Tom started it," I snapped. "I wasn't looking for a fight. He's the one that made a smart remark to me. I don't think I should have to go through this."

"He says you landed the first blow. By law we have to take you in. He's filed charges," he emphasized again.

In court the judge warned me about getting in fights, then released me on my own recognizance. I called Eddie to come pick me up.

On the way home we passed a phone booth. That gave me an idea. "Hey, Eddie," I said. "Go back to that phone booth so I can call Mr. Bear and see how the jerk is."

I could hear people talking in the background when the bear picked up the phone.

"Mr. Edwards," I said softly. "This is Don Dennis."

"Don Dennis?" he questioned.

"I'm the guy you met in the bar two nights ago," I explained with an angry quaver developing in my voice. "Remember? You filed assault charges against me."

"Oh?" he questioned.

"What's the deal? I don't have no money."

"You threw the first punch," he insisted.

"But you threw the first smart-alecky remark."

"That's no reason to beat someone up like you did."

"Well, I'll tell you, Mr. Edwards," I warned. "It probably will be worse on you later if you put me in jail. Have you thought about that?" There was dead silence.

"Mr. Edwards," I continued in a low, threatening tone, "why don't I let you think about it. I'll get back in touch with you tomorrow." I hung up before he had a chance to respond.

The next afternoon I called Edwards again and asked him how he was feeling. "Better," he replied nervously. "Don't worry," he continued quickly. "I've thought better about it. I started the fight. You don't have to pay."

"Then you're gonna drop the charges?"

"Yeah. I'll take care of it when I get out of here."

"Appreciate that, Mr. Edwards. Hope you get well real soon," I added with a trace of sarcasm.

Somebody told my parole officer about me drinking and getting in the fight. He called me up at work and told me to come in to see him the next day.

"I'm going to take you to court on violation of parole," he threatened me.

"Whata you mean?" I questioned.

"Well, you beat that man to a pulp."

"He dropped the charges," I protested. "He's a bully. Anyone in the bar could tell you that."

"That may be true. But you weren't supposed to be there in the first place. That's a violation of your parole."

"But my girlfriend was out of town. I was bored."

"I hear you've been smoking pot, too."

"Who told you that? It's not true."

"I have reliable sources. I can prove it. You don't have a leg to stand on. I'm going to send you up the river."

"What if I join the army?" I suggested quickly.

He leaned back in his chair. "I would approve that," he said thoughtfully. "The discipline would be good for you."

"Then I'll sign up tomorrow."

"Bring the papers by for me to verify. I need to know exactly when you're leaving and where you're going. And I need to put a copy in your file."

"OK. I'll do tha "

"No funny stu' now. I'm going to keep close tabs on you. It's about time you grew up." He paused, leaned forward, and looked me straight in the eye. "You do realize I'm giving you a break, don't you? I could throw you back in jail right now. Judges don't look kindly on parole violators."

"I know, Officer, and I appreciate it." I was lying.

I went down to the army recruiting office the next day. They said it would take a month to get my orders. While I waited to be called, me and Nancy decided to get married. I didn't tell her I was forced to join.

They sent me to Fort Ord, California, for basic training. Nancy stayed in Yakima with her folks. After basic I was stationed in Fort Lee, Virginia, then Fort Lewis, Washington. Nancy came to both places to be with me. Things were going good. I made sergeant in a short period of time.

Jail or Army

On guard duty I was assigned to Warrant Officer Bailey, who had a way of making his men want to excel. I worked hard to memorize the rules. Each day the soldier who knew the rules best and whose uniform looked best was selected as "soldier of the day." At the end of the month, the colonels and majors questioned the daily winners about the rules and then selected one to be "solider of the month." I was excited and honored when they picked me one month.

MaMa died while I was stationed at Fort Lewis. Barbie called to tell me. I felt guilty for all the trouble I caused her, but I did feel good that I was getting my life straightened out when she died. It terrified me to think MaMa wouldn't be there for me to talk to.

July, 1956, I received an honorable discharge. Me and Nancy moved to Whittier, California, to live near Uncle Cliff, Aunt Hazel, and Joycie. Within a week I went to work at International Paper as a machine operator. I was the youngest corrugator operator on the West Coast. I was proud.

At Fort Lewis me and Nancy were really close. But, when we moved to California, things changed. Free from the discipline of the army, it didn't take long for me to get back into my old habits of drinking and marijuana. Often on the weekends I stayed out with my buddies all night.

My behavior made Nancy start nagging about going back to Yakima. So, when her dad told me about a job possibility at the box plant, we moved there. Within a week I had the job. The second day on the job, the superintendent told me he didn't like the way I ran the machine. He said my way would make the machine wear out faster. "It's the only way I know how to run it," I told him.

"If you can't do it our way," the superintendent told me angrily, "you'll have to find work somewhere else."

"Then I'll have to find work somewhere else," I snapped back. The next day I got a job selling cars. Three days later I wrecked a car when I was showing it. I got careless and rolled it. Nobody got hurt, but I got fired. The boss smelled beer on my breath. Nancy was pretty disgusted.

While I was out of work, Barbie called to tell me that Granddad had died. His death hit me even harder than MaMa's, not because I loved her any less but because it was the end of an era. It terrified me to think that neither of them would be there for me to talk to. I wouldn't have anyone to love me like they did.

I started drinking more and more, going to bars without Nancy. She wasn't the party type. One night when Nancy went to see her par-

Breaking Crime's Vicious Cycle

ents, I picked up a girl in a bar and took her home with me. Nancy caught us. The next day her mom came over to help her pack. She filed for divorce. I knew I was letting a good girl go, but I didn't know what to do about it. I wasn't too interested in changing my habits.

After the divorce, I went to Kelso to cry on my mom's shoulder. Even though I didn't see her much, it seemed like the place to go. We got drunk together.

By now Cliff and Hazel had moved back to Longview. They invited me to move in with them. It didn't take long for Cliff to get itchy to move again. He asked me if I wanted to go to Santa Fe Springs, California, with them. He said he could get me a job at the plant where he was going to work. That sounded good to me. I was ready to move on, too.

Within a week after moving to Santa Fe Springs, I found a drinking buddy. This time it was Rusty, a guy I worked with. His wife had dumped him because of his wild ways. At a bar after work one day, two good-looking women kept glancing our way, smiling. We said hello and went to sit with them. "I'm Don," I said nonchalantly. "And this is Rusty."

The girl closest to us took the lead. "I'm Gloria, and this is Charlotte," she said. "She's my ex-husband's sister," Gloria added with a chuckle.

Gloria told us that she had worked in Las Vegas as a dancer. She bragged about gangsters and movie stars she knew. It was easy to believe. She was fast and pretty and dressed like she had plenty of money. I liked her style.

"I'm getting a divorce from Charlotte's brother," Gloria quipped. "We just can't get along."

Charlotte agreed that the marriage was doomed. "Just a bad match," she said.

Two days later Gloria took me to a bar to meet her ex-husband, Alex. He acted friendly and even asked for my telephone number. He called me the next day. "You better stay away from Gloria," he threatened.

"Gloria told me you two were getting a divorce."

"We were just having a misunderstanding."

"OK, Man," I said. "I don't want to come between you two. There's other fish in the sea."

Two days before Christmas Gloria called and told me that she and Alex were through for good and that she had moved into her own place. She wanted me to come see her. I hadn't been there five

Jail or Army

minutes when Alex came charging through the front door, waving a long knife at me. He pinned me down and stuck the knife at my throat.

"I saw your car out front," he yelled. "What're you doing here? I told you to stay away from her."

"She told me you were divorced," I explained pleadingly.

"She lied," he snapped. "She hasn't even filed."

"Don't worry," I said. "Let me up, and I'll go on."

Gloria looked scared and mad as I got to my feet and walked out the front door. I was good and mad, too.

I went over to Cliff's and borrowed his gun, then headed back to Gloria's. Standing at the bottom of the stairs outside the front door, I yelled for Alex. When he didn't come out, I fired the gun into the air. The next-door neighbors cautiously peeked out from behind the curtains to see what was happening. Alex opened the front door part way. "Calm down," he called to me. "The neighbors will call the police."

"Calm down?" I snarled, jumping up on the porch. "You're the one who started this." I pushed the door open and knocked Alex down on the floor, positioning the gun at his throat. "Here's a taste of your own medicine," I said through clenched teeth. "How's it feel, Alex?" I snapped sarcastically. "You want me to pull this trigger?"

"No, no!" he pleaded. "I didn't mean nothin'."

I stood up, placed a foot on each side of his waist, and pointed the gun straight at his heart. "You get outta here," I warned. "I don't want to see your face again."

The next day I moved in with Gloria and her three-month old baby. A month later we got married in Mexico. I never did feel right about shacking up.

Gloria took me to Las Vegas to show me around. I developed a skill for card games and made some pretty good money. From there we went to Redondo Beach, California. Gloria had friends there, too. It was fun being with Gloria. She knew all kinds of people who did all kinds of things.

One contact Gloria had was with check-forgery people. They helped me get some payroll checks and a check protector from a construction company. I got stolen credit cards from some other people Gloria knew. It made me feel good to be with the fast crowd who knew how to pull a good job.

The forgery and credit card schemes lasted a year. I cashed one check too many and got caught. I kept Gloria out of it. I told them she was an innocent partner. I spent six months in the county jail while waiting to go to Mira Loma County Farm. Gloria filed for divorce just before they sent me to Mira Loma. I really didn't care. I figured it wouldn't take me long to find someone else when I got out.

I met Dick Moore at Mira Loma. He was a dope dealer on the streets. After I got to know him pretty good, he told me his girl had a friend named Suzy who wanted to visit me. I told him to have her ask for me. "If we hit it off," I said, "I'll let her drive my car."

Suzy came with Dick's girlfriend on the next visit. I thought she was cute and fun to talk to. I gave her the address of the friend's house where my car was parked. All during the time at Mira Loma, the two girls helped smuggle dope into the prison. At a specified time, they threw tennis balls over the fence of the baseball field. The balls were filled with marijuana. The guards never caught up with us. They just thought we liked to carry tennis balls around.

Me and Dick got jobs at the officers' swimming pool. The first day on pool detail the officer told us not to bring anything into the pool pump room. We generally observed that rule. But one day Dick decided to take in some shoe polish and motorcycle magazines that he had gotten for his birthday. One of the guards, who had a special dislike for Dick, found an excuse to shake down the pump room. He discovered the magazines and confronted Dick. "Hey, Boy," he said angrily. "Are these your magazines and shoe polish?" He shoved the items in Dick's face.

"Yeah," he admitted. "I didn't think they could hurt nothin'."

"That's not the point," the guard replied. "You got to follow rules, if you want to work on pool detail. This is a privilege," he added, emphasizing every word. "Three days in the hole," he ordered, pointing in the direction of the isolation cell.

"That's my shoe polish," I yelled as they walked away.

The guard turned around and glared. "You trying to be cute, Dennis? I guess you want to go in with him?"

I stared at him with a smirk on my face.

"OK," the guard snapped, "I'm happy to accommodate."

Word got around real fast about me and Dick getting thrown in the hole. About an hour later, a friend sneaked candy, matches, and cigarettes into the cell. The guard on duty caught him as he was trying to slip out. He ordered him to get in the hole with us for being in a restricted area. The three of us shared the cigarettes and candy and took turns watching out for the guard.

Jail or Army

They kept me in Mira Loma for eighteen months. Suzy picked me up in my car. The first thing I did was have her stop at a phone booth so I could call Barbie.

"Hey, Barbie," I said. "What's goin' on?"

"Don," she replied softly, "it's funny that you would call just now. I have bad news. Mom died yesterday."

"Yesterday? Why didn't anyone tell me she was that sick?" I shouldn't have been surprised. She had been in and out of institutions for treatment of alcoholism for several years.

"We didn't know how to get in touch with you."

"Aw, come on, Barbie," I said. "Aunt Hazel had to know where I was."

"I'm sorry," she said softly. "Aunt Hazel's been sick. She doesn't write much. They're down in San Bernardino now."

"What's wrong? She was OK the last time I saw her."

"That's been two years, Don. She's got lung cancer."

"Is she going to be OK?"

"She has a fifty-fifty chance."

"I sure hope she makes it. She's my favorite aunt. When's Mom's funeral?" I asked, changing the subject.

"Tomorrow at two in the afternoon."

"In the funeral home at Kelso, I assume."

"Yes. The one down from the high school."

"I'll be there."

Suzy went with me to the funeral. On the way back to California, I got drunk and called my dad. "Did you know my mom died?" I slurred angrily.

"Yes, Barbie called," he replied softly. "I'm sorry."

"You know you killed her, don't you?" He didn't answer.

"Her blood is on your hands," I screamed into the phone. Again, there was silence on the other end. I slammed down the phone.

I took Suzy to Riverside and stayed with her for a couple of days, then drove to San Bernardino to see Hazel and Cliff and Joycie. Cliff told me they were hiring on construction jobs around Lake Arrowhead. I got a job there the next day.

Three months out of Mira Loma I linked up with Gloria again. She was still majoring on forged checks. I stole some checks where I worked, and she cashed them for me. She never had any trouble, I guess because she didn't look like a crook.

One night when Gloria wasn't around, I decided to cash one of the checks myself. I went into a bar and used an alias. The bartender didn't know me, but everybody else did. The cops picked me up at

Hazel and Cliff's two days later. Joycie watched sadly as they took me off in handcuffs. The look on her face made me feel bad. She was like a little sister.

When they were booking me, I asked the officer a question. "Is there any kind of help I can get to make me understand why my head's so messed up?"

"Gimme a break," he laughed. "You can't expect that kind of help in prison. Man, you've committed a crime against society." They sent me to Chino State Prison. I had now graduated from the county prison system.

I met some good men at Chino, at least by my standards. They weren't snitches. They didn't tell the cops anything helpful. They were loyal. They had respect for themselves, even though they were criminals. And they didn't cry about doing their time. It was at Chino that I picked up the motto, "If you're gonna play, you gotta pay."

Two interesting dudes I met at Chino were an old Italian named Joe and a big Jew named Mort. Joe had a nose like Jimmy Durante and a gravelly voice to match. He had been moving in and out of prison for many years. He and Mort walked the yard together almost every day. Walking the yard is a favorite pastime for prisoners. That's when you share your innermost thoughts with a friend.

Like Joe, Mort was a seasoned prison veteran. He had been going in and out of prisons for at least twenty years. A con man on the streets, Mort was a big-time gangster in L.A. He had a pretty wife Joy. I talked to her several times when she was visiting him. "Joy likes you," Mort told me one day.

"Really?" I questioned.

"I don't love her. You can have her."

"I couldn't do that," I insisted.

"It's OK," he insisted back. "Don't feel guilty. She's going to file for divorce. Here's her phone number." He handed me a piece of paper with the number scribbled on it. I put the paper in my pocket but made no commitment one way or other. My release time was getting close. I figured it would be nice to have a new contact on the outside.

A week before I was scheduled to be released, I walked the yard with Joe. He had some parting words of wisdom to share with me. "Don," Joe said, "have you ever heard about the two little birds that perch on my shoulder?"

"No," I chuckled. "Tell me about these birds, Joe."

"All my life I've had two birds that perch on my shoulder. One is a good little bird; the other is bad. When Joe goes to jail, the bad bird flies off, and the good bird lands on Joe's shoulder. He says to me, 'Well, Joe, here we go again, doin' time.' All through my prison time, the good little bird talks to me. He tells me to stay out of trouble, take a Bible study, get an education, learn a trade, work in a prison job, be nice to the guards, read positive thinking books, get ready to leave prison." He recited the list in singsong fashion.

"The good bird," Joe continued, "stays with me through all my jail time. Joe, the model prisoner, gets out in a minimum amount of time and walks out determined to go straight."

"And then what happens?" I quipped, anticipating what he might say. I had been around cons long enough to guess.

Joe flashed a bemused smile. "Right outside the gate, here comes the bad bird back. He lands on my shoulder and pushes the good bird away. He whispers all kinds of things in my ear—'Let's go get loaded, get some swingin' girls, get fast money.' A few months go by, and I'm back in jail! Off goes the bad bird, and here comes the good bird. It starts all over again." I don't know what happened to Joe. He was sixty then. He may be dead now.

Suzy offered to pick me up when I got out, even though she wasn't driving my car this time. She was sweet, but she didn't excite me all that much. I guess that's why I thought about Joy when I was filling out the final release papers. So, as soon as I finished the papers, I went to the pay phone and called her. "Hi, Joy, this is Don Dennis."

"Mort's good lookin' friend in prison?" she questioned teasingly.

"Yeah, that's me," I laughed. "One and the same."

"How're you doing?"

"I'm doing good. I'm getting out of prison in a couple of hours. Mort said you two were splitting up. I thought I'd see if you wanted to pick me up."

"Sure. I can get there before you get out."

After I hung up, I called Suzy. "There's been a mixup," I told her. "I'm not getting out today."

"I'm sorry. What happened?" she asked.

"It would take too long to explain. I'll be in touch. Thanks anyway. You've been kind."

"Let me know when you need me to come."

"OK. I'll do that. I'll give you a call."

I was standing out front when Joy drove up in her white Cadillac convertible. As usual, she was all made up and dressed in a classy outfit. She took me straight to her luxury apartment in a fancy neighborhood. The next day she bought me some clothes and a

Chevy convertible. She also got me a job in a men's clothing store.

Joy had lots of contacts. Right away, she put me in touch with the marijuana network. I started dealing about ninety kilos a week on the side. The money was flowing in. The bad little bird was whispering in my ear. Life was exciting again.

Our first family photo—Mom, Dan, and me in the buggy

Me and my sister Barbara in "the good ole days"

Thanksgiving in 1946 was happy—(left to right) Uncle Roy, Barbara, Mom, me, and Aunt Aggie.

That's me just out of the Army and about 23—thought I was the answer to "a maiden's prayer."

Man, didn't we look
happy in Soledad Prison?
Me and one of my good
buddies (1973)

This fellow inmate at
Walla Walla Prison
sported artistic tatoos, as
many of my prison
friends did.

Al Elliot of Prison Fellowship was with me on my first post-release visit to Walla Walla Prison. At first I hated going back, but now I love it because I'm carrying the gospel through the MasterLife discipleship program.

When I was ordained to the ministry, Barbara and my next-door neighbor, John, were among those present (1985).

Some of our adorable kids at Shawnee Baptist Mission

Chaplain Mike Fleming of Texas State Priston Beto II started me into the MasterLife program. What he began with me I am now trying to initiate in every prison where God sends me.

Now when I'm behind bars it's to preach and teach the only message that really frees a person—Jesus Christ who died, was buried, rose again, was ascended, who lives in our hearts when we trust Him, and who is coming again!

9

Mafia Connections

Me and Joy didn't last long. We got into an argument over some triviality, and I took off for Torrance to look up Dick Moore. I had the name of a bar where he hung out.

Lucky, the owner of the Soaring 60's, looked like a typical wheeler-dealer in his black, pin-striped suit and shiny shoes. He chewed on a cigar while we talked.

"You know Dick Moore?" I asked.

"Sure," he replied excitedly. "Is he a friend of yours?"

"Yeah, a good friend. Said you might have a job for me."

"Got any experience tending bar?"

"No, but I learn fast," I chuckled.

"You're in."

"Just like that," I teased.

"If Dick says you're OK, you're OK," he said decisively.

It didn't take long to figure out why Lucky was so quick to hire an ex-con. The first step in my job training was to learn how to water down the whiskey so no one would notice.

Lucky's crooked streak gave me an idea. While he cheated the customers, I would cheat him a little. I would hit the register like I was ringing up a sale but wouldn't record it. Instead, I slipped the bills in my pocket and the change in the register. I beat Lucky out of about thirty dollars a night. It wasn't enough to hurt Lucky, I figured, and it put a little extra in my pocket. Lucky never even suspected.

Armando, a lieutenant in the Cosa Nostra, was a regular at Lucky's. He fit the typical picture of a Mafia dude—short and stocky, dark brown hair, dark brown eyes. Lucky told Armando I was a friend of Dick's. He was impressed.

Armando introduced me to some of the Mafia boys and had me do business for him once in a while. I did work for him when his regular boys were tied up on other jobs. I had time to pull robberies on my

117

own. At Christmastime I pulled a good robbery and bought Armando and his wife Christmas presents.

On Armando's forty-first birthday his wife threw a party in the Soaring 60's. Armando waved me over to his table. "Look at this, Don," he said, opening a briefcase.

"Beautiful!" I exclaimed. Before me were glittering diamonds, so bright they made my eyes squint.

"How far you think you'd get if you took this case from me?" Armando asked.

"Not far," I said, smiling faintly. At least six of Armando's regulars were stationed at strategic points around the bar. I knew they were packing 9 mm's.

"Don," Armando continued. "I want you to go with Johnny to the body shop on Twenty-first and collect some money. The guy is way past due. OK? You wanna do that?" His dark eyes widened in anticipation of my reply.

"Yes, I'll go with him," I said quickly. "I'll drive him over." It was an offer I couldn't refuse. Johnny broke arms for a living.

"No, don't take your car," he said, "Johnny'll pick you up tomorrow afternoon at four. Be out front."

"I'll be there," I agreed, smiling broadly. I was ecstatic that a Mafia boss wanted me to do that kind of job for him.

At the body shop, I looked on with a threatening glare while Johnny confronted the owner in his office. "I come over here to get Armando's money," Johnny demanded.

A look of stark terror froze on the man's face. "I'll get it right now," he said, trembling. "Sorry I'm late." Armando was pleased with our success.

Another time when I was drinking beer with Armando, he pointed to a big Italian playing pool. "Don," he said, "go tell Big Al you need for him to go order a pizza for us and bring it back here. Combination with anchovies," he added.

I looked at Big Al and then back at Armando. Big Al didn't get his nickname for nothing. He was twice my size.

Armando impatiently waited for my reply. "OK," I agreed.

Buoyed by Armando's endorsement, I confidently walked over to Big Al. "Al," I said decisively, "You wanna go order me and Armando some pizza?"

He glared at me like he was going to kill me. I stood erect. Big Al glanced over at Armando. Armando moved his eyelids to confirm the order. Big Al turned back to me.

"Combination with anchovies," I said firmly.

Mafia Connections

He was on his way.

I met Jackie at Lucky's. She came to work there as a cocktail waitress about two weeks after he hired me. She was only twenty-two, but she knew her way around. A pretty bleached blond, she had a knockout figure to match her good looks. From the moment she walked into the bar, I was attracted to her. She felt the same way. A month later we got married.

I got Jackie mixed up in a forgery scheme, but they let her off when I pleaded guilty. When she visited me in jail, I cried on her shoulder about how sorry I was and how I wanted to go straight when I got out. She convinced my parole officer that I really wanted to straighten up, and he arranged for me to go back on parole.

Jackie kept hoping I would straighten up and quit drinking so much. When I got tired of her nagging, I hooked up with a girl named Susan. I was in a moving-on syndrome.

I kept bartending at Lucky's, doing work for Armando, and pulling armed robberies on the side. I pulled a big one in Long Beach. I bought clothes for Susan's two children with some of the money. Susan told me her friend, Janet, wondered where I got so much money and why I carried a gun. I told her to tell Janet to mind her own business.

Shortly after the Long Beach robbery, me and Susan were double-dating with Janet and Steve. Steve got stopped for speeding. While one cop was talking to Steve, Janet got out of the car and walked over to his partner. I thought she was trying to get them to go easy on Steve. When the cop turned around and gave me the once over, I knew she was snitching on me. I jumped out of the car and ran in the opposite direction. He ran me down, then searched me while his partner held a gun on me. They found what they wanted.

The cops took me to Torrance City Jail and put me in a cellblock with eight other prisoners. The next morning they took us to a day room because the cellblock was scheduled to be painted. We were all lying on the floor trying to sleep when a heavyset police officer walked up to the bars. His glasses undoubtedly were the thickest I had ever seen.

"Lawrence James," he yelled. We all looked up, but no one made a move toward the door.

"Let's go; you've got bail," he said impatiently, looking straight at me.

"Me?" I questioned sleepily, pointing my finger at myself.

"Yes, you," he snapped. "Do you want to go home or not?"

"I'm getting out?" I questioned again, standing up.

"Yes. Come on," he replied impatiently. "Your dad and mom put up the bail money. They're here now."

"It's about time," I said.

In the booking room, the sergeant handed me a bag. "Check to make sure everything is there," he advised.

The bag contained eighty-seven cents, a comb, and a pair of shoes. "Yeah. It's all here," I said smiling.

"Sign here," he said pointing to a line on the booking sheet. "Just like you did above," he added. I carefully copied the first signature. It was a close match.

"OK," the sergeant said, making sure I had signed in the right place. "Now make a print beside the other one."

The sergeant hurriedly checked the print. "OK," he said. "Put your shoes on, and you can go with your parents." I tried to get into the shoes, but they were too small. I quickly pushed the heels down. He didn't notice.

Holding the door open, the sergeant motioned to the bail bondsman. "Here he is."

"Your mom and dad are in the waiting room," the bondsman told me with a sense of urgency.

"I don't feel too good, Sir," I said, holding my stomach. "I need to get some fresh air before I talk to them."

"Make it quick," he urged. "They're anxious to see you."

"OK. I'll hurry," I said, then moved at a brisk pace to the front door, walking past several cops.

"Stop that man!" the bondsman yelled to the cops.

I kicked off the shoes, pushed the door open, and raced down the sidewalk. Two cops jumped into squad cars as I raced across Torrance Boulevard, then down a side street.

Blaring sirens moved closer and closer. I spotted a thick, waist-high hedge that ran across the front of a house. I eased behind the hedge and fell down flat against the house. Within a few seconds, cops were all over the street, walking door to door. My heart pounded out of my chest when two cops came to the door of the home where I was hiding.

"See any strangers, Ma'am?" one cop asked.

"No," the woman replied. "But I wasn't looking out."

"We need to check around the house, if you don't mind."

"That's fine," she agreed enthusiastically.

"See anything?" one asked the other when they met back in front near my hiding place.

"No, nothing. He may be on the next street."

When things got quiet, I decided to make a break for it. Slowly, I got on my knees and raised my head up over the hedge. A cop, sitting in his car, looked in my direction the exact moment my head came up. He jumped out of the car and raced toward me with his gun raised waist high. "I'm gonna blow your head off!" he yelled, aiming his gun at my face. "Get out of there, you punk! Move! Move!"

"Be cool," I called, moving out from behind the hedge with my hands up high. "I'm not armed. Don't shoot me."

"On the ground," he ordered angrily, "on your face."

I fell to the ground, hands stretched in front of me. The cop frisked me and put on the handcuffs, then helped me up and marched me to the squad car. At the station, they took me to the interrogation room. A detective came right in.

"How'd you get out?" the detective asked.

"That big sarge with the coke-bottle glasses asked me if I wanted to go home," I replied nonchalantly. "I said yes."

He got a bemused look on his face. "Put like that," he chuckled, "I guess I would have gone, too." He asked a few more questions about the circumstances, then called for a guard to take me to my cell.

Later, the big sarge came to my cell. "Dennis," he snarled, pushing me to the back of the cell. "I'm going to make Swiss cheese out of you, you low-life scum." He pushed me around some more, but didn't hurt me a bit.

When I went before the judge on the escape charge, he asked me how I got out. "Big Sarge asked me if I wanted to get out," I told him. "I said yes."

"Did you want to go home?"

"Sure," I chuckled. "I was facing the pen. What would you do?"

"I guess I would leave," he said with a bemused smile.

The judge gave me ninety days on the escape charge and informed me that I would be transferred to the Long Beach County Jail on the armed robbery charge. At Long Beach the police ran my picture by victims of unsolved robberies in the area. I was picked out by three different victims at three different supermarkets. They booked me on the charges and sent me to court. In court the judge asked me if I needed an attorney. "I don't think so," I told him. "I'm guilty." I didn't figure there was any point in wasting a lawyer's time.

Breaking Crime's Vicious Cycle

The judge gave me five years to life on the armed robbery charge and combined the sentence with the escape charge. They sent me to Chino Guidance Center for classification. There I met a lot of friends I knew from the night life in L.A. and Torrance and from county and state prisons. It was more like going home than ever before. We laughed, played dominoes, handball, and softball.

We walked the yard a lot, too, telling each other lies about the big money we made on the streets. That's a big thing in prison—telling about the women, the drugs, the money we had. After a few years, though, you know all the lies, and they get boring to tell and even more boring to listen to.

Periodically, lists were posted to inform prisoners about penitentiary assignments. There were lots of possibilities— CMC East, CMC West, Folsom, Soledad, San Quentin. Soledad was extremely volatile at the time. Most hoped to stay away from there. San Quentin had the worst reputation.

On a Tuesday morning I cringed when I found my name on the San Quentin list. Within a week, I was gone from Chino. About three in the morning of the assigned departure date, a guard went from cell to cell with a wake-up call for breakfast. After breakfast, they took us down to shipping and receiving to get papers and a receipt for any money that was recorded on the books. They then gave us a set of prison blues—shirt and pants. They asked us what we wanted them to do with our clothing—send it to our homes or give it to the Red Cross. I told them to give it to the Red Cross. I didn't know if I was ever coming out.

Before getting on the bus, they handcuffed each of us, put on leg irons, and chained us together by pairs. Luckily, I drew a friend from Chino. We had a long ride ahead of us, and it's even longer chained to someone you don't like. San Quentin is on the Oakland side of San Francisco Bay. On the rickety prison bus, it would take all day to get there.

Moving down the highway, the conversation was nonstop talk about the prison. "They fight all the time there," one said. "The Black Panthers are in control," another chimed in. "You can smuggle in any weapon you want," a glassy-eyed dude bragged. I knew what they said was true. Newspapers headlined one killing after another. We were sure it was plenty bad, but no one admitted he was scared. That's something you don't admit, even to yourself.

About four in the afternoon, the gates of San Quentin opened up to swallow us. The bus rumbled through the opening to the receiving center of that ugly, old, yellowed prison. Guards were everywhere, maybe twenty or thirty, yelling at us to "Hurry up; get off the bus; keep quiet."

A crowd of inmates came up to the bus and peered in the windows. Many were looking to see if any of their friends were on the bus. Some were just looking for a new face. A few were trying to spot young, weak, good-looking boys to make women out of. Some of these men had been lifting weights for many years. They were big, and they were tough.

East Block was home to the new arrivals. Five tiers high, it had at least one hundred cells on each tier. The bottom tier, reserved for new inmates, was called "fish row." A new convict is like a fish out of water—out of society. Inmate "tier tenders" stood at both ends of each tier. It was their job to pull the big lever to open and close the cell doors.

As the guards marched us to our cells, the prisoners above yelled wildly. "You're mine," they called to the "pretty" ones. "What'd you do, Man?" they screamed to others. While the cons yelled, guards, armed with .30-.30 rifles, patrolled the catwalk on all five tiers.

Close to chow time, the deafening sound started again. This time new inmates joined with the old in screaming for the tier tenders to open up the doors. No matter how much we yelled, they opened the doors at the same time. About fifteen hundred men were crowded into the chow hall at one time, all sitting in rows facing one way—toward the door.

The day after being admitted, they sent me to classification. They said it was routine. The receptionist led me to an inner office where a somber-looking man was seated behind a desk. Big and fat, he had puffy lips and buggy eyes. "Hello, Don," he said dryly. "I'm Henry Preston. I'm a counselor here. My job is to help you get adjusted in the prison. Have a seat."

I sat down across from Mr. Buggy Eyes, waiting for his words of wisdom. He picked up a wad of papers from a folder. "This is your record from other prisons," he said, waving the papers at me. He then started reading account of arrest after arrest and conviction after conviction. That was OK. I could take it. I knew what I'd done.

When Fatty got to the end of the list, he looked straight at me. "Your father's just a drunk, isn't he?"

"He drinks a lot," I admitted. "But he's always managed to hold down a job."

He looked skeptical, then moved on to his next point. "Your mother was practically a prostitute, wasn't she?"

"D— you!" I yelled, jumping up from my seat and shaking my fist at him. "You don't have no right to say things like that about my family." Before he could move, I shoved the desk to the wall, pinning him behind it. "I'll kill you, you fat slob," I screamed at the top of my voice.

Fatty frantically pushed a button on his desk. Three guards ran in, cuffed me, and marched me to South Block. There they stripped me and threw me in the hole. It was like the others. The commode was nothing but a hole in the ground about nine inches in diameter. I spent thirty days in there.

When they let me out of the hole, I was taken to a different classification section. They gave me a job in Education and told me I could move to North Block if I stayed clean for eighteen months with no write-ups for fighting, drugs, and insubordination. North Block was easier, with more time out of the cell and more TV watching.

Classification also said I would have a chance to move to West Block, the honor block, if I stayed clean for twelve months in North Block. In West Block, each inmate had his own padlock to the cell. This meant they had more freedom to come and go. I decided to work for that.

I worked in Education with Frank, a slick Italian from L.A. He knew Armando. At one time he was a lieutenant in the Cosa Nostra. Me and Frank got along real well. He helped me get to know a bunch more Italians. They all considered me a regular. "You've got a good 'rep' on the streets and in prison," Frank told me. "You don't snitch; you hate the cops; you'll fight in a minute for your friends; you'll loan money when you have it; and you'll share dope with your friends. You're OK, Don. You're one of us."

I had plenty of old friends in San Quentin, too. A bunch came up to see me when I was walking the yard. "Don't worry about nothing here, Don. You're covered," they assured me. Big Al from Torrance was in the group.

Bobby, a leader of the Mexican Mafia in L.A., was in East Block with me and about nine hundred men. I met him when I was dealing drugs for Joy. "Whata you need?" he asked.

"I'm dying for a smoke," I told him. All I had was a bag of Bull Durham and papers to roll my own. You get those when you first go in, if you don't have any money. "I'd like to have some coffee, too," I added, "and the other essentials."

That evening Bobby came to my cell with coffee, cigarettes, joints,

Mafia Connections

stinger—a homemade device to heat water, and a quart jar of pruno—
homemade beer. I gave the guy in the next cell some cigarettes to get
me snacks from the canteen. I was fixed, home, and comfortable.

"How would you like to be in West Block?" Frank asked me a week
after we started working together.

"I'd love to," I told him. "But I haven't been here long enough,
have I?"

"Time is no problem. You got cigarettes, you can move in. Seven
cartons of cigarettes for the captain's clerk will get you there. Three
more cartons will get you to the honor section." Since prisoners
processed the paperwork, it was prisoners paying off prisoners.

Frank helped me get fifteen cartons of cigarettes to move to West
Block. We paid the captain's clerk; then that clerk split it with another
clerk in East Block to alter my classification papers. In a few weeks I
was assigned to a cell in West Block. Frank was my cellmate.

Frank had big plans for me. He wanted me to be his lieutenant in a
drug ring. While walking the yard, he carefully explained the process
we would follow. "I don't want no one to know about me," he said.
"I'll order the dope from the outside. It'll be your job to get someone
to line up the distributors. You're my lieutenant. My captain will let
you know where to pick up the dope. The responsibility ends with
you. We won't talk about this again."

I got Smack to be my lieutenant. I knew him from Castlemont High
in Oakland and Chino Prison. I talked to Smack like Frank talked to
me. I explained the whole setup. He would get Black Panthers,
Mexicans, and others he could trust to distribute dope for him. My
captain would place an order for the drugs with his contact on the
outside. He would tell Smack where the drugs could be picked up.
Smack would then tell his lieutenant to line up someone to bring the
dope into the prison. That person could be a guard, someone on
seventy-two-hour furlough to get a job before being released, or any
other contact. A person would be designated to receive the dope.
That person would paper it up and give the joints to runners to sell. A
runner could sell as much as $1,000 worth of dope a day. Each person
in the distribution process, all the way up to Frank, got a cut. Me and
Smack saw each other in the mess hall but never talked again about
drugs.

George Jackson, the Black Panther leader, was in San Quentin
when I was there. A truly magnetic personality, he was making
moves to pull all the ethnic groups together to wage war over inhu-
mane treatment by the guards. I saw the guards kill George Jackson. I
was visiting friends and buying marijuana on the third tier of the

North Block when it happened. I heard whistles blowing. I looked out on the yard into the segregation unit where a lot of Black Panthers were put for causing trouble. I saw George running across the yard toward the library. Shots rang through the air. He fell to the ground. The guards claimed he was trying to escape. I wondered where they thought he was going.

When I had been in San Quentin for almost four years, Dad and Kathleen moved to Fremont, just south of Oakland. They came to visit me shortly after they moved. My dad had mellowed and was trying harder to be a good father. He was all torn up about my situation. "Don," he pleaded with tears in his eyes. "I hate it so much that you're wasting your life. You had so much going for you. Can't you see you need to make a change."

"Yeah," I admitted softly. "I really want to. But every time I get out, I just can't seem to change."

"We'll try to help you," Kathleen told me. "Jeanne Kay and Patti would love to see you. They really like you."

I promised that I would give the straight life a shot when I got out. They didn't visit again.

Early in 1972 they gave me a date to go home. Three months before my release date, they sent me to Chino for work release. I had a job in the free world during the day and returned to the prison at night. Since I worked at a corrugated box plant less than two miles away, I was able to walk to and from work.

Forty percent of my pay was deducted as the fee for processing the work-release program. That was a constant irritation. The irritation built up to a point that I decided to do something about it. One day on the way to work I stopped at a bar and got drunk instead of going to work. I called a friend who lived near Chino. "Jimmy," I began. "This is Don Dennis from L.A. County Jail. Remember me?"

"Sure, Don. How ya doing?"

"Good. But I'm tired of those guys taking most of my pay for running this penny-ante work-release program. I wanna get out of here right now. Will ya help me?"

"Sure, Don. Whata ya want me to do?"

I told Jimmy I was going to fix up my bunk so it looked like someone was in it. That way they wouldn't discover I was gone until count time. I was going to leave for work as usual but meet him at the bar instead. Jimmy said he would take me wherever I wanted to go.

"Where ya wanna go?" Jimmy asked when he picked me up.

"First, I want to go pick up the gun I bought a while back. I hid it under a rock on the way home from work. Then I'd like to go to Big D! I've always wanted to go to Texas."

"OK," Jimmy agreed, lightheartedly. "I know the way."

We laughed and talked, drank beer, and snacked on the food Jimmy's wife had packed for us. We got as far as Albuquerque when Jimmy remembered Texas was a dry state. "A dry state!" I exclaimed, holding up the beer can in my hand. "I don't wanna go to a dry state. I need that booze. Colorado's wet, isn't it, Jimmy?"

"Think so."

"Let's go there then. Let's head for Denver."

"OK," he laughed. "Denver, here we come."

Outside Albuquerque, Jimmy turned north on the highway to Denver. I was free! It was a good feeling.

10

On the Run

I took my gun out of its hiding place under the seat and waved it around, taking aim at the big Arizona saguaros. "This is a neat piece," I teased. I went through this routine at least once a day, usually when I was getting high from the beer.

Jimmy glanced anxiously at the gun. "Don, why do you want that gun?" he asked softly.

"Security. Protection," I slurred, laughing. "Lots of people out there wanna hurt you, Jimmy. You know that."

"Don," he warned, passing over my observation, "you're in big trouble if they catch you with that gun."

"Let's face it, Jimmy," I laughed. "I'm in big trouble already."

"You'll be in worse trouble if they catch you with that."

"Don't worry. I'll be careful. They won't catch me."

"Don," he urged. "Would you do me a favor?"

"Sure," I chuckled. "I'd do anything for a friend. Whata ya want me to do, Jimmy?"

"I just wish you would throw that gun away."

I took a long, hard look at Jimmy. He wasn't the same Jimmy I knew at Castlemont High and on the streets. He told me on the phone that he was married to a good girl, had a steady job, and planned to go straight. I was beginning to believe he meant it.

"OK, OK, Jimmy," I agreed light-heartedly. "If that's what you want. Pull off the road, and I'll throw it away." When Jimmy stopped, I wiped off the gun and tossed it in a clump of desert bushes. I don't know why I didn't argue with him. But, after all, he was doing a good deed for me.

In Denver, Jimmy booked me into a hotel room for a week under the name David Harrison. That was the alias I picked for a driver's license a friend of Jimmy's made for me. We unloaded the canned goods Jimmy's wife had packed, then drove around Denver just to see the city.

"Don, I need to get back home," Jimmy told me on the third day there. "I've got to get back to work."

"I know you have to leave, Jimmy, but I sure hate to be here alone."

Jimmy laughed. "Knowing you, Don, uh, David, I mean, you won't be alone long. You'll find a chick right away."

A feeling of loneliness mixed with sadness gripped me as I watched Jimmy pull out on the highway. He was a true friend.

That evening, with just fifty bucks in my pocket, I went from bar to bar to find company before that little bit was gone. At the third bar, I spotted a pretty brunette sitting at the opposite end of the bar. She looked lonely. So, when the seat beside her became vacant, I quickly moved next to her. "Hello," I said softly. "I'm David Harrison."

"Hi, David," she replied in a friendly tone, "I'm Linda." She took a good look at me. "I haven't seen you in this bar before. Do you live around here?"

"No, I just got in from California."

"Oh," she said. "What part of California?"

"Fremont."

"Oh, really," she said excitedly. "I go through there on the way to visit my aunt in San Francisco."

"Whata ya know," I said.

"What're you doing here?" she asked.

"I'm looking for a job."

"What kind of work do you do?"

"Running all kinds of machines in a box plant, selling men's clothing, bartending. You name it. I can do it."

Linda smiled. "If you can do all that, you shouldn't have any trouble finding work."

After shooting the breeze for an hour, Linda invited me to her house for a snack. On the way, she told me her ex-husband had been injured in a motorcycle accident, and they bought the home with the settlement money. When they divorced, she got the house.

Once inside, Linda proudly showed me her three-year-old twin sons. "They look so sweet when they're asleep," she quipped. "They're a handful, though. My mom baby-sits a lot. I don't know what I'd do if I didn't have her to help."

Me and Linda hit if off good. She was easy to talk to, and she didn't dig too deep into my background. I told her the good stuff about my relatives, like Uncle Roy and his high-powered job in education and Uncle Ray who worked in church. She was impressed. When she

Breaking Crime's Vicious Cycle

took me back to the motel, she invited me to come over the next night for supper. Her mother was taking the boys somewhere, so we would be alone.

After supper, I told Linda my money was running out. "Would you like to sleep on the couch?" she offered quickly.

"That would be great," I said. "Sure I won't be in the way?"

"No. Not at all. My mother has her own home. She just stays here when she baby-sits."

In a couple of days I got a job cleaning equipment for an asphalt paving crew. At first Linda drove me to work and picked me up. Later I took her to work and kept the car.

The first time I sat down for supper with the twin boys, I saw firsthand how much trouble they were. Without any warning, Tommy threw a spoon of food at Timmy. Back and forth it went. It was a war zone! "Do these kids always act this way?" I asked. "Or are they just showing off for me?"

A desperate look filled Linda's face. "I try, but . . ."

"Do you mind if I do something?" I offered.

"I wish you would," she said, tears forming in her eyes.

I got up from my seat, walked over to Tommy, leaned down to position my face in front of him, and looked him straight in the eye. I learned the strategy from prison life— find a way to control the worst troublemaker first; then the others will fall in line. "Tommy," I said firmly, "if you don't straighten up, I'm going to take you to the living room."

Tommy got quiet, and I walked back to my chair. The minute I sat down, though, the brat started laughing and throwing food and scuffling with his brother. I stood up again, calmly walked over to Tommy, and firmly planted both feet behind his chair. I then picked him up, tucked him under my right arm, and carried him to the living room.

"You stay here, young man," I said firmly, "until I say you can come back in." He stared up at me with his big brown eyes, trembling and sobbing. Tears poured down his cheeks.

I left Tommy sitting there alone for exactly five minutes, then went in to get him. "Will you behave now?" I asked.

"Yes," he sobbed, sniffling uncontrollably.

"Promise?" I questioned, handing him a handkerchief.

"I promise," he whimpered, looking up at me pleadingly.

"OK," I said softly. "Then you can come back and sit with us. But, if you act up again," I warned, "I'll make you sit here by yourself

On the Run

while we eat. It's your last chance." After that, mealtimes were fairly peaceful.

Me and Linda had some fun times together, but I was always on edge. Every time I saw a cop, I wondered if that would be it. A ringing phone made me jump. I insisted that the drapes be pulled at all times. Linda thought that was a little strange, but she went along to humor me.

On a Friday evening, exactly three months after me and Linda met, we went to the bar where we had met to celebrate our anniversary. While we were laughing and talking with friends, I noticed a man at one end of the bar staring hard at us. "Wonder what's with that guy?" I questioned.

"What do you mean?" Linda asked.

"He keeps looking over here. Is he an old boyfriend of yours?" I quipped.

Linda looked at him good. "I don't know him," she said. "I've never seen him in here before."

I breathed a sigh of relief when the man left a few minutes later. The relief was short-lived. In less than ten minutes, he was back with two friends. *Uh, oh,* I said to myself as the three men walked straight to our table. "Here they come," I said to Linda.

"Who?" she asked. Before I could answer, the three men were standing beside me. One stuck a detective's badge in my face. Linda's eyes got real big.

"Sir," the man said with an air of authority, "we need to see some identification."

"Sure. Be happy to," I said. I handed the detective my California driver's license with David Harrison on it.

My heart beat faster and faster as he carefully and slowly examined the license. After a few long seconds, he handed the license back and thanked me. "Sure," I said softly.

The three men huddled beside my table. I turned back to the table and picked up my drink, trying to ignore them.

The detective turned back to me. "Let's go outside, Sir," he demanded.

I turned around to face him. "For what?" I demanded.

"I think you're Don Dennis. I saw your picture in a wanted poster this morning."

"You're crazy," I sneered, standing up and looking him in the eye. "My name is David Harrison," I insisted. I motioned to Linda. "Ask her. She knows me."

Linda nodded in agreement, looking puzzled and concerned.

"I'm not going out of this bar," I snapped. The detective then grabbed me by the arm. At the same time, the other two men pushed me toward the door and out on the sidewalk. Linda followed close behind, standing just outside the entrance.

"Let's pull open his shirt," the lead detective said. "We'll see who he is."

While the men held me in place, the detective unbuttoned my shirt and pulled it open. "Lift up his arms," he said.

"So you're not Don Dennis," he sneered, pointing to my left side. "What about that scar under your arm?"

"So what?" I snapped. "I know plenty men who have scars like this."

"And that unfinished tattoo of a woman's face on your chest," he added, ignoring my remark. "It's just like the one Don Dennis has. Buddy, I've got you memorized."

"Lots of people have tattoos, Officer. You know that."

"Not with a scar like that, too!" he exclaimed, laughing sarcastically. "This coincidence is too much. You're Don Dennis! There's no doubt about it."

The detective turned to Linda. "Ma'am, this guy's a fugitive. He escaped from a prison in California three months ago."

"I can't believe it," she gasped. "He hasn't done anything wrong here. He's worked every day, and he's been so good to me and my kids."

"They can be real charmers some of the time," the detective chuckled. "They know how to con you. You're just lucky you never crossed him."

"I still can't believe it," she insisted. "Are you sure you have the right person?"

"Yes, Ma'am," he assured her. "We're positive."

Linda watched in stunned disbelief as they snapped on the handcuffs and led me to the car. "See you," I called to her.

"OK," she replied softly. "I'll come to see you."

They kept me in Denver City Jail while the papers were being processed for my return to California. It took three weeks. Linda came to see me almost every day. Just before I left, I finally admitted that I was Don Dennis.

The day I left for L.A., Linda promised to write and to wait for me. "Would you come to California and be a character witness for me?" I asked.

"Sure," she said, "if you think it will help. I know how you've acted for the last three months. Mom can keep the kids. She can't believe you're a criminal either."

On the flight back to L.A., I asked the cop how they happened to spot me. "It was a one in a million chance the detective would run into you in a bar," he quipped, a smile of satisfaction plastered all over his face.

"Yeah, that's my luck," I moaned. "I know how to mess up." In a way, I was relieved. The running was over.

On the plane I thought about why I was in such a fix. *If only my parents hadn't gotten a divorce, things would be different,* or *If my grandparents hadn't been so poor, I could have had better clothes,* or *The police are harder on me because of my criminal record.* Getting on the right track seemed beyond my reach.

Before I went to court, I wrote to Linda to tell her that there wasn't any point in coming to California to testify for me. "They already have their minds made up," I explained. As expected, the judge gave me two years for the escape.

Classification sent me to Soledad. I had plenty of friends there. I knew some of the black guys from San Quentin. And I knew white and Mexican dudes from the jails and on the street.

Linda wrote to me for the first six months. After I told her I wasn't getting out soon, the letters came less and less. When the letters stopped altogether, I got in touch with Maggie, a girl I met on work release at Chino. She came to visit at least twice a month and assured me she would be there for me when I got out.

Because of all the killings and knifings at Soledad, the inmates nicknamed it "Gladiator School." On a steamy August morning, three Mexicans were stabbed to death before breakfast. One had refused to pay a white dude for a pack of cigarettes. He was killed as a warning to others.

The violent atmosphere at Soledad made me stop and think. San Quentin was bad, but Soledad was worse. So many of the inmates were hardened, violent criminals, ready to kill on a moment's notice. I didn't dare admit it to anyone, but the place scared me. In every other prison, I figured my friends could take care of me. In Soledad, I wasn't so sure. I kept my eye on my back all the time.

An insensitive warden wasn't the problem. Mac had a unique way of communicating with the inmates. He would walk out in the yard alone and strike up a conversation. His outgoing and friendly nature combined well with a firm and tough approach. He was easy to talk to.

Mac had many good instincts. He once called 400 of us into one of the halls. He got in the middle of the crowd and angrily confronted us about the stabbings and killings. "If you men want to continue killing each other and don't want to get along, let's finish it today. You start killing now, and I'll bury the last one standing myself." He was sick of seeing so many young men die in his pen. Besides, it made him look bad. Things improved for a little while after his speech; then the killings were back up to the normal rate.

Maybe the situation at Soledad bothered me so much because I was getting older. I don't know for sure. But, whatever the reason, I was open to helping cool down the place when Mac asked me about that very thing. He called me and two other dudes to his office to look at the situation.

Buff, a tall, burly dude, was a leader among the Mexicans. He was tough as nails. Dancer, a muscular, black dude, was a former football player. His thick shoulders and hard-as-steel upper arms were a threat to everyone. And he looked plenty mean with his big teeth and dark, piercing eyes. Like me, Buff and Dancer both had long prison records.

Mac carefully explained what he had in mind for us. "I've called you in here," he said, "because of the killings and the racial conflict. We've got to cool things down in this prison. To do this, we're going to start a new program. We've called it a Catalyst Program. I want Don to be the catalyst for the whites, Dancer for the blacks, and Buff for the Mexicans. I selected you because you have a way of getting along with all the races. You're respected by the other prisoners. I think you can help us."

"What does a catalyst do?" Buff asked.

"You'll each be a go-between or liaison between the prisoners and the administration. You'll be the spokesmen for the inmates, kind of like a union negotiator. When they have a grievance or need some kind of special help, you'll sit in as an adviser. Each of you will need to let me know about current problems on the yard and trouble brewing that we may not know about. Whatever you can do to help ease the tension, we'll back you up 100 percent."

After thoroughly discussing our role, Mac asked, "Will you help?"

Me and Dancer and Buff were flattered by the warden's confidence. Still, all three of us had to think long and hard about the job. Before we would accept, we wanted to get one thing straight about our role as go-betweens. "We're not going to be snitches under any circumstances," Dancer told the warden. "We want you to understand that. We want the guards to understand that. And we want the inmates to know that, for sure." All three of us said we would try to spot trouble and help work things out. We also said we would personally quit pushing dope. But we wouldn't snitch on those who did. Mac agreed to the no-snitch rule.

"I'd like to make a suggestion," I said. "I think it would be good to have a meeting to let the inmates know exactly what we're going to do. I don't want any of these men to think that we're going to be snitches." The meeting idea was fine with Mac.

Soledad North had three halls with more than three hundred men in each hall. Mac called a meeting in each hall. He told the inmates what he proposed to do. At Lasson Hall where I would be the spokesman, I asked Mac to let me say a word. I directed my words to him. "Warden," I began. "I'll tell you this in front of these men. It's a thin line to run between being an informer and a liaison. I want these inmates to tell us how they feel. Do they want us to do this?"

"Tell us how you feel," Mac told the group.

"We want this," one after another agreed.

After the catalyst program was in place, whenever there was a killing, everybody would be locked up, as usual. Then we three catalysts would go from cell to cell to see what the problem was. We would ask questions like "How can we help?" and "What do you want us to say?"

One time a white dude informed me that a kid out front was about to be killed. "What's the problem?" I asked.

"They're trying to make a homosexual out of him."

When I got there, two big dudes had the young, good-looking kid pinned up against the wall. After reasoning with the big dudes about how hurting the kid would cause all kinds of trouble, they agreed to let him go.

The guards sometimes created problems by trying to get us to snitch on someone who was pushing dope. Or the convicts who didn't understand what we were doing would try to put "snitch jackets" on us. You can get killed real quick for being a snitch. From an inmates's point of view, a snitch can't be trusted. He is dangerous to everyone on the yard. He will tell about dope deals going on, killings that are going to happen, or anything that he thinks might help him get out of the joint sooner.

Because of my job as catalyst, the young guys looked up to me. They would come to my cell and shoot the breeze until lockup time. Rodney, a young kid from San Jose, came over almost every day. He would sit on the board I put across the commode and talk to me about

Breaking Crime's Vicious Cycle

life. He told me that his parents were divorced when he was thirteen and never had time for him after that. I could identify with his situation. It was a whole lot like mine. Rodney told me he had learned his lesson and wanted to go straight when he got out. I guess I was kind of a father figure to him.

Early Monday morning, just after the tier tenders had racked open the doors, an inmate frantically knocked on my cell door. "Hey, Don," he said, "Get up. Rodney got hurt."

"What happened?" I asked.

"I don't know. I just saw them taking him downstairs on a gurney. He had blood all over him."

Before the inmate could finish, Mac's voice came thundering over the loudspeaker, announcing a lockup. "Better get to your cell," I told him. "See you later."

Before I could get dressed, a guard was at my cell door. "Mac wants to see you," he said.

"What's happened?" I asked.

"A killing on tier 2," he replied. "I don't know any details." We walked silently to Mac's office. Buff and Dancer were already there.

"A young kid named Rodney got killed," Mac said somberly.

"Oh, no," I sighed.

"Someone went in and stabbed him," Mac went on. "You guys got any idea why anyone wanted to get rid of him?"

"He was a good kid," I said, a lump forming in my throat. "I have absolutely no idea why anyone would kill him. He minded his own business. Didn't cause any trouble. Didn't have any enemies that I know of." Buff and Dancer didn't have a clue either.

Mac took us to Rodney's cell. Blood was splattered all over the back wall. The bloody handprints that smudged down the wall graphically pictured the young kid's futile attempt to get away from his executioners. The scene sent shivers up my spine. I choked back the tears. "Looks like he didn't have a chance to get away," I said softly. "I cannot understand it. I simply cannot."

I grieved over Rodney's death, like he was my brother. By the grapevine I found out that he was killed by mistake. The killers got the cell numbers mixed up. Rodney was in cell 213. The intended victim was in 313.

Little by little, the catalysts gained a reputation of being good for the cons. When there was a legitimate grievance or when an inmate needed special help, we were there to help and encourage. We got good results. We didn't completely eliminate the killings, but we did cut down on them. Knifings were at an all-time low, too. We also helped to get better treatment for the cons from the guards and administration.

And we had our fun times. At Christmastime the three halls at Soledad North had a decoration contest. The prison furnished the materials, and we made our own decorations. It was announced that the winning hall would get to go to an extra movie. The prize that year was *2001: A Space Odyssey.*

In Lasson Hall fifty guys met to help make the decorations. We delegated various responsibilities. Some cut out bells and strung them from one side of the three-tier cellblock to the other. Some made confetti and put it in paper bags. On the long wall between the two sections of Lasson Hall, the Mexicans painted a mural of people walking to church in the snow. They painted another Christmas scene on the glass door of the phone booth in the hall. Without asking, we took three Santa Claus outfits out of the storage room in the gym. We wanted to have a black, white, and Mexican Santa Claus.

On Christmas Eve, Mac, his secretary, and other staff people came by to inspect the decorations. All the convicts were out of their cells, laughing and cutting up. When the inspectors came in, they were facing the phone booth. To the delight and cheers of everyone, the three Santa Clauses emerged from behind the phone booth and escorted the inspectors through the hall. Men stationed along the top tier poured confetti on the panel of judges as they walked toward the Mexican's mural. A black guy came out of his cell, playing "Silent Night" on a saxophone. No one came close to us for creativity. Our hall won the prize hands down.

Along with Buff and Dancer, I spent most of the last year in Soledad settling disputes between inmates and between inmates and staff. We were able to work with the authorities without losing the respect of the other inmates. I liked the job. I felt a sense of accomplishment about what was happening. For the first time in my life, I was making a positive difference. I was building up, rather than tearing down. It was a good feeling. Many times Mac let us know he appreciated our efforts.

I look back on the last year in Soledad as a time of charting a new direction. I looked forward to a fresh start in the free world. In my mind I truly had turned over a new leaf.

The middle of August 1974, three months after my dad's funeral, I walked out of Soledad a free man. The day I left, I gave my radio and TV to a friend. Freed prisoners do that sort of thing. It's an unwritten law. He needed them a whole lot worse than me. I was free. He still had time to serve. A duffel bag was all I needed to hold everything I owned.

Accompanied by a guard, I moved quickly through the cellblock to the administration building to check out. One friend after another called to me. "See you later, Don," they teasingly said.

"Yeah. Yeah," I teased back. *I hope it's not here*, I said to myself.

Like I told you earlier, I had good intentions when I left Soledad. Unfortunately, the good intentions didn't weather the storm.

11

Walla Walla

June 17, 1977. The gates of Walla Walla opened to let the Gray Goose rumble through. The judge's sentence still echoed in my mind—*life, . . . no parole*. What a California warden had called the "worst prison in the U.S." was going to be my home for the rest of my natural life, as the judge put it.

Right away I noticed a big difference from Soledad and San Quentin. Smiling inmates met us at the bus and ushered us into the administration building. Once inside, inmates took care of the classification details, distributed clothes, gave cell assignments. It looked like they ran the pen!

Later I learned why the prisoners were in charge. A warden in the distant past had established the system. Convicts were allowed to start all kinds of organizations—Mexican Club, Black Club, Indian Club, Motorcycle Club, Lifers' Club, to name a few. Each club had a designated meeting place. Motorcycle Club members worked on their motorcycles in the barnlike building where they met. They were even allowed to ride their bikes in the big yard.

After we received our prison clothes, two guards and four inmate helpers escorted us to our cells. One by one, they dropped us off at cells that already housed three cons. I faced three hostile cellmates, who moved quickly to stretch out on their bunks to claim their territory.

I looked for a spot to deposit my gear. The one unoccupied top bunk had clothing and blankets on it. I threw my duffel bag beside the pile and grunted a "Hi." When the greeting met with dead silence, I sauntered to the back of the cell, slid down beside the sink, and leaned against the wall. I looked straight ahead, waiting for someone to make a move.

Finally, a tall, lanky dude eased down off the bunk and stood facing me. "We own this cell," he said firmly and sharply. "We keep that one bunk free." The other two men enthusiastically nodded to agree with his declaration.

I looked him in the eye. "I'll try to find another place," I replied curtly. "But until then, I'll have to stay here."

"Just as long as you try," he agreed, still assuming the firm approach. His buddies nodded to second the motion.

"I will," I assured him.

After supper, I walked across the grassed area outside the mess hall to lean against the opposite wall. "Hey, Don," a deep voice resounded behind me. I quickly turned around.

"Hey, Eddie!" I exclaimed, extending my hand. "Man, you're a welcome sight. This isn't the friendliest place."

"Tell me," he sighed.

"How's things with you? I haven't seen you for a while."

"Not the best," he said with a serious look. "Let's walk the yard, Don. I've got something I want to tell you."

"Sure, Eddie," I said. "Let's go."

"What're you doin' here, Don?" he asked, as we moved into the big yard. Normally, prisoners don't ask questions like that. It was OK with Eddie, though. We went way back. He was one of my dope-smoking buddies at Chino. One time I got him a knife to help him escape. He got caught two hours later, but he never told on me. Eddie was one of those dudes who would rather die than snitch. He was my kind of guy.

"Same old thing, Eddie. Armed robbery. One big difference this time, though. They put the Big Bitch on me."

"The Big Bitch!" he exclaimed, obviously shocked. "You don't mean it. I thought they quit that."

"Guess not," I chuckled, spreading my arms wide open. "Here I am. I'm in this place for life."

"No recourse?"

"The judge recommended they never parole me. So, I'm here forever, unless a P.D. can get me out. And that's not likely. I haven't even heard from him yet. Probably thinks I'm hopeless," I added with a nervous chuckle.

Eddie moved his head close to mine, like one telling a secret to his best friend. "Let me tell you something, Don," he began. "This prison is not like any you've been in before. It's total chaos. San Quentin is tame compared to this place. It's filled with liars, snitches, and thieves. The cons steal from each other all the time. You can't trust no one. I mean no one," he added to emphasize his point.

Walla Walla

Eddie paused for a minute, looking around again, "Just checking on the guards," he quipped. "I've already killed a guy," he continued. "Wouldn't pay his debt. I gave him three warnings. Just thumbed his nose at me."

"They know you did it?"

"They suspected but couldn't prove it."

I didn't know if Eddie was telling the truth or just bragging. It didn't matter. It all came out the same.

"You got any influential friends in here, Eddie?"

"Yeah. I've been here a year. I've made a few friends. Why? Whata ya need?"

"I need a place to stay. These dudes they put me with say they own the cell. They don't want a fourth con in there. I need to move fast. Think you can find me something?"

"Probably. I'll see what I can do."

With the serious talk out of the way, me and Eddie reminisced about old times. We laughed about our escapades inside and outside the joint, smoking dope and not getting caught, girlfriends, all the fun times. We shot the bull until the announcement for count time.

As Eddie turned to go to his cellblock, he slipped me two nickel bags of weed. "I'll be in touch," he assured me. I didn't feel alone anymore.

The next day, shortly before supper, I took one of the nickel bags out of the hiding place in my pants. Based on the previous day's schedule, I figured I had fifteen minutes before the tier tenders would open up our cell. While my cellmates looked on curiously, I rolled a joint, lit up, and slid down beside the sink. I smiled as I took a deep drag. "You guys want to share this?" I asked with a bemused smile, glancing from man to man.

"Sure, sure," they said, almost in unison.

Huddling in the corner beside the sink, we passed around the joint. For the first time since my arrival, we laughed together. When the joint was gone, we teasingly blew talcum powder out the bars to kill the smell.

When they racked open the cells for supper, the three dudes waited for me. "We don't mind you staying here if you want to," the lead dude told me. "Yeah, Man!" the other two enthusiastically agreed.

"No, that's OK," I replied. "I'll be looking around. I've got friends here."

"Well, if you change your mind, it's OK," the lead man assured me.

Breaking Crime's Vicious Cycle

"Thanks," I said matter-of-factly. "I appreciate that." *Who would want to stay with fickle dudes like you?* I questioned to myself. *I certainly don't.*

Eddie delivered a week later. He found me a cell in Sixth Wing with two other dudes. One was an artist, a young kid. The other con was about my age. I already knew him. I met him during the classification at Shelton Prison.

It didn't take long to know that Eddie was right about the prison. Three days after I got there, a guy was stabbed and sent to the hospital. The second week an inmate was killed. The first year I was there, sixteen men were killed on the yard, many of them unprovoked killings. The club presidents did just about anything they wanted. They pushed dope. They let women into the prison. The homosexuals had a group dancing at the Mexican Club at two in the morning.

I went to work in the metal shop, operating a punch press. A big, muscular Indian named David worked there, too. Together we punched out license-plate numbers. We first met while working in the kitchen at King County Jail. A lifer like me, he wasn't a bad dude. He wasn't a murderer or anything like that. He just kept committing petty crimes that added up to something big.

"How ya doin'?" David asked me one day at break time.

"OK," I told him?

"Where ya livin'?"

"Sixth Wing."

"Like it there?"

"It's OK."

"Why don't you join the Lifers' Club?" he suggested.

"How can that help?" I asked.

"It might help you stay alive in this hellhole."

"I'll give that some thought."

I went with David to the next meeting of the Lifers' Club. I liked what I saw and decided to join. With 300 members, it was the largest club in the prison.

David lived on the Awareness Tier in the administration building. He told me it was heaven compared to the rest of the prison. The inmates were in one-man cells; they could come and go freely; and they got to eat first.

"Hey, Man, you've got to get me in there," I told David.

"Will you participate in the program?" he asked.

"Whata I have to do?"

"Read positive-thinking books like *How to Succeed in Business*," he replied with a chuckle. "And you have to lay off the weed."

"I can do without it if I have to. I'm not hooked."

Within a month, David got me a cell on the Awareness Tier. Right away, two dudes named John let me know they ran the Tier. John B. made it clear I would have to follow the rules if I wanted to stay. John H. told me about the self-improvement program that I would have to follow. "No problem," I told them both. "I'll follow the program."

On the Tier, life was good again. At night I could shut out the rest of the prison. The stabbings and the killings happened outside the Tier.

On January 6, 1978, just after breakfast, I got a call to go to the attorneys' meeting room. It was my P.D.

The bearded, bespectacled man seated on one side of the table rose to greet me, as the guard closed the door. His long hair, flowing down his shoulders, and his round, gold-rimmed glasses were straight out of the sixties. Short and thin, his head barely aligned with my shoulders. I guessed him to be about thirty-five.

"Hello, Don," he said softly, smiling faintly while stretching his arm across the table. "I'm John Ziegler. I've been assigned to move your appeal through the system."

"Good," I said, smiling cautiously. "I've been wondering what was happening. Braswell said someone would contact me."

"Sit down," he said in a friendly tone, pointing to the seat across from him. His relaxed manner put me at ease.

"Thanks," I said, pulling out the chair.

"Things going OK in here?" he asked.

"I'm still trying to adjust. This is a wild place."

"Yes, I know," he remarked matter-of-factly.

"I've just moved to the Awareness Tier," I added quickly. "Things are better there. I'm hoping it will help me."

"That's a good move. You must be making some progress for them to transfer you there."

"I think I am. Friends helped me get there, too. I'm trying hard. Going to work, laying off the dope. They'll kick me off the Tier if I don't stay clean."

"Just keep trying," he urged.

"Think I have a chance with the appeal?" I asked.

"We never know for sure, of course. It depends on so many factors. But I feel you have strong grounds for appeal."

"Is that so?" I questioned, excitement racing through my body. "I don't think Braswell thought I had a chance."

Passing over my last remark, Ziegler slowly opened the folder in front of him. He then looked across the table at me. "I've checked your record carefully," he explained, "and it appears you were not represented by counsel on two occasions. That is correct, isn't it?"

"At least twice," I chuckled. "I was so guilty I told the judge there was no point in wasting the state's money."

"Is that so?" he questioned with a bemused look.

"They caught me red-handed. I was ready to serve my time."

"That may work to your advantage now," he remarked.

Ziegler asked me about my family and how I was feeling about my life. He seemed genuinely interested in learning about where I was in getting my life straightened out. Right away, I was calling him John. And I was pouring out my hopes and dreams to him. "I've just got to get my life on track," I told him. "I'm getting too old for this stuff," I added with a chuckle. "I enrolled in junior college just before they let me on the Tier. I've finished one course so far. I'm enrolled in two more for the next go-around."

"Good," he said. "That certainly will help."

"I always thought college was just for rich kids."

"No, we're in America," he quipped. "All kinds go to college. It's the land of opportunity."

"I was a little afraid at first. Then, when I realized that some of the guys taking courses weren't any smarter than me, I decided I could do it if they could. I sure wish I had figured that out long ago."

Ziegler leaned back in the straight chair, balancing himself on the back legs. His expression changed from friendly to serious. "I know it's a jungle in here," he said kindly. "I'll do my best to get you out. In the meantime, you need to stay clean. If you mess up, it will make my job more difficult."

"I'll really try," I assured him. "I can't stand the thought of spending the rest of my life in here."

After meeting with Ziegler, I talked about him with some of my friends in the Lifer's Club. To a man, he was well liked. "John's a great guy," they all agreed. "If anyone can help you, he can. He understands how we feel, and he keeps at it." Their opinions gave me a glimmer of hope that I might get out of the joint some day.

After about a month on the Tier, a couple of Muslims started talking to me about the good, clean life they followed. They said they owed their new direction to the teachings of the prophet Muhammad. I was impressed with their life-style. They were the most decent men I had met on the yard. They didn't use drugs, didn't cuss, and weren't looking for trouble. After going to their worship services and discussion groups several times, I decided to join them. I thought the association might help me stay clean.

Walla Walla

Friends teased me mercilessly about being a Muslim—one white face in a crowd of blacks. I didn't care. I determined to be a good Muslim. I faithfully studied the Koran and observed the Muslim daily prayers and the Friday worship and prayer time. I did everything a good Muslim was expected to do. I even observed Ramadan, the Muslim holy month of daytime fasting and prayer. During Ramadan, the administration had special food for the fifty or so practicing Muslims and even set aside a special place for us to eat during the observance.

Every Friday, the Muslim imam came to the prison to conduct the prayer time. He talked in English and recited the prayers in Arabic. His messages moved me. I was inspired by his encouragement to live a good, clean life. I felt good about the direction of my life. I was proud to be a Muslim. From the time I joined them, I didn't use dope or drink pruno. It looked like Islam might just be the answer to my problems. I was anxious to tell Ziegler about my progress.

The first part of April 1978 Ziegler made his periodic visit to the prison to check on prisoners assigned to him. I got the call to go to the attorneys' room around ten in the morning. "How're you doing?" he asked, posing the routine, first question. Somehow, with Ziegler, it meant something.

"Fine," I replied. "I've joined the Muslims since I last saw you," I added quickly and enthusiastically.

"Oh?" he questioned, with a curious look.

"They're helping me keep decent," I explained. "It's a great bunch of guys. I'm keeping away from the dope, and I'm staying out of trouble. I'm doing good, real good."

"Great," he said, his voice filled with enthusiasm. "Are you still going to school, too?"

"Sure am. I'm taking English and psychology right now. I don't know what I'm going to major in yet."

"Keep at it," he said enthusiastically.

"I'm going to. Maybe it will help me get on track."

"It should help," he agreed. "Friends visiting you?" he asked, moving on to another subject.

"Friends from the street come once in a great while. Betty comes about twice a month."

"Who's Betty?" he asked.

"She's a kind woman I met in King County Jail. I helped her son out when he was in jail with me. She's been real good to me. Brings me cookies and snacks every time she comes. She even brought me an old TV and radio."

Breaking Crime's Vicious Cycle

"Any of your family visiting? Your sister?"

"She's not visiting, but she is writing. She and Jim have their hands full with four boys. My cousin's writing, too. She and her husband are trying to be family, but I think they're pretty disgusted with me. I can't blame them. I've put them through hell."

He did not respond to my admission one way or the other. He just listened with interest until I was through. He then proceeded to bring me up to date on my appeal. "I'm still trying to get your appeal through the courts. We'll have to take it to the state supreme court."

"Really?" I questioned.

"Yes. That's pretty standard for this type of appeal. They don't view this charge lightly. Going through the lower courts is a mere formality. It's going to take time. Try to be patient. I'll keep on top of it."

"I really appreciate what you're doing, John. I really mean it. But I've got to get out of here. I can't survive in this place. Being on the Tier helps. And I've got friends, but there's just so much friends can do."

"I know it's bad in here. The lawyers know it's bad, and the judges know it's bad. But there's no where else to send offenders. Do your best to stay out of the line of fire. That's the most useful advice I can give right now."

"I'll do my best. I'm minding my business."

Ziegler's visit encouraged me all over again. It made me even more determined to keep clean.

I only lasted about nine months with the Muslims. I started noticing their weak points and got disillusioned. They would bicker and fight over trivialities. When we went into the mess hall, they complained and threatened if everything didn't exactly suit them. It was embarrassing. Worst of all, one of the leaders got caught smoking dope. That was the last straw. I quit going to the meetings. I didn't want to be part of something that wasn't honest.

I was back to square one in my search for a solution to my problems. I wasn't giving up on my search, though. I moved from the Muslims to Eastern religion. It was popular then. I met a guy who had studied under a woman who was trained by an Indian guru. Extremely excited about his new faith, he helped me compose a letter to the woman. In the letter I told her that I was looking for answers about life and solutions to problems. "I've got to change," I said. "Life is a dead-end now." I asked for help.

The woman answered my letter within two weeks. She applauded me for my earnest search for meaning in life and stated that she had written to her guru, telling him about me and the depth of my search. She also said the guru had promised to get in touch with me in the near future. In the meantime, I studied books about Eastern religion a friend gave me and observed meditation times.

David and Joe on the Tier carried me high about my current pursuit. "Well, Don," Joe said, "you've tried college, the Awareness Tier, Muslims, and now an Indian guru. What are you going to try next in your search for the truth?"

"I don't know," I joked back. "What else is there?"

"Who knows?" he replied. "But I'll bet whatever it is, it'll find you." He let out a big laugh. I wasn't offended by the teasing. It was all in fun.

One evening, when most of the guys on the Tier had gone to a movie, me and David were in the recreation room playing chess. Since nobody else was there, we turned the radio high for background music. An hour into our game, John H. strode into the room. "What the hell!" he exclaimed, marching over to the radio. He turned it so low we couldn't hear it.

"What's the deal?" I snapped. "We can't hear it."

"You guys better keep that radio down," he warned, picking up a newspaper from the table and sitting down in a chair.

Me and David gave each other a disgusted look. I then strutted over to the radio and turned the volume back up full throttle.

John glared over at us. "Who turned that up again?" he snapped angrily.

I turned around in my chair to face him. "I did," I snapped back. "You ain't no cop. You're a convict just like me," I added, gesturing sharply to him and then to me.

"You better cool it, Don," he warned like a big brother.

"Yeah. Who says so?" I questioned angrily.

"Yeah," David mumbled in agreement.

John stood up, laid a newspaper on the end of the table, and strutted over to our table. "I want both you guys off this tier," he yelled, pointing to me and then to David. We both gave him a dirty look and returned to our chess game.

With his shoulders hunched in anger, John walked back over to the chair, picked up the newspaper, and sat down. The music blared across the room. Me and David tapped our feet to the beat and teasingly hummed the tune.

The next day we were assigned to Sixth Wing. Classification sent the word. No discussion. No hearing. Nothing. Just orders for me and David to leave the Tier. "Disgusting," I told David. "Why should those guys call the shots?"

"It is disgusting," he agreed. "But there's nothing we can do about it, right now at least. John's got the power."

The next day I quit college, with thirty hours behind me. I didn't tell my teachers. I just quit going to class. *If people are going to be like that,* I decided, *I don't care if I ever finish. I do not care. I do not care!*

On the yard after supper I got some dope. The next day I started dealing myself. Eddie lined me up. *So much for a new direction,* I thought. *It didn't work.*

12

Lockdown

John H. lost his power position on the Tier. He got too big for his britches, and they clipped his wings. David got back in first and asked me if I was interested in taking up residence there again. "Sure," I told him. "I miss the Tier." I was in my old cell when Ziegler came to visit.

"How're things going?" Ziegler asked as usual.

"I'm surviving," I replied. "This place is getting hotter and hotter, though. More and more stabbings and killings. You hear about the hostage incident?"

"Yes. Sure. Just lasted overnight, didn't it?"

"It was stupid. The five dudes grabbed some teachers in the Education Department, of all people. They're the best around here. Those crazy dudes didn't have a plan or nothin', just a vague demand for better prison conditions."

"You get caught in the yard?"

"Yeah. About five hundred of us were in the central yard screaming and yelling to get out. The National Guard finally herded us into the big yard. Stayed there all night, with the guardsmen's guns aimed at us. Kept warm by burning bleachers," I chuckled. "They didn't do nothin' about that."

"You in on it?" he questioned.

"No. Just happened to be in that area when they decided to light them up. I was cold. I was glad they did it."

Ziegler looked puzzled but said nothing.

"Think you can get me out soon?"

"Looks like we're going to beat it. I don't know how soon, though. I'm in the state appeals court now. After that, I'll get a date before the state supreme court. It's moving."

"John, I've got to get out of here. I've got friends in here, but I don't know how long I can last. These aren't run-of-the-mill cons. They kill for no reason. Look at the wrong dude cross-eyed, and he'll get you killed."

"I know it's tough. Just be patient. The wheels of justice move slowly. You still going to college?"

"I'm taking two classes. I had a run-in with a bully on the Tier and got disgusted and laid out for a while."

A concerned look flooded Ziegler's face. "Everything's OK now," I said quickly. "I'm back on track, studying hard."

"Good. Just hang in there and stay out of trouble. We're going to beat it."

"I'm counting on that."

In the inner recesses of my mind and heart, I wondered if Ziegler was just a bunch of hype. I hoped against hope that he could deliver. In the meantime, I had to concentrate on survival.

The warden used the aborted hostage-taking incident to take away privileges and secure a tighter grip on the inmates. He let us keep our club meeting places with the understanding that guards would conduct regular rounds to check on the activities.

The Indian's clubhouse, located across from the mess hall, was used for both recreation and worship. They had decorated the meeting place in bright colors and were really proud of it. They even carved the name "Indian Club" on a piece of wood and nailed it over the entrance.

We teasingly called the Indian Club the "Sweat Lodge" because of a religious ceremony they had in there several times a week. For the ceremony, they heated rocks and sat on them. They claimed the ritual brought about a spiritual cleansing. Naturally, the experience made them sweat a lot.

On June 15, 1979, the Indians' cleansing ceremony took place at noon. That day, the Indian Club was on Sergeant Cross's beat. A burly white dude, Sergeant Cross had straight, thick, dishwater blond hair and piercing blue eyes. His bottom lip always protruded slightly, a mark of his surly outlook on life.

Sergeant Ross, Cross's partner, wasn't as muscular as Cross, but he was equally hostile toward inmates. The hostage-taking incident was all the excuse they both needed to come down harder on the convicts. After that incident, they were on our backs for the least misdeed.

Generally, the guards walked around the clubhouses and peeked in the windows, if they didn't have a tip that something was going on. That day Cross was in the mood to do more. "Ross, you want to see what these sweat hogs are up to?" he teased.

"They're deep in worship, no doubt," he teased back. "Sure. Let's check it out."

Cross defiantly pranced up to the entrance. He took his billy club from its holder, raised it high, and landed a hard blow on the door. Before anyone had a chance to answer the knock, he pushed the door open and stuck his head in. Five Indians seated on the coals meditating looked up, surprised and irritated at the intrusion.

"What a sight," Cross joked. You guys are gluttons for punishment, making yourselves sweat on a day like this.

Ross moved up beside Cross and stuck his head in. "Yeah," he teased sarcastically, "you can get just as clean with a shower and soap. And you don't have to suffer like that." Together, they let out a loud roar.

"You don't understand," one Indian protested softly. "This is our worship."

"Worship?" Cross jeered. "Yeah, I bet. Sure you aren't making pruno in there?"

"No. No," the Indian replied quickly. The Indians were notorious for stealing sugar from the mess hall to make the homemade beer. Many times they had been caught with sugar in their cells. But the authorities never had found any in their clubhouse. All the inmates were careful to keep their clubhouses clean, so they wouldn't lose the privilege.

"This is a holy place," a second Indian protested. "We don't do pruno here. You know that."

"Oh yeah, we understand about your worship," Cross jeered, putting a special emphasis on the word *worship*. "You're just having worship."

The man moved toward Cross in a threatening stance. A buddy stepped between them. "Cool it, Johnny," he advised.

"Make sure you keep it clean," Cross warned, looking from Indian to Indian, "or we'll take this privilege away from you." He paused, then added condescendingly, "You do realize this is a privilege, don't you? Cons in other prisons don't have these prima donna clubs."

"Sure. Sure," the lead Indian grudgingly acknowledged.

Cross lifted his billy club in a good-bye gesture. "See you around," he said, reaching for the door knob. He shut the door firmly, then returned the billy club to the holder. "No good Injuns," he sneered to Ross, loud enough for the Indians to hear.

"Yeah," Ross agreed.

The Indians watched through the window until the two men were

Breaking Crime's Vicious Cycle

out of sight. "That no-good slob," one sneered. "He don't have no respect for no one. He'll be sorry."

Buzzy was an Indian friend of mine on the Awareness Tier. "You hear what that buggy-eyed Cross did at the sweat lodge today?" he asked me on the way to supper.

"No. What?"

"That big fat slob and his partner went over there and stirred things up. A bunch were in the middle of their meditation time. Cross and his buddy just barged right in. They made fun of them for their cleansing ritual. Cross accused them of making pruno in there, too."

"They're just little boys trying to show their power," I said sarcastically. "Take that gun and stick away from them, I could lay 'em low in two seconds."

"You sure could," Buzzy agreed. "You've got the muscles."

"You could, too, Buzzy," I said, teasingly reaching over to feel the muscle in his arm. "Man, you're like steel."

"From what I hear, they really went overboard," Buzzy went on, an angry quaver developing in his voice. "I'm not into that sweat ritual," he explained, "so I don't care one way or the other. But those guys are mad as h—. The guards better cool it, or they'll make them wish they had."

"Cross is always lookin' for someone to run over," I sneered. "I'd sure like to waste him." I emphasized my point by making a fist with my right hand and hitting the palm of my left with it.

"They're all dogs," Buzzy sneered, "pushing us around all the time. This is a hellhole." He had a special kind of sneer. After each declaration, he shut his mouth tight and then lifted the right side of his top lip to expose his teeth. I never knew anyone to sneer quite like that.

Since it was a special worship day for the sweat-lodge Indians, they all sat together in the mess hall during supper. They looked plenty mad, glaring at one guard, then another. They quickly finished eating and went outside. When me and Buzzy came out, seven or eight of them were huddled together in the middle of the grassed area.

"Something's going down," I murmured to Buzzy. "Got any ideas?"

"No, but I want to see what happens."

"Me, too."

Me and Buzzy walked straight ahead to the building on the opposite side of the yard and leaned against it. We kept our eyes on the Indian huddle about thirty feet away.

Suddenly, three guards flew out of the mess hall and took positions about five feet away from the huddle. "Injuns, come on over here," one of the guards demanded, motioning wildly with his left arm. "We want to talk to you." It was Sergeant Cross.

The Indians didn't look up. The other convicts moved back toward the buildings that framed the open area.

"You Injuns, come here," Cross demanded again. "Bring that sugar over here."

The Indians laughed among themselves, still ignoring the order. Cross clenched his teeth, raised one shoulder and then the other, and charged toward the huddle. Ross and Carter stood in place, keeping an eye on the huddle.

The Indians closed the circle together. Cross took his billy club from its holder with his right hand, while grabbing an Indian by the shoulder with his left to force open the huddle. He then plunged in the middle of the huddle. Cross and the billy club disappeared from sight. Ross and Carter instinctively blew their whistles, raised their billy clubs high, and rushed toward the huddle. The Indians scattered, hurriedly moving back to the side building. Cross, covered with blood, staggered forward two steps and fell to the ground.

"A gurney! A gurney!" Ross yelled, rushing over to Cross's motionless frame. He stooped down to touch his neck. "He's gone," he said quietly, looking up at Carter.

Ross jumped to his feet, waving his arms wildly. "Get the Indians!" he yelled to a band of guards who, by now, had descended on the yard. "Get the Indians!" he yelled again, his voice cracking. "They did it! They did it!"

We watched in stunned silence, as the guards cornered the Indians, handcuffed them, and marched them out of the yard.

Suddenly, a voice boomed over the loud speaker. "Count time in every cellblock. Return to your cells immediately. Return to your cells immediately." It was the warden.

Me and Buzzy headed for our cells in the Awareness Tier as the warden repeated the announcement over and over again. "I want to tell you, Buzzy," I said, walking at a brisk pace, "this prison will never be the same. Those dudes killed one of them. We are in for it."

"Yeah, I know. It's all over but the shouting."

"Yeah, it's a sad day. We deserve better than this."

Once inside the Awareness Tier, we didn't look to the right or left. We went straight to our cells. I locked myself in and waited for the announcement. Secretly, I was relieved. The prison was out of control.

The clanging sound of one set of cells after another being locked echoed from cellblock to cellblock. This time guards did the racking down, rather than inmate helpers. Every convict was in a cell.

Breaking Crime's Vicious Cycle

We all started yelling wildly at the guards and at other convicts. When one inmate stopped yelling, another took over to keep the roar at a high pitch. "What's happening?" we kept asking. "What'd we do?" The guards did not reply.

The warden got on the loudspeaker again. "You will be confined to your cells until further notice," he said dryly. He repeated the announcement twice with no commentary.

That night we laughed and talked from cell to cell until lights-out. We speculated what they might do to us. "Oh, it will blow over," John B. in cell 10 predicted.

"Yeah," Al chimed in. "They'll punish those Indians, and we'll go back to business as usual."

"Yeah," I agreed. "They can't keep us locked up forever. Who'll do the work?"

"Yeah, yeah," convicts chimed in from cell to cell.

"We didn't do nothin'," I yelled loud enough for the guard to hear. He ignored me.

Early the next morning they brought us breakfast in TV-dinner containers. It was the bare minimum—coffee, juice, and a sweet roll. "Can't work with a breakfast like this," I remarked when the guard came by.

"You may not have to," he quipped right back and moved on down the tier.

After breakfast, club leaders started yelling to the guards. As an officer in the Lifer's Club, I felt it was my duty to join in. "Why do you lock us down just 'cause someone gets killed?" I asked.

"Yeah," another dude chimed in. "We didn't do nothin' to anyone. Make those guys pay, not us."

"You haven't seen the half of it yet," a guard sneered back. "Cuss all you want, but we're in charge now. Party's over, boys." His partner joined him in jeering laughter.

At noon and at supper, they brought us meals in TV containers. Not one cellblock had yet been racked open. Another lights-out came and went. Nothing changed. We speculated about what happened to the Indians. We figured they shipped them out to another prison, and the lockdown would end soon. The yelling got louder and louder.

"When're we gonna get out?" I asked the guard when he strolled by.

"Maybe never," he snapped.

I cringed at the sound of *never.*

Two weeks into the lockdown, about an hour after lights-out, the door to our cellblock creaked open. Two oversized guards moved

Lockdown

through the door leading ten handcuffed inmates. Two guards followed the pack. I recognized the inmates as they passed by my cell. They were high-spirited dudes from cellblock 8. They kept that cellblock stirred up all the time.

The guards herded the men to a room at the end of the hall, turned on the light, and lined them up with their faces to the back wall. The lead guard positioned himself behind the first inmate on the row. "We're gonna teach you foul-mouthed slime how to respect authority and property," he yelled. "We're sick of you cussing at us and destroying this place." He clenched his teeth, reared back, and landed the first blow with his billy club, then another, and another. He moved down the row, landing blow after blow with the full force of his weight.

One by one, the other guards followed. Each guard landed at least five strikes on each inmate. The inmates refused to beg for mercy. After all the guards had a good turn, they herded the limping and battered inmates back down the hall past our cells. They threw them into the main recreation yard to spend the night.

The next day we learned why the guards beat the men. They incited the men in cellblock 8 to pull out all the plumbing to protest not being allowed to take a shower in two weeks. The entire cellblock had to be moved to the main recreation yard while repairs were made.

On Monday of the third week, about twenty guards marched into our cellblock and announced that we would be allowed to take a shower. They let us out in groups of twenty-five and gave us two minutes to run to the shower room, soap up, rinse off, and dash back to our cells to dry off. This shower detail was repeated every two weeks. In between we took sponge baths with the water in our toilet tanks.

After the beating of the ten, the cursing of the guards came to a halt, with a few stubborn exceptions; but we kept asking when we would get out. The guards kept telling us to shut up, if we knew what was good for us. The days dragged by. We traded reading material and tapes to pass the time. Nobody was able to get a weed or pruno. The addicts were getting jittery.

Tuesday night of the fourth week of the lockdown, I heard an uproar outside the tier, like pushing and shoving. Shortly, fifteen white guards, wearing black gloves, moved into the hall, pushing along six white dudes. They were handcuffed and dressed only in shorts. One kid with bleached-blond hair was about twenty years old.

The guards shoved the men into a room at the end of the hall near three small strip cells. They switched on the light and left the door open. I quietly positioned my mirror on a bar of my cell so I could see what was going on. I recognized the men. They were from cellblock 8. *What did they do this time?* I wondered. *They never know when to quit.*

The guards stripped the men and threw their clothes into a big pile in the middle of the room. One by one they raised up the convicts' arms and positioned the handcuffs over pegs on the wall. The fifteen guards proceeded to land blow after blow on the men with their billy clubs. "You guys don't know when to stop," one guard screamed with a high shrill in his voice, delivering a blow to the inmate's back.

Each guard took turn after turn. The hits went on and on with increasing intensity. The beating sounds, mixed with the pleas of the convicts, echoed down the tier. The convicts cried and screamed and called for their mothers.

Finally, it was over. The guards lifted the handcuffs off the pegs, removed them, and threw the men into cells. Each convict fell to the floor, sobbing uncontrollably.

The young kid with bleached-blond hair was the last to be taken down. On impulse, the guard positioned his billy club under the kid's rectum, and gave it a hard push upward. "Maybe that'll teach you," he yelled.

The kid let out a blood-curdling shriek that brought every convict in the cellblock to his feet. The guard threw the kid into a cell. I quickly pulled back the mirror and moved quietly to my bed, sitting on the edge.

As the lead guard strutted back down the hall past our cells, he held up his billy club and pointed it threateningly from cell to cell. "If anybody in here wants the same treatment," he shouted, his voice cracking with rage, "just keep causing trouble." Following his lead, the other guards made threatening gestures with their billy clubs, pointing from one convict to the next. We sat on the edge of our beds in stunned silence as the guards filed out the door.

The muscles in my stomach tightened into a hard knot. My palms were wet. My throat was parched. I fell back on my bed in desperate disbelief. "My God, what is happening?" I whispered. "Will I be next?" I lay motionless, staring up at the ceiling. I was afraid to go to sleep.

Two hours later, Del in the next cell called to me in a hushed whisper. "Don," he said, "John B. recorded all that." We quietly passed the word from cell to cell.

When I finally dropped off to sleep, the men in the strip cells were still sobbing and moaning. The young kid woke me up several times during the night, shrieking out in pain.

By law a nurse had to be let in to see anyone who was hurt. The administration was careful to observe that requirement. Early the next morning, a male nurse was escorted past our cells to the isolation cells. The kid was still crying. Blood was splattered everywhere.

The nurse stayed in the isolation area for at least an hour. When he emerged with the guard and went past our cells, John B. called to him. "Did you see what happened to that kid?" he asked quickly in a low voice.

"Yes, I saw it," he replied, shaking his head back and forth in dismay. "And I'm going to have something done about it," he added confidently. We never saw that nurse again.

A couple of days later, John asked to see Father Bey. He told the guard he wanted to see if Father Bey could get him something to read. He wasn't the least bit suspicious, because Father Bey was chaperone of the Awareness Tier. Prisoners have the right to ask to see their clergyman.

"How're you doing?" Father Bey asked.

"OK," John replied. "I was wondering if you could get me some reading material. I need something to lift my spirits."

"Sure," he replied, flashing his ever-present smile.

Father Bey had a kind and gentle manner. He looked tough, though, with his big hands and firm arm muscles. He worked out in the gym every day, keeping his body in good shape. He was a match for any convict. Except for the bald spot on the top of his head and his thinning hair, he appeared much younger than his forty-five years.

When the guard was out of sight, John slipped the tape to Father Bey. "Take this and listen to it, Father Bey. Don't say nothin' now. Just put it in your pocket."

The next day Father Bey made copies of the tape and took one to a radio station in Seattle. They played it over and over. The administration had no choice but to suspend the fifteen guards. They probed some to find out who smuggled out the tape, but everyone was tight-lipped.

A week later, just after breakfast, the warden came on the loudspeaker to announce a cell check. Guards went in pairs from cell to cell, removing items of value. They took my TV, pictures of my sister and cousins, my extra blanket, my homemade heating unit, knickknacks I had accumulated over the years—everything that was an extra. It all went into a giant garbage container on wheels.

They got to Father Bey, too. About a month later, during his regular visits to the prison, somebody planted booze and drugs in his car. He was taken into custody and formally charged with smuggling the contraband into the prison. He successfully fought the charges and stayed a couple of years. But, from that point on, a cloud hung over him. The kid with the bleached-blond hair was another casualty. He committed suicide a year later.

About three months into the lockdown, I got a letter from the guru in India. "Dear Mr. Dennis," he wrote. "Miss Singa has told me about the depth of your search for meaning in life. I want to help you in your search. I am coming to America in 1980. I will try to visit you then."

"I can't believe it," I yelled out, jumping off my bed. "Hey, John B.," I called at the top of my voice.

"What's happening?" he asked.

"Would you believe I got a letter from a guru in India! Hot dog!" I exclaimed.

"You're kidding," John yelled back.

"No, Man, I'm not kidding. I've got it right here."

"You're pulling my leg. Why did he write you?"

"I don't know. I can't believe he's coming to see me. I'm going to send it down to you."

The guys passed the letter from cell to cell. After the letter went past Art in cell 12, he yelled to me. "Hey, Don. I'm shooting you down a kite."

"OK, I'll read it."

Art's message was scribbled on notebook paper, folded like notes we passed in school. My name was written in big letters on the outside.

Hey, Don—Since you got some spare time (ha! ha!), why don't you pick up a Bible and read about Christ Jesus and His ability to change people—if you're looking for a change in your life?

I know you've been studying with a guru in India searching for the truth. If you'll look in the Bible, you'll be able to find out that Jesus Christ is THE truth. Read Romans 4, 5, 6, and 7 about how Christ came into the world for dudes like you and me.

Art was a college graduate. About thirty-five, he was tall, muscular, and good looking. His dark brown hair receded a bit, but that didn't hurt his looks. His big problem was raping women. That's the reason his wife divorced him. Since coming to prison, though, he had made a big change in his life. He was the chaplain's clerk and helped in chapel. He really seemed determined to get his life straightened up.

I read the note two or three times, then lay back on my bed, thinking. *THE truth, he says?* I questioned silently.

Lockdown

Art's message made me recall how the guys teased me about searching for *the* truth. *Well, here comes another possibility,* I thought. *I've tried different concepts, different religions. Now what about this? Is it just another trip? I'm more confused now than when I started searching.*

Childhood memories flooded in. I mused about going to Sunday School with MaMa and Barbie and Aunt Aggie and Uncle Ray. I thought about the time when I told the preacher that I wanted to let Jesus come into my heart. I was just nine then. I thought about my baptism and how I liked to memorize Scripture for a long time after that. It had been so many years since I had consciously thought about Jesus.

I went to my cell door and yelled to Del in the next cell. I knew he had started going to church a while back. "Del, you got an extra Bible?" I asked.

"Yeah. Sure."

"Let me read one."

"You *are* getting desperate," he joked, handing the Bible to me through the bars.

I had no idea where Romans was and was too ashamed to ask. I used the table of contents to find it. With the Bible opened to Romans 4, I sat on my bed, leaned against the wall, and started reading.

In verse 25 of Romans 4, I read about how Christ came to earth to die for sinners. In 5:1 I read that one can find peace through faith in Christ. I paused there to contemplate that possibility. *Peace,* I sighed silently. *How desperately I need peace. I am so torn up inside.* Exhilarated by the possibility of finding peace, I moved on.

In Romans 5:7-8 I read that one would hardly die for a good man, but Christ died for sinners. I hooked onto verse 8—"While we were yet sinners, Christ died for us." *What a tremendous thought!* I exclaimed silently. I read the verse over and over.

Romans 6:17-18 told me that a person is set free when he accepts Christ. *Set free!* That possibility gripped my heart. I read those verses several times, too.

Peace. . . . Freedom. . . . Maybe this has been the answer all along, I thought.

A prickling sensation like goose bumps rippled through my body. A lump formed in my throat. I choked back the tears. "If this is the truth, God," I whispered softly, "I pray I will understand that it is."

I kept reading. Verse by verse, truths jumped out at me.

"Chow time," the guard yelled, interrupting my thoughts. I laid down the Bible and picked up the meal. I quickly finished it, anxious to get back to my reading.

As I read, my thoughts kept moving back to the time when the

Bible was so important to me. I thought about Mrs. Slottin and how she hugged me when I told the preacher I wanted to be baptized. I thought about MaMa and how she loved me so much and tried to help me be a good boy. I never once told her that I was sorry I hurt her. I was amazed that she never quit loving me. "This is the answer," I whispered. "This is it!" The realization overwhelmed, thrilled, and challenged me all at the same time.

If Jesus Christ is the answer, I concluded, *if this Bible is true; then what I need to do is get back with God and being a Christian and really make Christ my Lord.*

I read until lights out. Then, when it was quiet, I got down on my knees beside my bed. "God," I prayed softly, "if you're for real; if Jesus Christ is your Son; if He came on this earth for sinners; if He died on the cross for people like me"—the tears began to flow. I couldn't hold them back any longer—"I want to know that truth for myself, God," I sobbed. "Please reveal that to me."

The answer came quickly, echoing inside my mind—"This is the truth! This is the truth!" Oh, God didn't speak out loud or anything like that. But, if He had spoken out loud, it couldn't have been more real. The still, small voice deep within me made it crystal clear. I knew I had found the answer. I knew Christ wanted to come into my heart.

"Christ Jesus," I sobbed, "I ask you right now to come into my life and change me."

Tears of relief and joy trickled down my cheeks. In an instant I felt a deep peace within my heart. The feeling raced joyously through my whole being. Enclosed by prison bars, I had found the truth, and the truth had set me free.

October 2, 1979. I slept like a baby that night, content and secure.

13

A New Beginning

October 3, 1979. I woke up early to a new world and a new beginning. I lay there for an hour or so, musing about the previous night's experience. It seemed like a dream.

When the first light of dawn reflected off the catwalk, I called to Del. I had to tell somebody. "Hey, Del," I said in a hushed whisper, leaning against the bars. "You awake?"

"Sure," he whispered back sleepily.

"Know what happened last night?" I questioned excitedly.

"Whata you mean?" he replied curiously.

"I accepted Christ."

"Really!" he exclaimed, bounding out of his bed and leaning his head against the bars. "I saw you in my mirror last night, reading that Bible pretty hard."

"First time I've read it since I was a kid. Art told me what to read."

"So that's what his note was all about."

"Yeah. It's for real, Del. I feel great."

"Hallelujah!" he exclaimed. "This is cause for rejoicing. Man, let's pray."

"You pray," I said lightheartedly. "I'm not very experienced at this yet."

"Sure," he agreed like a benevolent older brother.

With both our heads bowed, Del began to pray. "Thank you, God," he said in a reverent, soft tone, "for saving Don. I know that this is the most important decision anyone can make. And I know it is so hard to be a good person. Give him the strength to live like a Christian should. Help us both to do your will every day. Thank you, Lord, for your love and your understanding. In Jesus' name, amen."

"Del, thank you. I wish I could pray like that."

"You can. Just relax and tell God how you feel."

"Can I keep your Bible for a while?"

"Keep it as long as you like. I've got another one."

Breaking Crime's Vicious Cycle

After breakfast, I stopped the guard when he was making his rounds. "Officer," I called to him politely.

"What do you need?" he asked dryly. He moved toward my cell, stopping a few feet from the bars.

"Would you tell Jacobson I want to see him?"

"Sure thing," he replied, continuing the dry tone.

Within an hour Jacobson was at my cell door, dressed as usual in a sport coat and dress pants. Tall and thin, he held his head erect like a man who was confident but not arrogant. "The guard said you wanted to see me," he said politely but cautiously. "What can I do for you?"

"I know you think I'm a rabble rouser," I began in a low tone, "always pushing for inmate rights and running around with murderers."

I paused, looking Jacobson in the eye. A questioning frown formed on his face.

"I've made it clear that I didn't want anything to do with your brand of religion," I continued. "I've been rude to you. I'm sorry for that."

"You certainly haven't offended me," he said softly.

"Now," I said, "I am interested in your brand of religion. I wanted you to be the first to know. I do respect you. I want to get baptized when I get out of here."

"That's wonderful!" he exclaimed, the frown disappearing. He moved closer to the bars, still maintaining eye contact. "I'm so glad to hear that, Don. How did you come to this decision?" he asked with a smile.

Jacobson listened intently as I told him about my experience with God the night before. "You'll never regret this decision," he assured me when I was finished. "I praise God for helping you see what you needed to do."

"I'll tell you, Chaplain, I should have done this long ago. I know I've found the answer to my problems."

"It's not an easy decision to make," he assured me. "You've made the decision. That's the important thing. Now, you can move forward. The apostle Paul said it quite well, 'Forgetting those things which are behind, I press forward.'"

Jacobson talked with me for a long time about what it meant to accept Christ as Lord and Savior and how I needed to learn more about Christ.

"Will you baptize me?" I asked quietly at a pause in the conversation.

A big grin spread across his face. "Certainly. I'd be delighted. You understand, of course, that we'll have to wait until after the lockdown?"

A New Beginning

"I figured that. Have any idea when it will end?"

"No. 'Fraid I don't know any more than you do."

Jacobson quickly moved on to another subject. "I've been bringing some Bible study materials to Art and Del," he said. "Would you like for me to bring some to you, too?"

"Sure. I'd like that very much."

"OK. I'll get them to you right away." I was thrilled with Jacobson's loving, caring response. He did just like God—he wiped the slate clean.

That afternoon, Jacobson brought me a legal pad, a couple of pens, a Bible, and two books. He told me they were mine to keep. I gave Del's Bible back to him and carefully printed my name in the new one. I didn't put an address.

After supper, me and Del started studying the Bible together. Jacobson suggested we do that. Since Del was more experienced in Bible study, he was the teacher. He would pose questions, then tell me to read certain verses to find the answers. He had a workbook full of questions.

"How do you get strength enough to overcome bad habits?" he asked, reading the question out of his workbook.

"Considering my situation," I quipped. "That's a good place to begin."

"Find the answer in Philippians 4:13. Read the verse out loud."

Del patiently waited while I looked in the table of contents to find Philippians. "It says," I began, " 'I can do all things through Him who strengthens me.' "

Del pointed out that "Him" referred to Christ. Then he told me about times Christ had helped him resist temptation. Like me, he came back to Christ in prison. We studied together practically every day. He took special delight in being the teacher.

Less than a month after my cell encounter with Christ, we got word that the lockdown was being lifted. There was no formal announcement. They just let out a section at a time for short periods. The kitchen help in Fourth Wing were first. They let them out for a few hours a day, mostly to help in the kitchen, along with exercising. The Awareness Tier was next. They let us go to the big yard to exercise.

The path to the big yard led through the large grassy area outside the mess hall where Cross was killed. The first time I walked into that yard, I could not believe my eyes. The entire area was solid cement. Not one thin blade of grass anywhere! "Would you look at this?" I gasped to Del.

"Why'd they do this?" I asked the guard politely.

Breaking Crime's Vicious Cycle

"Why do you think?" he grunted. "To keep you guys from digging tunnels and hiding weapons in the dirt."

"Oh," I said, moving on across the concrete lawn. "Punish sixteen hundred because of a few," I mumbled to Del.

"Don't get all wrought up, Don," he cautioned. "Remember. They've got the power."

"Yeah. I know. They can lock us up in a second."

Everywhere we went grassed areas had been cemented, and a maze of chain-link fences partitioned once-open areas. The big yard was the one exception. It still had grass.

The voice over the loudspeaker was different, too. A new warden was in charge. Stricter policies were in force. We were informed that we would walk the yard by sections at designated times, rather than as we chose.

Jacobson came to see me before the lockdown had ended completely. He had already selected a date for me to be baptized. "How about November 11?" he asked. "Is that OK?"

"Sure. Sure," I replied. "I'm anxious to do it. That's just two weeks away."

"Right. Sunday after next."

Jacobson also told me that Chuck Colson and his prison ministry staff were coming to Walla Walla within a week. They know about the lockdown and the other problems, he said. "They want to help in this adjustment period."

"It's hard to believe someone like that could help us," I told Jacobson.

"What do you mean?" he asked.

"He was so arrogant in the Watergate hearings? It looked to me like he was one of the worst of the bunch. He wasn't a bit sorry for what he did."

"At the time, he didn't think he had done anything wrong," he explained. "He's a different person, now." He paused, smiling. "You know how that can happen, don't you?"

"Yeah," I reluctantly agreed.

The advertisement about Colson's visit that was posted on the bulletin board indicated he was going to give his personal testimony. The news spread fast, with mixed reactions. Some were skeptical, like me; others were intrigued that such a popular personality was visiting the prison. Many couldn't have cared less, simply because he was a religious figure now. Most thought his visit wouldn't do any good.

About a hundred and fifty men gathered in the auditorium to hear Colson's testimony. He spoke in a conversational style as he told us

A New Beginning

how God put a ministry on his heart while he served time in prison. "I was in prison like you," he said, "when I turned my life completely over to God to do His will. From that point on, life was different."

Colson said he knew how prison conditions were because of his own experiences. He wanted to help us cope with the problems in prison and with life on the outside when we were released. At the end of his speech he invited us to a Christian Bible study that would begin in a few days. I was touched by his testimony.

"Don," David whispered to me as things were winding up. "Talk to him for us. Tell him how bad it is in here."

"OK, if you want me to, I will," I said confidently, flattered that he wanted me to be his spokesman.

David followed close behind as I caught up with Colson in the open area outside the auditorium. "Mr. Colson," I called. He turned around to face me, then moved closer.

"I'm Don Dennis," I said, extending my hand.

"Hello, Don," he said in a friendly tone, while shaking my hand. "How are you?"

"Fine," I replied with a faint smile. I took a deep breath, stood up straight, and looked him in the eye. "Mr. Colson, let me ask you a question, " I said nervously.

"Certainly," he said. "What is it?"

"Are you for real?" I blurted out, a trace of hostility unconsciously surfacing.

"Yes," he replied decisively. "God has changed my life," he explained. "I'm on the right track now. It's taken a while, but, with Christ's help, I'm moving in the right direction." He smiled, waiting for my response.

"Prove you're for real," I challenged him. "I dare you to go out and tell the public how bad it is in here. When one guy does something wrong, they punish all of us. There's some men who have been in segregation for two years. I dare you to tell them the truth. Tell them how they treat us."

"I will," he promised. "I'm going to be speaking in Walla Walla tonight. I'll tell them what you said."

"I'll appreciate that." David smiled approvingly.

"You did real good, Don," David said excitedly, as we walked back to our cells.

"I like his straightforward manner," I said. "He seemed sincere. Now, we'll see what he does."

"Yeah," David agreed, with a trace of skepticism.

A week after Colson's visit, George Soltau and Al Elliott from his staff came to Walla Walla. The advertisement said they would lead a Bible study in the chapel.

"You going?" David asked.

"Sure. Looks like we can trust Colson. Jacobson said he talked to the people in Walla Walla. He promised the Bible study, too, and here they are," I quipped.

Before the Bible study, George and Al mixed with the inmates gathered in the chapel. Jacobson made a special point of introducing me to George. "Here's a convict who's made a complete one-hundred-eighty degree turnaround," he began. "He was one of the worst convicts at San Quentin and other prisons. He's been a convict leader in every prison he's been in. Now, he's going to be a leader for Christ."

George's face lit up. "Wonderful!" he exclaimed, greeting me with a warm, firm handshake. "We praise God for what has happened in your life." He reminded me of Santa Claus, with his red nose, beard, jolly nature, and chubby build.

"He's going to be baptized a week from Sunday," Jacobson told him.

"Oh," George said. "I plan to be here then. I'd like to participate in the service."

"How about that, Don?" Jacobson said excitedly, turning to me, a big smile filling his face.

"Sounds great!" I exclaimed. I could hardly believe what I was hearing. A man like that anxious to participate in my baptism! My heart beat furiously.

After the Bible study, George stopped me as I was going out the door. "Don," he said, "do you know any convicts who would come to a meeting to talk about solving some of the problems here?"

"Sure," I said. "I know a bunch who would like to talk about the problems."

"Would you get the word out for us? Some of these men can help you," he said, pointing to the inmates standing near me.

"Sure. Sure I will. Here's one who can help," I said, pulling Del over to talk to George. After George explained what he had in mind, Del enthusiastically agreed to help.

A time was set for the meeting, two days away. Working with Jacobson, me, Art, Del, David, and John B. got a commitment from ninety of the most outspoken convict leaders. We contacted them at work, outside the mess hall, playing handball, walking the yard—wherever the opportunity opened up. They were skeptical that any-

A New Beginning

thing could be done to help the situation, but they were willing to give it a try.

The meeting was held in the Education Building in the room where I went to the college classes. Everyone who had promised to come showed up, anxious to give their opinions about what was needed to solve the problems. Seated in a big circle, along with ninety inmates, George introduced himself and Al and then proceeded to explain why the group had been gathered together. "We're here representing Chuck Colson," he began. "Some of you may have heard him give his testimony a couple of weeks ago."

A number nodded to indicate that they had heard the testimony. George smiled, encouraged by the response.

"Colson and the rest of us in the prison ministry," he continued, "are interested in making conditions better here. We'd like to know what you think we can do to help."

George paused to glance around the circle. The group was strangely silent as he made eye contact with one inmate after another. "We know you experienced a lot of heartache when they threw away things that were special to you," he went on, the group still staring at him in stony silence. "We know there's a hit list to get rid of six guards. We want you men to voice your grievances, and then we'll see if we can find ways to work out peaceable solutions. We sincerely want to help ease the pain."

George paused to give the inmates an opportunity to speak. No one said a word. I had already told him what I thought. I wanted someone else to speak up. He held his ground, refusing to move on until someone spoke.

Suddenly, as if ignited by an inaudible signal, one inmate after another let go. "They didn't have no right to beat those men like that," one yelled. "It was inhuman."

"Yeah," several yelled to agree.

"They destroyed every photo I had of my family," a young dude screamed.

"We can't replace them," someone added.

"That nurse in the hospital treats us like slime," a Hispanic dude yelled. "She's like the hag nurse in that cuckoo-nest movie."

The complaints overlapped into a spontaneous, violent upheaval. It was like a dam breaking and the water pouring out in uncontrollable rage.

George and Al listened patiently, as the inmates yelled and yelled. When the roar was winding down, George moved to gain control. "OK. OK," he said, raising his hand. "We can understand why you feel this way," he assured us. "We must do more than yell, though. We need to take definite measures to solve the problems. We need to discuss your complaints with the administration."

George paused and took a deep breath. All eyes were glued on him. "Would you men be willing to pick ten or twelve spokesmen to represent you to the warden?" he asked. "These men will talk to the warden in a reasonable manner. We'll arrange a definite time and place for the meeting."

"Sure, sure," one after another agreed.

"Would you men pray with us about this matter?" George asked.

"Sure," several said as the others nodded in agreement.

"Let's stand and join hands in unity," George requested.

Al stood up beside George, reaching to take his hand. The two then held out their hands to the men standing next to them. One man after another linked hands to form a circle.

"While Al voices our prayer," George said, "let's all ask God to help us select the men to talk to the warden."

After Al prayed, George told us to talk among ourselves about the men who could represent us best. We all agreed that we needed to have representatives from all the races and from all sections of the prison. Me and David B. were among the twelve selected.

After the meeting, George and Al met with the elected representatives. They guided us in developing a plan for presenting the problems to the administration. The plan included immediately setting up meetings to let all the convicts voice their complaints and to discuss the problems. George and Al got approval from the warden to hold the meetings. They counseled with us through the whole process.

After the meetings with the convicts, the twelve of us, along with George and Al, met with the warden. The warden listened sympathetically as we openly voiced the main grievances that came up over and over again. We told him we didn't think it was fair for the entire prison population to be punished for the actions of a few. We said the guards had no right to harass us. We demanded that the guards who inflicted the savage beatings on the eight men be dismissed. We asked that they return our TVs and other belongings.

The first good-faith gesture came two days after the meeting. Guards went from cell to cell, delivering our confiscated belongings. I got back my TV and radio. None of us ever got our pictures back.

George and Al were both there for the scheduled baptismal observance. Jacobson baptized Del. George baptized me. Coming up out of the water, I whispered a prayer, "God, please make me a strong Christian."

A New Beginning

After the baptismal service, George preached a sermon to more than one hundred inmates gathered in the chapel. At the close of the service, he asked me and Del to stand in front. Everybody came up and hugged us and wished us the best. It was exhilarating to have so many friends propelling me forward. I had a new family.

That night in my cell I fervently prayed my own prayer of dedication. "God," I said, "please help me overcome my bad habits. I don't want to be a phony Christian."

George and Al spent most of the month of November preaching and leading Bible studies at Walla Walla. I attended every service. I was amazed that these two men would give that much time and effort to solving our problems. I was captivated by the way they helped the inmates feel good about themselves and how they helped them plan to do better when they got out. "I wish I could work like you do in the prison ministry," I told George after chapel one Sunday.

"That would be good," he said, smiling broadly. "You understand how these people feel, and you relate well to them. They look up to you. When's your release date?"

"I don't have one," I chuckled. "Maybe never. I'm hoping my P.D. will be able to get me out sometime."

"Oh?" he questioned.

"I still would like to help, whether I get out or not. We've got to get hold of this and turn it around. There are too many repeat offenders like me," I added.

"I'll talk to Colson about your interest," he assured me. "I can tell him how you've helped us here."

"I appreciate your confidence. Please do tell him."

A month later I received a letter from Colson expressing appreciation for my interest and telling me he felt there would be a place for me in his ministry when I got out. I showed the letter to David and Del. "Whata ya think, Men?" I joked. "Pretty safe to make that promise to a man serving a life sentence, isn't it?"

"Still good to hear, though, isn't it?" David observed. I hoped for more, but I didn't know exactly what.

About fifteen of us started getting together for prayer every day after lunch. That made some of my dope-smoking friends put it on me pretty heavy about going to chapel all the time. Eddie was right in there with them, teasing me mercilessly. We were still friends, but he let me know he wasn't interested in the religion stuff. "You might be interested sometime," I told him.

"No, I won't," he responded decisively.

"It's sure helped me, Eddie."

"We'll see, Don. Bet you get tired of it, too, just like the Muslims and the Eastern religion stuff."

"I think you'll be surprised this time," I assured him.

The skepticism and teasing weren't anything I couldn't handle. All I had to do was think about what life was like before I wanted to go to chapel all the time. I'd take the trade-off any day.

In the midst of all the changes in my life, Ziegler made a visit to the prison. It was his first visit to see me since the lockdown was put in place. He stopped by to let me know the status of my appeal. "You doing OK?" he asked, as I sat down at the table in the attorneys' room.

"Doin' good," I replied. "Things are a little better in here now. Guess you've been hearing about this place."

"Sure have. Front-page news. I would have been by, but there was nothing new to tell you. I know it was hard, penned up for so long. Almost five months, wasn't it?"

"Yeah," I sighed. "Something good did come out of it, though."

"You mean the negotiations for better conditions?"

"That's one thing, but it isn't what I had in mind."

"Oh?" Ziegler said, questioning.

"I got baptized," I blurted out, smiling broadly.

"Really?"

"Yes. I accepted Christ."

"Oh, you're one of those Christians now," he said with a bemused look on his face.

"Yeah. I got dunked. It's for real this time, John, not like my other ventures. I should have done this long ago. If I had, I wouldn't be in this mess now."

Ziegler smiled faintly. "I have some good news, too."

"Really? What is it?"

"The state supreme court has agreed to hear your case."

"You don't mean it!" I exclaimed. "When did you find that out?"

"Got the notification two days ago. The verbal argument is scheduled to be heard in two weeks."

"Just like that," I said excitedly. "Still think we have a good chance?"

"Yes, I do. Other cases like this are getting favorable rulings. As I told you before, I'm basing the appeal on two convictions when you were not represented by counsel."

"Like I told you before, John," I warned, "both times I told them I didn't need a lawyer. I didn't see any point in wasting their time. They caught me in the act."

"That doesn't make any difference," he said decisively. "They're

A New Beginning

supposed to follow the law, and it's a violation of your constitutional rights to be without counsel."

"What about all the other things I did?"

"If those two convictions are set aside, they don't have enough for the habitual criminal ruling to hold up."

"Man, we really do have a case!" I exclaimed.

"Sure we do," Ziegler replied firmly.

"I thought maybe you were just blowing smoke," I quipped. "Guess I was afraid to get my hopes up."

"We're not there yet," he cautioned. "Even if the habitual criminal conviction is overturned, you'll be resentenced on the armed robbery charge. That's standard procedure."

His warning jarred me. My emotions were moving up and down like a yo-yo. "So there's a chance I will serve some more time, depending on the judge," I questioned somberly.

"Yes. I can't promise that you'll get out. I'll know more after the verbal argument."

"There's a good chance, though?" I questioned, refusing to accept the negative.

"I can't say that. Just try to go on as usual. Don't get your hopes too high for release right away," he advised.

"Will you let me know about the verbal argument as soon as you know?"

"Yes. I'll be here the minute I get the word. Good or bad," he added.

Ziegler's caution had brought me back to reality. I left the attorneys' room a bit dejected.

"How'd it go?" David asked on the way to lunch.

"Ziegler had pretty good news," I said matter-of-factly.

"What kind of good news?"

"The supreme court is going to hear my case."

"Great!" David exclaimed.

"Calm down now. Ziegler told me not to get my hopes too high. I still may do more time, even if they set aside the Big Bitch. So don't tell everybody I'm getting out."

"OK, Man," he said, enthusiastically patting me on the back. "But you'll have to admit that it does sound good."

"No guarantees, David. I may be here a while longer."

"Yeah," he smiled. "You're just trying to be cool."

"I just don't want to be disappointed."

"OK, OK. I'll wait to celebrate."

By supper time the news was across the Tier. They all had me paroled already. I persisted in playing it low-key, but I couldn't help daydreaming about what might be. It was a long, long two weeks.

Ziegler came straight to Walla Walla after the hearing. Sitting in his usual place at the table in the attorneys' room, he had a neutral look on his face. "I've got pretty good news, Don," he said calmly.

"I've been hoping and praying," I said softly. "What did they decide?"

Ziegler smiled broadly, his brown eyes gleaming. He couldn't hold it back any longer. "The court overturned the habitual criminal conviction," he said excitedly.

"Great! Great! Great!" I exclaimed, jumping up out of the chair, then quickly sitting back down to face Ziegler. "My prayers have been answered!"

"But, as I told you," Ziegler explained, "you'll have to go to court to be resentenced on the robbery charge."

"I've prepared myself for that. You've warned me good."

Ziegler took a deep breath and smiled broadly. "Just between you and me, Don," he began, "I think you can plan on getting out."

Before I could respond, he added another word of caution. "Remember. Still be prepared to serve some more time. You never can tell what the judge will do."

"OK. OK. I'll try. But you're driving me crazy."

"I just want to prepare you."

"Is the judge tough?"

"Pretty tough."

"When do we go to court?"

"February twenty-fifth."

"That's just two weeks from today. It's happening fast!"

"That's right. When things move, they move fast."

On the way back to work, I stopped at a pay phone to call my cousin, Joycie.

"Hi, Joycie," I said lightheartedly.

"Don!" she exclaimed. "Where are you?"

"Where do you think? Walla Walla, of course. I may get out of here pretty soon, though."

"Really? When?"

"If everything goes OK, I'll be out February twenty-fifth."

"The twenty-fifth?" she questioned. "Today's the eleventh. Hey! That's just two weeks away!"

"My P. D. thinks they'll let me out. They've overturned the habitual criminal conviction. Now it all depends on what the judge does with the armed robbery conviction. I've kept clean in here. I'm hoping that'll make a difference."

"Want us to pick you up?"

"I'd sure appreciate that. But what if I don't get out?"

"We'll just drive back home," she said with a chuckle. "But I'm going to plan on you getting out."

"Me, too. I figure everything will be wound up by noon, one way or the other. Why don't you just meet me in the lobby of the courthouse?"

"OK. Danny and I will be there and the girls, too. They talk about you all the time, Don. They really want to see you. I'm sorry we haven't been to see you."

"I understand. I've put all of you through a lot, Joycie," I added. "I'm gonna make it. Things are really different this time."

"Good. Good. Let's plan on it. I believe you will."

"See you later."

I quietly put the phone back in place and went back to work to punch out some more numbers.

That night in my cell I went through the little address book I kept in my billfold. I knew I would need contacts on the outside. Folded inside the book was a letter from Melody, now frayed on the edges from carrying it around. It was the one memento I had managed to save. Lying down on my bed, I read it once again:

Dear Uncle Don,

I am going to miss you very much. And I hope you come back real soon. I didn't tell you this before but you're my best uncle I ever had and will always be. My mom and sisters will never stop love'n you and that includes my daddy. . . . I wish you could stay till Monica got home but you're leaving today. Eat alot of peanut butter & jelley & you'll be strong like usual.

Love, Melody

Tears eased out the side of each eye, trickling down my cheeks to the bed. *I'm so sorry I've hurt those sweet girls,* I sighed silently. *I hope I can make it up to them.* I prayed that God would help me.

14

Breaking the Cycle

As the squad car pulled away from the gate with the two escort guards in the front seat, I refused to look back at the old, gray, ugly prison. Moving down the highway, I speculated about what might happen in the courtroom, both good and bad. The best scenario, of course, was that I wouldn't see ugly Walla Walla again.

Braswell, the P.D. who unsuccessfully tried to limit my conviction to the Little Bitch, was there with Ziegler when the guard brought me and the other prisoners into the courtroom. By the time my turn came, the tension had built up inside me at a fever pitch. My head was whirling from the endless scenarios running through my brain. Heart palpitations erupted when the court clerk finally called my name.

With Ziegler on one side of me and Braswell on the other, we walked forward to face the judge. For a few long seconds, he examined the form in front of him.

"Mr. Dennis," he began, peering down at us over his half-moon reading glasses, "the State Supreme Court has overturned your habitual criminal conviction." His expression was emotionless, neutral.

I smiled faintly, trying to maintain court reserve.

"Consequently, that sentence will be set aside," he continued. My smile broadened. I couldn't hold it back.

"On the armed robbery charge," he went on, "I am going to sentence you to three years in prison."

A deep, sinking feeling gripped my stomach. My smile faded. In an instant Walla Walla passed before me. *Three more years! Three long years! I've got to go back to that place, after all!* The reality paralyzed me.

The judge paused to clear his throat. "This sentence will be commuted to time served," he explained, still maintaining the neutral tone. "With five years probation," he added.

My heart pounded joyously out of my chest. *Time served! Probation!* I exclaimed silently, the smile back in place.

"You will be released today," he stated.

I turned to Ziegler, not sure what I dared do to celebrate victory. "We won! We won!" he exclaimed, waving his arms wildly and jumping up and down. He excitedly reached out to hug me. With tears flowing freely down our cheeks, we hugged each other, sobbing unashamedly and joyously.

"I knew you could do it!" I exclaimed through the tears.

Free! Free! The words bounced off the courtroom walls, as me and Ziegler sped down the aisle and out the door.

"After we sign some papers, you're free to go," Ziegler told me. "Your family's here, aren't they?" he questioned.

"My cousins should've been in the courtroom. They're supposed to meet me out front after I sign the papers."

"I want to meet them."

Ziegler excitedly guided me through the paper-signing. We then went to the reception area where me and Joycie had agreed to meet. The girls spotted me first. "Uncle Don," they called, almost in unison, running to hug me.

"Don," Joycie said hugging me. "This is a miracle. I'm so glad." Tears ran down her cheeks.

"Me, too," I said. "I still can't believe it."

"Welcome home, Don!" Danny exclaimed, shaking my hand.

"Did you see it all?" Ziegler asked excitedly.

"Sure," Joycie said. "It was exciting!"

After a few minutes of small talk, we said our good-byes. "I wish you well," Ziegler assured me. "You're going to make it this time."

"Thanks, Man. You're a lifesaver."

Since my release was so sudden, I was probated to Longview. Joycie and Danny gladly invited me to stay with them. Shelley gave me her room and moved in with Monica.

"Barbie and Jim are anxious to see you," Joycie said.

"They haven't given up on me?" I chuckled.

"Not yet," Joycie teased back.

Barbie and Jim came right over when I called. It was a fun evening. Joycie fixed a really nice meal. We laughed about the good times. And everybody was interested in what I was going to do. I felt good about the future.

The next day Joycie dropped me off at the probation office. My parole officer was a young woman about twenty-eight years old. In a very businesslike and decisive manner, she explained the conditions of my parole. "One condition," she said, "is that you use no drugs or alcohol. Your record indicates that alcohol abuse is one of your biggest problems. For this reason, you will be required to take antiabuse pills. The pills are effective for about three days; so you'll need to come in here on Tuesday and Friday to take a pill."

"How long do I have to do this?" I asked.

"For the duration of your parole. Five years."

Five more years of control, I thought. *What a drag.*

"Don," she continued, "I want to impress upon you the consequences of drinking when you're on this pill. If you take any alcohol, you'll become deathly sick. It could even kill you," she added, looking me in the eye.

"I want to stay clean," I said softly.

"You will report to me once a week for six weeks and then monthly. If you have to relocate for a job, you are required to inform me. Do you have any questions?"

"No. I think I understand everything."

She wished me good luck in getting a job and resettling in society. "If there's anything I can do to help, feel free to call," she said, a smile finally breaking through.

After I left the probation office, I went to the state employment agency to sign up for work. They said they didn't have anything with my job skills but would call when something came up.

Barbie took me around to the paper mills in the area. Many weren't even taking applications. Two weeks later Danny told me they were taking applications at Reynolds Aluminum where he worked. He said the competition was keen, that I needed to be there early in the morning.

I got a folding chair from Joycie, a blanket, a thermos jug of coffee, and got in line at the plant the night before. I was tenth in line with forty other guys.

"Don't call us; we'll call you," they told me the next morning after I filled out the application. With my record I figured I could forget about that job.

Every Tuesday and Friday, Joycie drove me to the probation office to take my pill. The girls went inside with me and watched as I downed the pill. I started teasing them about not taking it. I would put the pill under my tongue and show it to them. "Uncle Don," Melody always pleaded, "take your annabuse; take your annabuse." Monica and Shelley chimed in with the same plea. I would then take some more water and swallow the pill. They always smiled approvingly.

Joycie and Barbie were practically working full time to get me settled in society. Barbie made an appointment for me to meet with her pastor at the community church where she attended. Sitting in the pastor's plush office, I told him I had just gotten out of prison and that I had been going to chapel in prison every Sunday. "I really want to make it this time," I told him.

"That's what it takes," he responded.

"But I'm so scared inside," I confided to him. "I don't know if I can handle the streets. When my drinking friends see me on the street, they try to get me to join them. My old, wild girlfriends are starting to call me."

"I know how difficult it must be," he replied.

"I need to find some Christian friends," I continued. "And I need a job to buy things like my own shaving stuff."

"I understand," he said. "And I am sorry, but there's no help available here. I honestly don't know anyone with your background that you can relate to. The people in this church have been here a long time. They have their friends and their ways. Barbara can tell you that. They would have a very difficult time relating to your situation. I know it shouldn't be that way, but I'm just trying to be honest."

"Well, thanks for listening," I said quietly. "I better be on my way. I need to look for a job."

"I wish I could be more encouraging," he replied. "I'll be praying for you."

"You do that," I said with sarcasm. *Brother, I'll catch you later,* I said to myself. *I don't need the kind of words you have for me.*

"How'd it go?" Barbie asked, as I got in the car.

"Man, Barbie, this isn't right. He's telling me I won't fit in here. If a preacher can't overcome the barriers, how can anybody?"

Over lunch Barbie tried to make me feel better. "I realize how the people are in that church," she began. "They're basically good people, but they are locked up in their own little world. They don't know how to respond to any kind of outsider, much less one in your situation. I was hoping the pastor would be different, though," she added softly.

As always, Joycie tried to cheer me up when I told her what happened. "Didn't you say Charles Colson said something about a job possibility in his prison ministry?" she asked.

"Yes, he did," I replied. "But that was when I had a life sentence on me."

"He probably meant it. Why don't you give him a call?"

The next morning I called the Prison Fellowship and asked for Colson. Since, he wasn't in, the receptionist gave me one of the administrators.

"Hello, Don," the man said pleasantly. "How can I help you?"

"I met Chuck Colson when he came to Walla Walla about six months ago," I explained.

"Oh, is that so?"

"Yes. He said there would be a place for me in the Prison Fellowship when I got out. I was released earlier than I thought and was wondering if anything is available now."

"This comes as a surprise," he replied. "I don't recall Chuck saying anything about a job for you. Right now, nothing is available, but something might open up later on. We are expanding our ministries all the time."

"Do you think the ministry could loan me a couple hundred to help me get started. I've been looking everywhere, but the job market isn't very good here."

"Let me double check with Chuck about the job, and I'll call you back right away."

"I'd appreciate that."

The man called me back the next day. "Don," he began, "no positions are available at the present time, but we would suggest that you go through the placement process with the Fellowship. Then, when a job opens up, you'll be ready to step in. We'll send you the two hundred as a loan while you're going through the placement process."

"That sounds great!" I exclaimed. "I really want to work with your Fellowship."

"Right now, I would like for you to get in touch with our contact in Longview." I wrote down the name.

The contact turned out to be the pastor of the church where Joycie attended. She gladly made an appointment for me to talk with him and drove me to the church.

"What can I do to help?" the pastor asked.

"I accepted Christ in prison," I began, "but I haven't gotten much encouragement from Christians so far. The pastor at the community church gave me a pretty cold shoulder. He didn't want to be bothered." My voice choked with emotion, so unlike me to let down in front of a stranger.

"I hope we can help you," he said quietly.

I showed him the letter from Colson, telling me he would see about placing me in a job in his organization when I got out of prison. "I'm mainly looking for a job to fill the time, so I won't walk the streets. I need a place to stay, too. My cousins don't act like I'm in the way, but I know its hard on them with an extra person in the house. It's pretty crowded. I'm hurting. I desperately need a job and a place to call my own."

He got right to the point. "I'm going to tell you the truth, Don. I just don't know where you can find a job. The job market just isn't very good in this area right now."

"Aren't you the Prison Fellowship contact?" I asked impatiently. "Can't you help me?"

"Most of the money available for our ministry is targeted to help people before they get out of prison—Bible study and that sort of ministry. We just don't have any money to speak of for aftercare. You'll certainly be welcome in this church, though."

"Until I get me a suit of clothes or a pair of slacks and a dress shirt," I began, my voice cracking. "'I don't think I'll feel like coming to church."

Passing over my emotional declaration, he asked me to pray with him. "Yes," I agreed quietly, with little enthusiasm.

He fervently prayed that God would help me get settled into society and into a church where I could be happy. The prayer made me cringe. *Just prayer. No help,* I thought. *What good does that do?* His supposed piety was disgusting.

As I walked out the door to his office, the pastor patted me on the back. "I'll keep you in my prayers, Don. I know how difficult it must be for you."

I grunted a feeble "thank you" and went to meet Joycie.

"How'd it go?" she asked.

"No help there," I said dejectedly. "He doesn't know about any job or resources. He just prays," I added, with a trace of sarcasm. Joycie looked disappointed but did not pass judgment on the preacher.

The two hundred dollars came with the job application from the Prison Fellowship. I completed the application and sent it right back. Barbie put me on to a temporary job in a supermarket bagging and taking out groceries. They needed some extra help while they were changing to a computer system. Most of the baggers were teenagers. People looked at me like, "What's this guy doing here?"

I was relieved that the bagging job only lasted three weeks. It was demeaning for someone my age. After that, I signed up with a temporary job service. They managed to keep me working almost every day.

I started walking downtown in the evening to get out and to give Joycie and Danny some privacy. The first three or four times I went out, I passed by the bars without even thinking of going in. One

Friday evening I thought it might be nice to have one little beer. I couldn't give in, though; the antiabuse pill stood in the way.

I decided to do something about the antiabuse pills. I told Joycie that my parole officer had changed the time for me to take the pill. I gave her a time when the girls would be in school. The next time I went to take the pill, I faked a swallow, put the pill under my tongue, and spit it out in the restroom before I went outside to meet Joycie. With no little girls to check on me, it was easy.

Three days later I stopped at a bar while taking my evening walk. At first, I just drank a beer or two and tried to stay away from the action. Then I ran into Mae, the wildest of the wild. We started going out almost every night. When Barbie found out I was going with her, she came by Joycie's to talk to me. "Don," she pleaded. "You're going with those wild girls again. If you want someone to talk to, come over to my house. You're going to be right back in trouble again. Something's wrong with that Mae. I don't trust her. She's got a glassy look in her eyes, like she's on drugs. Is she?"

"I don't know really," I lied. I did know Mae was on drugs, because we smoked weed together.

One Friday night, on an impulse, me and Mae got married. The next day I moved my things into her place. I didn't bother to tell Barbie. I let her find out from Joycie.

In no time I was locked into my old life-style. Things were different this time, though. The guilt was driving me crazy. Before, I enjoyed smoking weed and running around with wild women. Now I was ashamed and guilty. I couldn't do anything without feeling guilty. Still, I didn't let the guilt feelings stop me.

The day after our month anniversary, I got mad at Mae and moved back in with Joycie and Danny. Before long, I started going with a girl I met at Longbell Lumber where I had a temporary job. She was a decent girl. She told me that a girlfriend of hers had an older car up on blocks. The tires were gone, and the battery was dead; otherwise it was in good shape. Danny bought tires for it and charged up the battery. Now I had wheels and could go anywhere I wanted.

I decided to go to L.A. to visit a Mexican dude named Jose that I met at Walla Walla. I had his phone number in my address book. He was in the pen for drug dealing and got paroled about two months before me. I knew he had a bunch of big-time connections.

I called Jose from a phone booth. I didn't dare call from Barbie or Joycie's house. They would ask a lot of questions about making contact with someone in California.

Breaking the Cycle

Jose remembered me well. "How you doing, Buddy?" he asked. "What's happening?"

"Hey, Jose," I replied, "I need to make some money."

"Come on down to L.A. I can put you to work. There's plenty of money here."

"Sounds terrific, but I'm broke. I don't even have the money to get there."

"I'll send you the money," he offered quickly. He wired the money to me the next day.

Jose had a place for me to stay when I got to L.A. The next day I started selling dope he supplied. Me and his cute sister-in-law, Cindy, started going together right away, but the romance didn't last long. When I had a little money saved up, I lost interest in Cindy and the dope selling. I had moving-on fever. The day after Mount St. Helens blew up, I went back to Longview and moved in with Joycie and Danny.

Danny told me about work at the dam by Mount St. Helens. I got a job there making about six hundred dollars a week. Things looked good. It beat all the guilt that went with selling drugs.

On my own, I quit smoking weed and drinking. It was the first time I had ever really tried. The alcohol ban lasted a month. I couldn't quit completely. I just didn't have the strength. The booze drew me like a magnet.

Mae called me up at Joycie's, and we got back together. It scared Barbie and Joycie. "Oh, Don," Barbie said, "I sure hope you don't go back to jail."

"'You've got to slow down," Joycie urged. "You've got to stay away from your wild friends."

I didn't tell Barbie or Joycie or anyone else, but I had come to the conclusion that I could not make it as a Christian. *Who am I trying to kid?* I decided. *I'm just not cut out to be a Christian. That's for goody-goody people. Why fight it? Why try to be something I'm not? I believe in Christ, but I can't really live like that.* On the surface, I pretended to be having fun. Deep down, I was tormented, dismayed at my weakness. I was drinking because I had to, not because it was fun.

September 4, 1980, I was in a bar drinking with Mae, laughing and talking aimlessly, as usual. At a lull in the chatter, I took a swig of beer and glanced across the table at her. *She looks like a tramp,* I thought. All of a sudden it seemed that Mae's hard living had caught up with her. She looked stale. Her glassy eyes made me cringe. An empty, eerie feeling gripped me. I looked around the room from table to table. The place was packed with people laughing and talking. Strangely, I felt totally alone, trapped.

I glanced back at Mae. She still looked like a tramp. "I've got to go for a walk, Mae," I said nervously. I was roaring inside like a lion pushed into a corner by a threatening tamer. I had to get out of there.

"OK," she said, with a puzzled look on her face. "You want me to go with you?"

"No. I need to go alone. I'll see you later." I looked back at the table, as I walked out the door. Mae was still watching me with that puzzled look. Disgusted with me, she left town the next day.

I walked south a couple of blocks, thinking about life. I thought about MaMa and going to church with her. I thought about that night in the cell, alone with God. Chuck Colson's Prison Fellowship came to mind. I recalled my conversations with George Soltau about living like a Christian inside and outside the pen.

I stopped at a phone booth and dialed information in Texas. "What city?" the operator asked.

"Richardson," I replied. "George Soltau. S-O-L-T-A-U."

The operator keyed in the recording. I wrote down the number, then dialed the operator. I told her I wanted to call collect. When George answered, I nervously waited as the operator asked the big question, "Will you accept a collect call from Don Dennis?"

"Yes, of course," he said, without hesitation. I was tremendously relieved.

Before George could say anything else, I told him about our meeting at Walla Walla and how I had wanted to be involved in the prison ministry. "What's going on?" he asked.

"To tell the truth, George, things aren't going too good."

"What's the problem?" he asked in his gentle, caring tone.

"I'm back to my old ways, George," I sighed, "smoking dope and drinking and running around with wild women. I've just about come to the conclusion that there's no hope for me out on these streets. I'm gonna get me a gun and just go for what I know, and I'll be back in the pen."

"I don't think you'd be calling me if you didn't think there was hope. Don't get a gun, Don. There's hope for you."

"I don't know whether it's worth the effort. At least I have friends in prison and a roof over my head."

"Give it a little more time," he urged.

"George, I've given it almost six months. I'm worse off now than when I first got out. There's no decent jobs here. I don't have any decent friends. It's just no good."

Breaking the Cycle

"I'll tell you what," George offered, "if you can get the money together to come to Texas, I'll help you get a job and find a place to stay."

"That would be good," I said softly.

"Don, let's pray about this," he suggested. "Would you like for me to do that?"

"Yes, George, I would like that."

George thanked God for me and for giving me life. He fervently asked God to give me the strength to get out of Longview and come to Texas. His warm, caring prayer made me feel God's presence in a special way. At that moment, God was standing right there beside me.

I kept George's offer to myself. I didn't want anyone to pressure me into a decision. And I wasn't ready to leave Longview to go to a place I didn't know anything about.

A week later, when my car broke down, I decided to take the bus to Portland to see Mae. A friend told me she had moved there. She was glad to see me and invited me to stay. The harmony didn't last long, though. The day before Thanksgiving we got into a big fight. On Thanksgiving morning I angrily stuffed my clothes and other belongings into my badly worn duffel bag and a cardboard box. With rain pouring down, I started walking the fifty miles to Longview. *What a sorry piece of luck,* I thought. *The first Thanksgiving out of prison and here I am all alone. No one should be alone on Thanksgiving.* The desperate longing for family sent a dull pain through my body.

A mile down the highway, I stopped at a phone booth to call Barbie. I was relieved when she accepted the collect call. I half expected her to refuse. "Barbie," I said, trying to be upbeat. "I'm on my way to Longview. Could I come stay with you for a few days?" A deadly pause followed.

"I'm sorry, Don," she sighed impatiently. "I just can't. I've tried with you. Everybody's tried with you. They've all lost their patience. Jim's disgusted. He doesn't want you around anymore. It's not good for the kids. They've seen enough of your antics. I just don't feel like I should let you ruin our holiday."

"I understand, Barbie," I said quietly. "I can't blame you."

I called Joycie, Aunt Eleanor, and every relative I could think of. Everyone was gone. I stepped out of the phone booth into the rain and continued walking toward Longview. I didn't know any where else to go.

Another mile down the road a car pulled up beside me. Inside was a young couple. The woman rolled down the window. "Where are you going?" she asked, smiling broadly.

"I don't know," I replied. "I guess I'm heading for Texas." I didn't know why I said "Texas." The name just flew out.

"We're going to Longview. We could take you that far."

"That would be great!" I exclaimed. "I have relatives there."

"I'm Don Dennis," I said, once inside the car.

"Sally and Jack Morris," the young man said.

"This was so nice of you. I am drenched to the bone."

"We never pick anyone up," Jack explained. "But you looked so cold and wet. We just felt God wanted us to pick you up."

"Really?" I questioned. "I'm thankful for that." *Maybe God is still in my life, after all,* I thought.

"We're going to our parents' home in Longview for Thanksgiving," Sally said.

"What's their name?" I asked.

"Robert and Virginia Hale," she replied.

"I don't recognize the name. Have they lived there long?"

"About ten years."

"Oh, I haven't been back much in the last ten years."

"Do you go to church?" she asked.

"I have, but not lately."

While we rode along in the rain, I mused about the possibility of moving to Texas. In my heart, I knew I had to let go and put Longview and all my wild friends completely behind me. Also, in my heart, I hated to let it all go—the known for the unknown.

I asked the young man to let me off at a phone booth on the main highway just outside Longview. "Be happy to take you to your relative's house," he offered.

"No. This will be fine," I insisted. "I need to call first. You've been very kind." I had a good feeling inside as I watched the young couple move on down the highway.

Joycie answered on the first ring. She said she would pick me up. She told me Barbie and Jim were there.

After Joycie fixed me a turkey sandwich, Jim and Danny went in the living room to watch TV. Sitting across the table from me, Barbie and Joycie turned serious. It looked like my final hearing. "I've decided to go to Texas," I blurted out nervously before they could say anything.

"What are you going to Texas for?" Barbie questioned.

"A friend said he would help me get a job and a place to stay."

Breaking the Cycle

"What kind of guy is he?" Joycie asked in a suspicious tone. It was so unlike her.

"Is he a crook?" Barbie questioned sharply.

"No. He's a Christian. He works with Chuck Colson in the prison ministry. I told you about him. He said he would help me if I could get the money together to go down there."

"I hate for you to leave," Joycie said softly. "But I do think you need to get far away from this area."

"I don't have the money for the bus ticket. Maybe I could work at Longbell long enough to save it up."

"No," Barbie said decisively. "You need to get out of here now." She emphasized the *now*.

"Let's go see Aunt Eleanor," Joycie suggested. "Maybe she can help?"

The three of us walked across the street to see Aunt Eleanor. Sitting around the kitchen table drinking coffee, Joycie told her what I planned to do. Aunt Eleanor got all excited and called up Aunt Virginia and told her what I wanted to do. She was there in ten minutes. The two aunts talked together in the bedroom, then came into the kitchen. "We want to help you, Don," Aunt Eleanor said. "But we don't have much money. We both live on fixed incomes. I can give you fifty dollars, and Virginia can give you fifty."

"I would appreciate that very much," I said, touched deeply by their gesture.

Joycie and Barbie quickly offered to give me the rest I needed for the ticket. Barbie got the bus ticket the next day. I called George from Joycie's and told him when the bus would arrive.

The Tuesday after Thanksgiving, Barbie, Joycie and the girls went with me to the bus station. Melody made me promise to write. "Sure I will," I told her.

A twinge of sadness gripped me as the bus pulled out of the station. I waved good-bye to the little band of family. Barbie and Joycie looked hopeful. I thought I saw a tear trickle down Melody's cheek.

As the bus moved through the center of town, one lone tear trickled down my own cheek. I wiped it away quickly.

God, I prayed silently, *please make it better this time*. I looked forward to yet another fresh start.

15

One More Day, Lord

December 7, 1980, the anniversary of the infamous attack on Pearl Harbor, the bus pulled into the depot at Dallas. It was six in the morning. We had been on the road five long days. With my cardboard box in tow, I jumped from the steps to the pavement. Except for six, one-dollar bills and a little pocket change, everything I owned was in the box.

George answered on the first ring. "George," I said, "this is Don Dennis. Hope I didn't wake you up."

"No problem," he assured me cheerily. "I've been waiting for your call. My son delivers papers, so I always get up early. It will take about a half hour to get there."

I was finishing my second cup of coffee when George pulled up to the curb. He walked right over to the bench where I was sitting. "Hello, Don," he said pleasantly, smiling through his thick beard. "It's good to see you."

"So you recognized me," I quipped, standing up to shake his outstretched hand.

"Sure did," he replied with a smile. "Ready to go?"

"I'm ready. This is all the luggage I have," I said, picking up my cardboard box from under the bench.

Along the way to Richardson, George pointed out sights he thought were interesting. "I know you're going to like it here, Don," he said, his voice filled with enthusiasm.

"I hope so," I said softly. At that moment, I couldn't share his enthusiasm. Compared to Longview, the place was so bare—so few big trees. And, the minute we drove into Richardson, I was intimidated by the affluence of the town, with its big brick homes, finely manicured lawns, and expensive cars parked on the long driveways. I didn't say anything to George, but I wondered how I could possibly fit in.

The Soltau house was big, but not as showy as some we had

passed. George's wife, Lennie, was at the door to greet me. She was at least ten years younger than George, her dark, bouffant hairdo attractively framing her olive complexion. She was short and petite like my sister, Barbie. "Hello, Don," she said pleasantly, extending her hand. "Come on in."

The place was buzzing with activity, with children running in all directions getting ready to go to church. Lennie showed me to her son's room. "This will be yours while you're here," she said. "I know you're tired. Make yourself at home. We'll have breakfast in a few minutes." I was relieved that she didn't notice the cardboard box.

I put the box on the bed and opened it up. Along with some toiletries, I had three shirts, a pair of jeans, a pair of corduroys, a jacket, and tennis shoes. Before I had time to put anything away, George knocked on the door, telling me it was time for breakfast.

Six of us gathered around the big table. George remarked that it was a small crowd compared to the ten they used to have. They had eight kids between them, five now scattered to "their own pursuits," as George put it. Both their spouses had died some years before.

Christmas carols provided a festive background for our conversation. I found out later that the beautiful classical soprano voice on the recordings belonged to Lennie.

One by one everybody left to finish getting ready for church. With just me and George sitting there, he invited me to go to church with the family. "Sure, I'll go with you," I replied, although I really didn't want to. I just felt obligated after all George had done for me.

While getting ready I glanced at myself in the mirror. My washed-out look was shocking—no haircut, faded plaid shirt, weather-beaten corduroys, worn-out shoes. *It's the best I can do,* I sighed. Feeling totally inadequate, I went into the family room to visit with George.

"Don," George said kindly as we talked, "I just pray that you'll be able to make it here. There's lots of work in this area. Our church has a good deal of money. A man in the church owns a car lot, and I know he'll work with you. I think the church can get you a little car, and you can pay it off. I'll do all I can to get you the help you need."

"I sincerely appreciate what you've done already, George. There was no hope for me in Longview. I'm homesick already, but I know I wasn't going to make it there."

"All I ask from you, Don, is that you don't come home drunk or use drugs."

"I do want to change, George. I really do. But, right now, I don't feel I have the strength."

"Don," he continued seriously, "I think God has His hand on you. I really do. What we've got to do is stay in prayer. And you should think about getting in a church where you can meet Christian friends."

"Maybe that will help," I agreed. Silently, I was saying, *I don't think I can make it. I'm too weak. I don't believe anything good is going to happen.*

"Is that the only pair of shoes you have?" George asked cautiously, pointing to my worn-out dress shoes.

"Other than tennis shoes, they are."

"Try these out," he suggested, taking a shiny brown shoe off of his right foot and then the left.

My feet slipped right in. "I can't believe it!" I exclaimed. "They're an exact fit."

"They're yours."

"Thank you, George! Thank you very much!"

As we went out the door to leave for church, George grabbed a Bible off a side table. "Here, you'll need this," he said, handing it to me.

We all piled into the van to go to Town North Presbyterian Church. Driving into the parking lot, I could easily tell what kind of people were in the membership. Lincolns, Cads, and Oldsmobiles were everywhere. *How can I possibly fit in here?* I wondered again.

Lennie led the way to their regular pew. Self-consciously, I moved in behind George, desperately hoping no one would notice my clothes. *What is this ex-con, shaking alcoholic doing here?* I thought to myself. *I do not fit in. I do not fit in.* How I wished I had said no to George's invitation.

 With great enthusiasm, the song leader announced the number of the first hymn. He made me want to sing. After a series of songs and announcements, the pastor stood up to deliver the morning message. About forty, he looked every bit the clean-cut, polished gentleman, with styled hair and dressed in the latest in men's clothing.

The pastor asked everybody to turn to James 2. "I will read verses 1 through 6," he announced while I was still searching for the passage. I picked up at verse 2: "If a man comes into your assembly with a gold ring and dressed in fine clothes, and there also comes in a poor man in dirty clothes, and you pay special attention to the one who is wearing the fine clothes, and say, 'You sit here in a good place,' and you say to the poor man, 'You stand over there, or sit down by my footstool,' have you not made distinctions among yourselves, and become judges with evil motives?" In keeping with the emphasis of the passage, he preached about the Christian's responsibility to help those in need.

I caught the preacher's eye. He turned beet red, but quickly moved on in his sermon.

One More Day, Lord

When I walked out the front door of the sanctuary, the preacher was there to greet me. George introduced me as "the man I told you about."

"I guess I preached about you this morning," he said good-naturedly.

"I guess so," I chuckled.

"We're glad you came to worship with us. Come back again soon." I liked his warm, friendly style.

After lunch I went through the job listings in the paper. I circled several possibilities and showed them to George. "Don't get frustrated if you don't get a job right away," he advised. "You're welcome to stay here as long as you need to." They were a kind Christian family. But all the friendliness in the world couldn't keep me from feeling out of place.

After church that evening the pastor talked to me and George in his study. George told him about meeting me in prison and how I had worked as a coordinator for the Prison Fellowship Ministries while I was in Walla Walla.

"How can our church help you?" he asked.

"The main thing I need," I replied, "is a car and a job, so I can get on my own."

"Let me see what I can come up with. I feel sure there are people in our church who can and will want to help."

On Monday George drove me around to find a job. I put in several applications, but none really fit me. In the afternoon I went with George and Lennie and the kids to find a Christmas tree. The kids picked out a big one.

It was fun to watch George, Lennie, and the kids decorate the tree. They invited me to help, but I told them I would rather watch. The last tree I decorated was the one my dad threw out the front door.

The next day I called Joycie collect. I was desperately homesick. She told me Mae had been looking for me. That made me more homesick.

In the evening the preacher came by to bring me a suit, a gray glen plaid, that looked brand-new. "It's one my father gave me," he said, "but it doesn't fit me very well. I thought maybe you could use it."

"Sure could," I said. "I really appreciate this."

The suit was a good fit. George gave me a black pair of shoes to go with it and money to get a haircut, with a little left over for spending money. I felt better.

Four days before Christmas George told me he was going out of town after Christmas. Anticipating the trip, he had located a halfway house I could live in. It was in the upper part of a hotel that had been donated to a Catholic church. An ex-con ran it, with some supervision from the nuns. George thought it would be a good spot for me to be while I looked for work. "And," he said, "I think you will be a great influence there."

"That sounds fine to me," I agreed, trying to be enthusiastic. I knew I needed to get out of George's house, but it scared me to be put in downtown Dallas with a bunch of losers. *George may be right,* I reasoned. *Maybe, I can help some people.* No matter how much I told myself that, I found it hard to believe. I wasn't stabilized myself.

George took me to the halfway house and introduced me to Kenny, the guy who was in charge. About fifty-five, he had a gentle, yet effusive manner. His ruddy cheeks and watery eyes identified him as a recovering addict. He shared a room with a prissy young man about twenty-three.

Kenny put me in with a guy named Red, who was a little older than me. His bloodshot eyes matched the red of his hair. Kenny warned me that Red had a drinking problem but said he was required to lay off the booze while he was there. I assured him I could handle alcoholics. "I've had a good deal of experience in that area," I told him.

In all there were a dozen guys in the house. Kenny tried to set strict rules, but nobody paid attention. He had a ten o'clock curfew, but nobody came in on time. Red wasn't supposed to drink, but he sneaked beer in. Kenny simply didn't have the ability to make the men follow the rules.

George picked me up at the halfway house Christmas morning to have dinner at his house. It was a fun time, eating a delicious meal and singing Christmas carols around the tree. And they had gotten me a Christmas present.

After George took me back to the halfway house in the evening, I discovered that the nuns had brought us presents and cookies and candy and some nice clothes. Red sneaked in a six-pack. I was propped up in my bed reading the paper when he smuggled it in, wrapped in his jacket. He threw the jacket on the bed and set the booze down on the table across from me. I resisted about five seconds.

"Give me one of those beers, Red," I said, as he took one from the pack for himself.

"Sure," he said cheerily, glad to have drinking company. It didn't take long for me and Red to down all six.

The Monday after Christmas I resumed my search for a job. Three things were against me. People weren't hiring; they weren't interviewing until after the first of the year; or I didn't have the job skills needed. It

One More Day, Lord

was discouraging. Each morning, I got up later and later to hit the pavement looking for a job.

New Year's night George came by to check on me. When he realized how discouraged I was, he asked me if I would like to go home with him and have a snack. I said I would.

Sitting at the table, George asked me how I was feeling about things. "To tell you the truth, George," I replied sharply, "I'm getting pretty disgusted with Texas."

"Oh, don't get impatient, Don," he urged kindly. "Give it some time. It's better than where you were. At least you're not thinking about getting a gun."

I gave him a blank stare.

"Are you?" he questioned, opening his eyes wide.

"Oh, no," I assured him. "I wouldn't do that."

"The people at church are looking out for you."

"Are they?" I questioned, a touch of sarcasm slipping out. "I'm broke. I need to borrow some money."

George gave me a what-are-you-up-to? look.

"Well, I can't get a job until I get a car," I snapped. He promised to check on the car first thing in the morning.

George gave me ten dollars when he let me out at the halfway house and said he would pick me up for church Sunday morning. On Sunday he told me he had arranged a meeting for me with a radio preacher named Chaplain Ray. He thought Ray might have a place for me in his organization. He had a prison ministry radio program that was based in Garland, Texas. Through his program, Bibles and Christian reading materials were sent to prisoners. It seemed like a ministry I would like to be involved in.

Friendly and outgoing, Chaplain Ray was about sixty. He was short and slender, with his bald head covered by a toupee that looked like it was going to take off and fly. When he showed me around the building that housed his program offices, radio station, and mailing room, I soon discovered why he was so successful. He really believed he was helping people through his ministry. Coupled with this was an obvious gift for organization and leadership. And he knew how to cut corners in running the program.

Sitting in Chaplain Ray's office, George told him about my background and how I was struggling and looking for work. Chaplain Ray looked me straight in the eye and asked, "Are you wiling to go to work for three dollars an hour?"

"Yes," I said quickly.

Breaking Crime's Vicious Cycle

"I'm willing to take a chance with you, then. You'll be working with Jack putting together mailouts."

Jack was a sweet-natured, all right guy. He was about twenty-five and single. He liked being the boss man on getting out the mail orders for Chaplain Ray's ministry and seemingly had no ambition beyond that. He worked hard. I found out later that Chaplain Ray paid him five dollars an hour.

For a month I rode the bus from the halfway house to work. In February the church bought me a '72 Chevy, light blue. I agreed to pay fifty dollars a week. That left me fifty bucks for everything else. But, even with just fifty dollars left over, I was able to save a little.

Because things weren't working out right at the halfway house, the Catholic church decided to discontinue the ministry. When I told Chaplain Ray that I would have to find another place to live, he offered to let me stay in the warehouse. They had a little room in the back with a bed and bath. It had a striking resemblance to a prison cell.

Even though the office was only a block away from the warehouse, I drove to work. I liked to have a car parked outside. Every day after work, I drove to the warehouse, watched TV alone, went to bed, and then back to the office the next morning. The schedule was desperately monotonous.

I quit going to church when I went to work for Chaplain Ray, so I had very little contact with people other than those at work. When George offered to pick me up for church, I told him I was going to one in the area.

After work on the last Friday in February, I drove the block to the warehouse, as usual, and sat down in the chair facing the TV. I looked around the room. *Nobody to talk to,* I sighed. *I can't stand to spend the weekend like this,* I decided. *I'm going to get me a drink and see some people.*

I drove to a bar in Garland, had a few drinks, and chewed the fat with guys who dropped in after work. I wasn't lonely anymore. I started going to the bar after work most days.

One Saturday morning I had a few drinks at the bar, then drove to Richardson to see George. I wanted to talk to him about my job and my living conditions. "I'm fed up with working for three dollars an hour," I told him. "And I don't like living in that warehouse."

George said he understood how I felt and asked me what kind of job I wanted to look for. "I think I better concentrate on corrugated box plants," I told him. "That's the only job skill I have. It's more interesting than what I'm doing, and it pays better."

George suggested we look through the yellow pages. We circled all the container plants in Dallas, Fort Worth, and Arlington. I picked out six I thought were good possibilities and started calling. Two said they weren't hiring or taking applications. Three said they weren't hiring but were taking applications. The last one I called was PCA—Packaging Corporation of America—in Arlington.

When I told the woman in the personnel office that I was an experienced machine operator, she told me they did have a couple of openings. "Could you come out here Monday at two o'clock?" she asked in an unusually pleasant tone.

"Sure," I replied, my heart racing with excitement.

Early Monday, I called Jack and told him I wouldn't be in. Concerned about getting to my interview on time, I drove into Arlington around noon. To take up the time, I stopped at a bowling alley and had a couple of drinks. From the bowling alley, I went to a bar and kept drinking. By five I was good and drunk. At seven I was disgusted with myself.

I remembered a business card a preacher gave me when he visited Chaplain Ray's place. It was still in my billfold. I decided to call him. "Hank," I said with a drunken slur, "this is Don Dennis from Chaplain Ray's. I'm the ex-con. Remember me?"

"Oh, yes," he said. "How are you doing?"

"Not too good, Hank. I was supposed to go for a job interview in Arlington today, and I missed it. I'm disgusted with myself."

"Are you drinking now?" he asked.

"Yes," I said, trying not to slur.

"Do you want to come over here?"

"Yes, but I don't know how to get there."

"Can you quit drinking?"

"I think so."

"Would you like for me and a friend to come over and guide you to my house?"

"Yeah, I would."

"We'll be right there."

I was sitting at the bar with a drink in front of me when the two men walked in. I took one last swig for the road. Hank was right there beside me as I was setting the glass down on the bar. He angrily reached for the drink, moved it well away from me, then turned around to face me with his hand braced against the edge of the bar. "That's the end of that," he snapped in a decisive tone that matched his tall, lanky, muscular frame. He reminded me of Ichabod Crane.

I glared into Hank's angry face.

"Come on, come on, let's go," he said like a parent to a stubborn child. I reached over his arm, grabbed my drink, and took another swig.

"I guess you didn't hear me," he snapped, reaching for the glass.

I grabbed Hank's arm. "I want to tell you something, Mister," I mumbled angrily. "I don't want this. If I needed someone to talk to me like this, I'd call the police."

Hank turned around, hunched his broad shoulders, and marched toward the door. His friend followed close behind.

"I'm sorry," I called to him in a drunken yell. He slowly turned around and walked back to the bar.

"I don't want to go back to my room," I moaned.

"Come on then," he urged, tugging at my arm.

When we got to Hank's house, he introduced me to his wife and four of his eight kids. His wife gladly fixed me a pallet on the floor.

At the breakfast table the next morning, I told Hank I wanted to change. "I want that job in Arlington," I said.

"Why don't you call them and see if you can set up another interview?" he suggested.

"You think they'll let me come in?"

"Sure. Just say you got tied up."

The lady at PCA happily set another appointment for two o'clock. Hank offered to drive me there. Before we went in, he asked if I would like to pray. I told him that it was fine with me. "I'll pray and then you pray," he suggested.

Hank prayed that God would help me get the job if it was His will. I prayed the same prayer, copying his words.

The receptionist was as pleasant in person as she was on the phone. "Oh, yes, we've been expecting you," she said when I told her my name. She then gave me an application.

About halfway through the application, I came to the question, "Have you ever committed a felony?" I painfully checked yes.

"If yes, state the type of conviction," was the follow-up. The instruction jarred me. For a minute or two, I stared into space, considering what I should do. I decided to go for broke. So, in big, bold letters I wrote, "THERE'S NOT ENOUGH ROOM FOR THE FELONIES I'VE COMMITTED." *I don't want this stupid job anyway,* I cried out silently.

With a dejected look on my face, I gave the application to the receptionist.

Shortly, the receptionist led me to an office down the hall. The tall, thin lady stood up and came around her desk to greet me with outstretched hand. I guessed her age to be about forty-five. "Mr.

One More Day, Lord

Dennis," she said with a pleasant smile, "I'm Elaine Baskin. Have a seat," she added, pointing to the chair in front of her desk.

"It looks like you've had a good deal of experience in this line of work," she observed.

"Yes, I have. Been running the machine since I was in high school," I bragged.

"I see you've had a felony conviction," she said, maintaining a businesslike demeanor.

"Yes, I have," I replied nervously.

"How are you doing now?"

"Pretty good."

"Do you plan to stay in this area?"

"Those are my plans. I'm here from now on."

She smiled approvingly. "I need to take your application to the plant superintendent," she said, as if informing me of a routine step in the interview process. "You can wait here until he calls for you."

After taking the application to the superintendent, Mrs. Baskin came back to talk to me. At first, it was small talk. She asked me where I was originally from and where my family lived. Then she began to probe a little deeper. "Are you a Christian?" she asked, looking me in the eye.

"Yes, I am," I replied, touched by her interest.

"Do you go to church?"

"I have gone some but not to any particular one."

"You ought to come to my church."

"What one is that?"

"Northside Baptist in Arlington. It's a friendly, caring church."

"I may do that sometime."

The receptionist stuck her head in the door. "Mr. Simmons would like to talk to you now, Mr. Dennis," she said, smiling. "I'll take you to his office."

"Have a seat, Don," Simmons said, pointing to the chair in front of his desk. Like everyone else I had met in the company so far, he had a pleasant and friendly manner.

"I see you've got a lot of experience in corrugated box work," he said, pointing to my application.

"Yes," I said decisively. "My dad had the job you've got. I've run a corrugator, press, slitter, the stitchers. I can drive a forklift. I've worked in shipping. Whatever job opening you've got, I can do it," I added with a chuckle.

"I tell you what," he said with a twinkle in his eye. "I've decided to hire you."

Breaking Crime's Vicious Cycle

A burst of excitement surged through my body.

"Fifty percent," he continued, "is for experience. The other fifty percent is because you told the truth."

"I appreciate that, Sir."

"Can you take the physical today?"

"Sure!" I exclaimed softly. "I sure can."

"Can you begin work tomorrow?"

"Sure. I'm ready."

"I'm starting you as a press helper. The beginning wage is $5.64. You'll have to work your way up. Before you can start, you'll need to buy a pair of safety shoes."

"I don't have money to buy shoes," I said quietly.

"We've got an arrangement with a shoe store on Randol Mill Road. You can get a pair of shoes there, and they'll bill us for them. We'll take the cost out of your paycheck."

"I appreciate that," I said, tremendously relieved.

Simmons stood up to walk me to the door. "Don," he said, "we look forward to having you as an employee."

With a lilt in my walk, I went to the reception area to meet Hank. I didn't have to tell him what happened. It was written all over my face. "It's almost twice as much as I'm making now," I said excitedly as we walked to the car. "And they seem like such nice people."

Before we drove off, we both thanked God for the job.

"I've got another problem now," I told Hank.

"What's that?"

"I don't know where I'm going to live. I can't stay in the warehouse."

"I have a friend who's a builder in Arlington," he said quickly. "He helps in the prison ministry. He might have a place for you to stay."

The minute we got back to his house, Hank called Jim, the builder. He told him about me and how I was trying to get on my feet. Jim said he had an apartment building that was partially finished. Part of it didn't have a roof on it, but there were appliances in the covered part that I could use and he knew where he could get me a mattress. He said I could stay there for the next two or three months. "We can help each other," he told Hank. "I'll furnish a roof over his head, and he can be a watchman for me."

"Sounds great to me," I told Hank. I was ecstatic. Making a good salary and having a free place to stay! I was sure I could save some money and get ahead.

I thanked Hank for all his help and went back to the warehouse to pack up my things. The next morning I told Jack I wouldn't be back. He said he understood how I felt and would tell Chaplain Ray for me.

I then went to Arlington to get the safety boots. At three-thirty that afternoon, I started work at PCA.

A week later I ran into Mrs. Baskin in the break room. "How are you doing?" she asked.

"Fine. I'll just be glad when I get a paycheck," I said with a nervous chuckle.

"I keep my lunch in here all the time. Would you like for me to bring you a lunch until you get your first regular paycheck? They'll hold back a week at first," she warned.

"Sure!" I exclaimed softly. "That would be nice."

"I'll put your name on it, then."

"Thanks. I really appreciate that."

Every day for the next two weeks the big, delicious lunch was in the refrigerator. I ate half at work and took half home when I got off work at midnight. It was a lifesaver.

The day I got my first paycheck I went to the Exchange Bar after work to find some friends. Even though things were working out, I started drinking more. I drank before I went to work in the afternoon and then after work. And I drank even more on weekends. Feeling extremely guilty about being so weak, I started praying about my problem. "Oh, God," I pleaded. "Please help me quit drinking. I know I'm getting old, and this is my last chance. I'll be back in the pen if I don't settle down." Most of the time I ended the prayer sobbing quietly.

Along the way, I added a new petition to my prayer: "Please send me a Christian woman." While I waited for God to come through, I spent most of my spare time at the Exchange Bar.

One Sunday afternoon, as I was sitting on a bar stool at the Exchange, I noticed a woman about my age on the other side of the room. Her tinted, light-blond hair, pretty blue eyes, and soft features caught my eye. Almost at the same time, she looked my way. Since she was sitting alone, I decided to ask her to dance. On the dance floor we introduced ourselves as Carol and Don, no last names. When I took her back to her table, she invited me to sit down.

"I've been coming to this bar for the past month, Carol, and I've never seen you here. Where you been keeping yourself?"

"Guess I've come at different times," she replied. "But I really don't go to bars very often."

"Well, I'm glad you decided to come," I said. She smiled sweetly.

For more than two hours we talked. I found out where she worked, that she had been divorced for several years and had a son named

Breaking Crime's Vicious Cycle

Greg. "Let's go get something to eat," I suggested about five o'clock. That sounded good to her, so we went down the street to Jo Jo's.

"I know those people in that bar have been talking about me," I told her. "What've they been saying?"

"They said you've been in prison," she replied softly.

"That's right," I admitted. "I've been out about a year and a half. But some of those guys have the wrong idea about me. They think I'm a killer. I'm not. I was in for armed robbery. Anyway, I'm straightening up now."

"That's good. The bartender said you were an OK guy."

"Did he really?" I replied, surprised that she had talked to him about me.

On the way back to the Exchange parking lot, I asked Carol to come back there the next night. "I don't think I will," she replied with a decisive tone in her voice. "I don't do this often. I'm not a barfly," she added.

"You ought to come on. What's your phone number?" She wrote it down for me.

On the way to my apartment, I stopped for a cup of coffee at Denny's. Walking to my car, I impulsively moved toward the phone booth to call Carol. "Hi, this is Don," I said softly. "How're you doing?"

"I was praying you would call me," she said.

"You're lying," I quipped.

"No. I'm not kidding. I really did."

"OK. I believe you."

At work the next day I kept thinking about Carol. I called her at seven-thirty during my supper break. "Would you like to go out again?" I asked.

"That would be nice. Where are we going to go?"

"Let's go to the lake."

"Sounds like fun. When?"

"How about Saturday?"

"That's fine."

"I'll pick you up about two."

Me and Carol went to the lake and had a delightful time. The next Saturday we went out again. After that date, we each assumed we would go out every weekend. Everything seemed to fall into place. Me and Carol got along really good, and I got along with her son, Greg, too. So, on June 26, 1981, we got married and celebrated at the Exchange.

Even before we married, me and Carol talked about how much I

One More Day, Lord

drank. I told her I wanted to cut down. Still, we went to the Exchange every weekend. Carol would sip a drink while I drank five or six. When she tried to cut down on the trips, I started going there alone. Every Saturday I would go to the bar and come in late.

On October 31, 1981, just after our four-month anniversary, I came home drunk. I was in the kitchen trying to find something to eat when Carol walked in. "Could I help you find something to eat?" she asked, her voice cracking.

"Oh, yeah. I guess you really want to help me, don't you?" I snapped sarcastically.

"Don, you're killing yourself," she sighed, tears welling up in her eyes. "I can't stand it."

I reached out and pushed her against the wall. "Don," she gasped, moving to the doorway.

I drunkenly lunged at her again. As she eased out of the way, I fell face down on the floor. When she tried to help me up, I angrily told her to get away. I then pulled myself up and staggered to the bathroom..

Bracing myself against the sink, I looked at my reflection in the mirror. "What a monster," I sighed. "Carol," I called.

She stood in the doorway, looking disgusted. "I've got to quit drinking," I told her.

"You've been saying that week after week, Don. I hope you do."

I stayed home Sunday night, fighting the urge to go get a drink. Carol quietly encouraged me. I got through Monday, Tuesday, Wednesday, then Thursday. "Lord," I prayed. "If I can just get through Friday, I think I can make it. I beg you to help me one more day."

Two weekends went by, then three. Each one got a little easier. We didn't go near the Exchange. We took Greg to the lake. We went on picnics with friends. We went to the movies. I wanted a drink less and less.

Three days after Thanksgiving, I circled the date on the calendar to mark one month of sobriety. To celebrate, we went out to eat at our favorite restaurant. Before I dropped off to sleep that night, I thanked God for the month and prayed for "one more day, Lord."

16

Reaching Out

Pastor Weir asked how long I had been in Arlington, where I worked, and where I was from. After the second question, the nervousness began to build. In my mind, his interest was taking on the character of an interrogation. My heart pounded furiously. My palms moistened.

"I've been out of prison less than two years," I blurted out softly. I wanted to get it all out in the open.

Carol's mouth flew open. The deacon's mouth froze in disbelief. I sat silent, waiting for a reaction.

"Where were you in prison?" Pastor Weir asked, not betraying the least bit of shock.

"Walla Walla was the last place," I replied.

He looked puzzled. "It's in Washington State," I explained. "I was in San Quentin and Soledad, too."

It was Monday-night visitation. Pastor Weir and a deacon were welcoming me and Carol to Northside Baptist. We had joined the church the Sunday before. After visiting several churches, Northside was our pick. The lady at PCA was right. It was a friendly and caring church. I fit in. Pastor Weir's reaction was one more reason to like Northside.

I proceeded to tell the two men how I came to know Christ in prison and that I had been baptized there. "It hasn't been easy adjusting to life on the outside," I said.

Pastor Weir asked about my plans for the future. This time it didn't seem like prying.

"For now I'm going to keep working at PCA." I began. "But I feel the Lord has something more for me to do. I would like to find a way to help men when they come out of prison. I know how difficult it is to reenter society."

His face lit up. "I think there are people in our church who would be open to getting involved in a prison ministry."

"Really!" I exclaimed.

"Yes. Our congregation has a strong sense of ministry. We have ongoing ministries to troubled teenagers, the homeless, nursing homes, and many others. I think the first thing we need to do is form a prison committee. We'll have a meeting to talk about it."

"That sounds great!" I exclaimed.

Pastor Weir went into action. By the next Tuesday he had arranged a meeting. We met in the mission house by the church. Seven were there: Pastor Weir, Carol, me, and two couples. We talked about the best approach to take in developing a prison ministry. I told them that I would like to help men and women find jobs when they got out of prison. I suggested we contact George Soltau for advice about establishing the ministry. They liked that idea and asked that I get in touch with him and report back to them.

I called George the next day. He said he would be happy to come to the meeting. Before the meeting, me and Carol bought a typewriter as the initial capital investment in the new venture. Together, we developed a proposal for the prison ministry. The proposal included things we thought we could do for prisoners in an aftercare ministry.

About fifty people showed up, mostly from Northside Baptist and people they knew from the Arlington area. George Soltau told the group how he had met me and what I hoped to do to help prisoners. After he spoke, we made assignments and set a time for a second meeting.

My assignment was to contact the prison chaplains and let them know how we wanted to help. I also was going to call companies to see if they would hire ex-cons. George was very encouraging. "Don," he said. "I think we've got enough here to do something meaningful."

George came back for the second meeting. About twenty-five showed up. Among them was Charlie, a leader-type businessman from Arlington. He was married to a woman who had an alcoholic son that had been in and out of prison. Charlie suggested that we form a board and incorporate. The group overwhelmingly favored incorporation.

We agreed on a name: Interdenominational Prison Ministry. Everyone wanted the ministry to include all denominations. A board was elected, made up of both men and women. Bill Nevins, a CPA, volunteered to file the papers necessary for incorporation. We were still in the talking stage, with the idea that I would take the responsibility for keeping the work going and enlisting volunteers. The next step involved getting the necessary financial support. Charlie had already developed some ideas for getting funds for the ministry. We asked him to draw up a plan to implement his suggestions.

While plans for the prison ministry were developing, me and Carol met Bob and Ida Davis, missionaries on furlough from Hong Kong. Pastor Weir introduced us one Sunday evening. As we were walking out the front door after the worship service, Bob said, "Don, the pastor has told me about you. I would like for you and Carol to come to our house on Thursday." He slipped an envelope in my pocket.

When we got home, I opened the envelope. It contained a printed invitation: "We would like for you to come to our home on Thursday, January 27, to introduce you to MasterLife, a discipleship program that will change your life."

"How about that, Carol!"I said teasingly. "At least it isn't Amway."

I called Pastor Weir the next day to ask him about MasterLife. "I know about that," he said. "Bob Davis asked me to pick out eight people I thought would be interested."

"Then you think this is something good?" I questioned.

"Yes, I do. I want to warn you, Don," he continued with a note of seriousness in his voice. "The program requires a great deal of time. But it's worth the effort. We get good reports about how MasterLife is changing people's lives."

Pastor Weir's endorsement really made me and Carol feel special. We were so hungry for acceptance. Getting involved with a group of people like that sounded exciting.

At the organizing meeting for the MasterLife group, Bob let us know that it was a demanding commitment. The training extended over a three-month period and involved at least an hour of individual study every day, five days a week. In addition, we met as a group for two hours once a week to discuss our assignments for the preceding week.

The MasterLife study really helped me understand and express what it meant to be a Christian. For the first time in my life, I was deeply involved in applying the basics of the Christian walk.

MasterLife also helped me and Carol focus on what God wanted us to do with our lives. One evening we got down on our knees and offered our lives to God in a way we had not done before. We made a deep commitment to do whatever God chose for us to do. From that point on, we knew God had something definite for us to do; we just didn't know exactly what it was. We did feel sure that our involvement in the prison ministry was a step in the right direction.

I prayed constantly about what God wanted me and Carol to do. While I worked I prayed. After I got off work, I prayed. I told friends and coworkers about the possibilities for the prison ministry. People began to respond to the ministry with time, action, and support.

Reaching Out

They called us for committee meetings about the prison ministry. Every weekend a prison ministry volunteer went with me to visit in the prisons. We got calls from chaplains about prisoners they wanted us to help. The activity increased day by day.

On the way home from work one Friday, I turned the radio to a religious station. Joe Danada was preaching. He said something about a prison ministry. Then he gave a challenge. "If you're thinking about going full time into a prison ministry, don't be afraid. God will take care of you."

His powerful words sent a thrill through my body. "God," I blurted out loud, "please make it happen."

The next day I called Danada's home and asked his wife to tell him how his message had touched my heart. She was thrilled that it had helped and said she would tell him.

Things started moving from seemingly unrelated sources. I got a phone call from Al Elliott of Colson's Prison Fellowship Ministries. He asked if I would like to go to Walla Walla and give my testimony. "Would I!" I exclaimed. "You bet I would! This is an answer to prayer." Al said he would send me a plane ticket. Within two weeks, I was on my way.

As Al drove into the prison grounds, a sinking feeling gripped my stomach, much like what I felt the first time I saw that gray, ugly prison—the time I thought it was going to be my home for the rest of my life. The imposing wall and the massive gates intimidated me all over again.

When I signed in, I could tell the guard thought he knew me. "Yeah, it's me, Don Dennis," I chuckled.

"What are you doing here?" he asked.

"I'm here with Colson's Prison Fellowship. I'm going to give my testimony about what Christ has done for me."

"Well, I'll be darned!" he exclaimed, a smile spreading across his face. "You never know, do you?"

"Yeah," I agreed. "You never know."

Inside, guards escorted us to the warden's office. I stood face to face with Larry Kinchloe, the same warden who was there when I was paroled less than two years before. "Don," he said. "I'm so happy things have gone well for you."

"Thank you, Sir. I appreciate that."

Our next stop was the chaplain's office. Jacobson was still there. "I knew you would make it," he said excitedly. He was tremendously pleased that I was involved in the prison ministry.

Jacobson had arranged a chapel service for interested prisoners to come and hear my testimony and get infromation about the after-release ministry. About two hundred men filed into the chapel in their prison blues. Many were old prison buddies. Del was still there. I fought back the tears. I wished he could be free, too.

I told the crowd how God had changed my life and how I wanted to help ex-cons adjust to society. I could see the hope light up in their eyes when I told them the details about the after-release ministry. Many stayed after the service to ask questions.

From the chapel service, me and Al went from cell to cell to visit with prisoners. I told one after another what was happening in my life and how God had used many people to help me get on my feet. I visited with a man on death row. There's not much you can say to a man in that situation. You just let him know that God will forgive him, if he is truly sorry. I told him what a difference Christ made in my life when I turned myself over to him. As far as I know, he's still on death row.

The next weekend me and Carol went to a prison ministry conference at First Baptist Church, Sherman, Texas. A man named Bill Whitehead was responsible for the program at the conference. His son was a member of Northside Baptist and had told him about me. He asked me to give my testimony during the conference. I shared the podium with a policeman and a judge. On the front of the program we were billed as "A judge, a cop, and a con."

Standing at the podium, I directed my first remarks to the judge and the policeman who had preceded me. "It sure feels good to be following you guys rather than you following me," I laughed. The remark brought down the house.

Me and Carol spent all day Saturday at the conference. That night we stayed in Sherman with the Whiteheads. Sunday morning Bill took me to the county jail. Sunday evening, I gave my testimony at his church. After church, we talked and talked, mostly about the possibility of me going into the prison ministry full time. At three o'clock Monday morning, me and Carol pulled into our driveway, tired but excited about getting more deeply involved in the prison ministry.

As a union representative at PCA, I always made sure I was never late for work. But Monday morning I simply could not drag myself out of bed on time. At 5:30 I called to tell the superintendent that I would be thirty minutes late. He wasn't there, so I talked to his assistant. "What's the trouble?" Wes asked impatiently.

"We went to Sherman this weekend for a prison conference," I explained. "Didn't get in until three this morning."

"Is that right?" he said dryly, then cleared his throat. "Don," he continued in a big-brother tone, "I think you should really think about what you're going to do with your life. I know you've been talking about that prison ministry to several of the guys. You need to make a decision about whether you want to work here or in the prison ministry. Running these big machines takes a lot of concentration, as you know. One mistake means many lost dollars."

"Well," I said quickly. "I choose the prison ministry."

"OK, if that's what you want to do," he said sharply. "That's your decision."

"I'll talk to you later, Wes," I said, responding in the same sharp tone, miffed at his impatience.

I went in at ten and talked to the superintendent about what had happened. I told him I felt I should go into the prison ministry full time. "It's too big a job to do part time," I said.

He didn't try to talk me into staying. "If it doesn't work out," he said, "you're welcome to come back here, if we have an opening. You do good work."

A week later Carol quit her job. We both decided that, if we were going to live on faith, we should live totally on faith. I don't know what I expected to happen to keep us going; but, whatever it was, it didn't happen. Our meager savings evaporated in a very short time. In six weeks the gas was turned off, and we lost our car. The people at church were shocked that we both had quit our jobs, but they still helped us. A kind man helped us keep the electricity and telephone in service. We used our Mr. Coffee to heat water for a bath. It took eighteen fillings for each bath.

Pastor Weir gave me a job painting the fellowship hall at Northside. That provided enough money for basic supplies. I kept going to the prisons with members of the prison committee and volunteers. We were having good results. On Thursday nights, we had a group of ex-cons—both men and women—in our home for Bible study. Prison chaplains asked us to help convicts that were in our area.

After four months of the hand-to-mouth existence, I knew I had to give up the idea of working full time in the prison ministry. When I let Pastor Weir know how I felt, a deacon at Northside offered me a job on the lawn crew at a hospital supply company. The next week Carol got a job in an office in Arlington.

At noon, the lawn crew ate in a shed on the hospital grounds. We had a table, chairs, and a radio in there. Some of the guys played cards while they ate; some listened to the radio; some talked. Most of the time I studied my Bible.

One day a radio news item drew me away from my study. The

newscaster reported that the state law had been changed to allow for more executions for capital crimes. A young punk at the card table had a quick response. "Good," he snarled at the top of his voice. "I hope they kill them all."

I slowly raised my head to see him glaring straight at me. Still looking in my direction, he continued his tirade. "They ain't nothin' but a bunch of rapers and baby killers."

I bit my tongue, trying to keep my mouth shut.

He raved on, glancing back and forth from his friends to me, obviously baiting me.

That snotty-nosed brat, I thought. I stood up, laid my Bible on my chair, and walked over to the table. I stood beside the young punk and glared down at him. "I don't want you talking to me no more," I snapped. "Don't you dare get in my face, or I'll make you wish you hadn't."

He glared defiantly up at me. The look made me explode inside. I looked around the shed for a weapon. Spotting a bar of steel propped against the wall, I angrily picked it up. With a firm grip on the bar, I reared back and threw it in the direction of the young punk. The four men at the table froze in fright as the bar flew over the punk's head and hit the back wall.

For several seconds nobody moved. Nobody said a word. I marched angrily over to my chair, picked up my Bible, and continued reading the Gospel of John. The chatter resumed.

The next day before starting time, I went into the foreman's office and told him I wouldn't be back. He didn't argue. He agreed that I might be happier somewhere else.

I drove straight over to PCA to see if they would rehire me. The superintendent gladly took me back, telling me again that he liked my work. At the same time, he made it clear that I would have to work my way up again.

That night I made a promise to God. "Lord," I prayed. "I'll never quit a job again until You show me I should. I want to take care of my family." I continued to do the prison ministry part time.

Two months later, on a Saturday, four men came to my home. Seated in my living room, they told me they knew of my involvement in various types of prison ministries. They wanted me to know they had enough money for me to go into the ministry full time, if I were still interested. During the conversation I discovered that they had already formed an interdenominational board of prison ministries. I told them that me and Carol would pray about it.

That evening me and Carol prayed together earnestly, pouring out to

Reaching Out

God our hopes and dreams and asking Him to show us the direction we should go. The next day we prayed together at breakfast and in the evening. By the next morning we had come to the conclusion that the time, indeed, was right to go into the ministry full time. I called Wilburn Carter, chairman of the board, and told him I was ready to go. On Monday the board rented an office and furnished it for me. The middle of November 1982, the Interdenominational Prison Ministry became an established reality!

In my new office, Wilburn filled me in on the details about support for the ministry. He told me that Highland Park Presbyterian church had made a commitment to provide a certain amount each month toward the expenses of the prison ministry. Individual wealthy persons were committed to providing the balance needed.

We sent out a newsletter to persons interested in prison ministries. Through the newsletter and personal contact, we enlisted a corps of volunteers. I was on the phone every day getting jobs for ex-cons and places for them to stay. Prison chaplains were told about the ministry. News spread by word of mouth. A chaplain in Fort Worth regularly called to tell me about any Christian who was being released. I contacted each prisoner and let him know that we would help him get a job and a place to stay. During a six-month period we placed more than three hundred ex-cons in jobs and housing.

While the prison ministry was going full steam, Northside built a satellite church in another part of town. George Turner, a deacon in the church and a friend of the prison ministry, asked Carol and me to join the church. We made the move partly because Rick Lineberger, the pastor, was enthusiastic about the prison ministry.

Lamar Baptist, as the church was named, had an unusually good basketball team, made up of adult men between the ages of twenty-five and thirty-five. I got the idea to take the basketball team into the prisons to play against the inmates. The team was excited about ministering that way; and the church was open to the idea. As a regular part of the event, I was given an opportunity to present my testimony to the several hundred inmates who came to watch the games. I told them what had happened in my life and the ministry that was available for them on the outside.

Through the grapevine, I became a magnet for ex-cons in the Dallas area. Word spread that I cared about them and could help them. Almost every Sunday an ex-con or two went to church with me and Carol. But the people in the congregation were not as comfortable with them as we were. The Sunday School teacher let me know, in a nice way, that the ex-cons and their wives didn't fit in. He personally wasn't uncomfortable, he said, but class members had expressed concern about the situation. "We just aren't talking about the same things," more than one said.

At first, I was irritated and hurt by the teacher's suggestion. At the same time, I was reminded about how I felt when I went to the church in Richardson. I came to the conclusion that the ex-cons probably were as uncomfortable as the other people. Me and Carol decided to expand the Thursday-night Bible study in our home to Sunday morning Bible study and worship. I let the pastor know that we would still be linked to Lamar Baptist.

The Sunday morning service grew fast. Within a month we had sixty in attendance. At Thanksgiving we had almost a hundred. When the group got too big for our home, I looked for alternatives. One morning, while having coffee at Denny's, I ran into James Weir. He suggested that we meet in a little building behind South Park Baptist Church in Grand Prairie. I contacted the pastor and told him about Weir's suggestion. He was happy to let us use the building.

Before I moved our Bible study group to South Park, Rick Lineberger suggested that I be ordained. Although I was giving my testimony every opportunity that opened up and was leading the Bible studies and worship services, I hadn't thought about being a preacher. He was suggesting it, he said, so that I would have definite validation for the prison ministry.

On May 12, 1985, at Lamar Baptist Church, I was ordained to the gospel ministry. After the usual process of questioning about beliefs, Lineberger preached the ordination sermon. I had taken another big step forward in serving God.

On the first Sunday in the building behind South Park, the entire basketball team and their wives joined the church. Some of the ballplayers took on the responsibility of acting deacons. Their wives were involved in teaching and other ministries.

About six months after starting the church, James Weir took me to a pastors' conference luncheon in Dallas. There he introduced me to Joe Mosley who was director of special services for the Baptist association. When Weir told Joe about my involvement in the prison ministry, his face lit up. "Don," he said excitedly, "you're just the kind of person I need to help develop an inner-city ministry. There are so many ex-offenders in the area. I think you can help." We set a time for me to come to Joe's office and talk about the possibilities.

When Joe described what he wanted to do in the inner city to help ex-cons, I knew it was something I would like to do. Although I hated to leave South Park, I was excited about the possibility of a ministry more closely related to my main interest.

We found a building in the black ghetto of South Dallas that had been used by a black seminary since the sixties. The building was owned by the Dallas Baptist Association, and they were delighted to put it to good use. The large, flat-roofed, red-brick building had eight large rooms. There was adequate office space and a chapel that would seat a hundred.

Carol picked a name for the new church: Beautiful Gate. The setting reminded her of the healing of the lame man in Acts 3:1-11. We arranged for someone to put a neon sign on the building with that name.

Since I was going to be sponsored by the Dallas Baptist Association, I decided to sever my connection with the Interdenominational Prison Ministry. In my mind, I planned to continue the ministry but in a different form.

Me and Carol found a house about a mile away from Beautiful Gate. The next Sunday we announced to the South Park church that we were going to South Dallas and asked for volunteers to go with us. Not one person volunteered to go. "Too much crime and violence," a few said frankly. "Too far away," others said. Me and Carol were on our own.

Little by little, word got around about the church. People came from the halfway houses and the neighborhood. Eventually, it became more of a neighborhood church rather than a ministry to ex-cons. When I saw that happen, I began thinking in terms of turning the ministry over to a black preacher who had joined me as associate pastor.

I was open to the possibility of renewing my relationship with a board that wanted to concentrate on prison ministries when I got a visit from Joe Mosley and Ben Beltzer. They told me about a ministry to help ex-cons get housing and to teach them good work habits. I told him I would like to get involved in that type of ministry. A board was formed with me as the main worker. The new ministry was called "Exodus" to emphasize the aftercare concept of the founders.

Me and Carol moved from the ghetto to a house outside Ennis to once again concentrate on the prison ministry full time. Along with visiting in the prisons, we had Thursday-night Bible studies in our home, and we gave shelter to one ex-con after another.

Ray was one of the first to come our way. When he was only two years old, someone dropped him off at a doorstep in New York City. He was raised by the state. At the time we met him, he didn't know the identity of his parents and never expected to find out. He came to us from Angola Prison in Louisiana. A big hunk, weighing about 270, they called him "animal" in prison, because of his hairy body and ferocious nature. Out of prison, he broke arms and legs for a living.

Soon after he hit Dallas, Ray called me from his apartment. He said he had sixteen thousand dollars in his pocket. A week later he called and said he was dead broke. He was so drunk he could barely talk. "Don, you gotta come and see me," he slurred. "I'm gonna kill myself."

"I'll come to see you, Ray," I said calmly. "Give me the address."

Carol was alarmed. "You don't know what condition he's in," she warned. "He's drunk and probably has a gun."

"Probably. But I have to go, Carol," I explained. "He needs me."

I didn't admit it to Carol, but I was uneasy, too. I prayed the whole way to Ray's apartment. Psalm 23 came to mind— "The Lord is my shepherd. . . . Thy rod and Thy staff, they comfort me." Reciting the psalm helped to calm my fears. I felt God's uplifting, protective presence.

At my knock Ray called to me with a drunken slur. "Com'n in, Don. Door's open."

Slowly, I opened the door to see Ray sitting at the dining room table. In front of him were two liquor bottles. In his right hand was a .357 Magnum.

"Sit down, Don," he slurred, dangling the gun toward the chair across from him.

"Whata you doing, man?" I asked softly.

Without answering, Ray spun the barrel of the gun around and held it to his head, then pointed it in my direction. Bracing his right hand with his left, he took aim and pulled the trigger. My heart raced madly at the click of the gun.

"Man, Ray," I urged. "I don't want to die. I didn't come over here to die. I came to pray with you."

"Is that a fact?" he chuckled. "Jus' a minute. I gotta go to the bathroom. You stay here."

"Don't worry, Ray," I assured him. "I'll stay here."

He staggered to the bathroom, leaving the gun on the table with the barrel pointed toward me. I grabbed the gun and removed the one Russian-roulette bullet. I then positioned the gun as it was and threw the bullet under the couch.

When Ray came back, I grabbed the gun, spun the barrel around, and held the gun to my head. With a smile on my face, I pulled the trigger. Ray's eyes got big as saucers. The color drained from his face.

Reaching Out

"That ain't nothing," I quipped, spinning the barrel again and holding the gun to my head. While Ray watched in disbelief and horror, I pulled the trigger. I then calmly set the gun aside and fixed a pot of coffee.

After shooting the breeze for a few minutes, I suggested to Ray that he go home with me. He seized the opportunity. Two days later, I placed him in a job. He lasted a week or so, then moved on. Within a year he was back in prison.

David, a friend from the Awareness Tier at Walla Walla, stopped by for two weeks. A guy with no legs stayed a week. I got them both a job and a place to stay. Sally, just released from the women's prison, came to us with a drinking problem. She left before I could get help for her.

Fifteen waking hours a day our lives were consumed with helping ex-cons—men and women. The need was overwhelming and heart-breaking. Each ex-con would make it for a short while and then drift back into the old pattern of drinking and crime. Gradually, I came to the realization that what we were doing wasn't working.

When I told the Exodus board about my frustration, they were astonished. "Don," they assured me, "you're doing a great job. The ex-cons are coming for help. You're getting them jobs and places to stay. We're reaching more than we ever dreamed possible." The main difference between the board and me was that they weren't involved in the ministry twenty-four hours a day. They didn't see the ex-cons come for help, stay straight for a relatively brief period of time, and then revert to their old habits. They just saw numbers on a report form. And those numbers were increasing.

In my heart I knew there wasn't enough money in this world to rehabilitate people if they aren't changed on the inside. Without that change, I knew they had no real, lasting chance.

I prayed and searched for understanding and a better way to help ex-cons. I was sure the answer was out there somewhere. "But where?" I kept asking.

17

A Handle on Life

Bob Juliuson invited me to give my testimony and tell about the prison ministry at a Saturday morning prayer breakfast in his church. After the breakfast, I invited him to visit in the prisons with me. Later, he did just that; and, little by little, his interest in the ministry grew.

A retired businessman with a big heart, a gift for music, and a patient nature, Bob became my main volunteer in the prison ministry. On June 12, 1988, he went with me to sing in the chapel service at Beto II prison near Palestine, Texas. Before the chapel service, we talked with Mike Fleming, one of the chaplains in the prison.

"These guys sure do need some intensive Bible study, don't they?" I remarked to Mike.

"They sure do," he agreed. He paused thoughtfully, then asked, "Are you familiar with MasterLife?"

"Sure. I've been through MasterLife I. The study really helped Carol and me to grow. It made me develop the disciplines I needed to get going in my Christian life. I haven't had any fears of backsliding since then."

"I'm not surprised. It's a great program."

I stared at Mike with a puzzled look. "I've been coming here for two years now, Mike," I began. "I'm wondering why you haven't mentioned MasterLife before this."

"I just got certified to lead a group myself about six months ago. And, to tell you the truth, Don, I didn't know how it would work with inmates. Now I have two who have completed MasterLife I. The discipline of that program has made a tremendous difference in their lives."

"It is amazing what the study can do, isn't it? Look at incorrigible me," I chuckled. "If it can get me on track, it can help anybody."

Mike got quiet, as if suddenly gripped by an idea. "Say, Don," he said excitedly, "after you give your testimony, why don't you mention how MasterLife helped you? Then you might ask if any would like to participate in a MasterLife group."

"I'd love to do that! Honestly, Mike, I don't know why I never thought of this before. Hey, this is exciting!"

The inmates filed into the chapel, dressed in Texas prison whites. For a few minutes, I mixed with the group, greeting those I already knew and meeting new people; then me and Bob took our places on the front pew. Just before I got up to speak, Bob sang a touching rendition of "At the Cross."

My Bible text was Philippians 3:13-14: "One thing I do: forgetting what lies behind and reaching forward to what lies ahead, I press on toward the goal for the prize of the upward call of God in Christ Jesus." I challenged the inmates to put the mistakes of the past behind them. "Quit blaming your background, other people, and the system for the fix you're in," I urged. "Let God help you get going in the right direction." I was speaking from vast experience in the blame game. I knew how easy it was to blame others, to refuse to accept personal responsibility for my actions.

After the sermon, I told the group about MasterLife and how it could help them. "I want you dudes to know this," I began, "MasterLife is a tool to help you develop your walk with Christ. It will help you live good right now; and it will prepare you for life on the outside. It will truly give you a handle on life. That's what it did for me. MasterLife put me into the disciplines I needed to overcome those bad habits I had developed over the years."

I paused, slowly looking from one side of the chapel to the other. "MasterLife isn't easy," I emphasized. "You'll have to work hard at it. To do it right, you'll have to spend at least an hour a day on your studies, and you'll have to practice what you learn during the day. I'll guarantee, though, when you're through, you'll have something that no one can take away from you. Right now, I'd like to know how many of you think you would participate in a MasterLife group if we started one here at Beto II."

A hand in the back went up first, then one after another all over the chapel. Within a few seconds, twenty-five inmates had raised their hands. All twenty-five stayed after the service to learn more about MasterLife.

"I can't believe it," Mike told me in his office afterward. "I could only get two men to show an interest, and you get twenty-five! Don, you ought to get certified, so you'll be ready to lead a MasterLife II group here. After the two of us finish these MasterLife I groups," he added with a smile.

"I'd love to do that! How do I get certified?"

"They'll have a week-long certification workshop in Garland in October. It's grueling. You go from early in the morning into the evening."

"OK by me," I said forcefully. "I can do that."

"I'll get the information for you, then."

"Man, this is great!" I exclaimed. "It's an answer to prayer. I've been asking God to show me something more I could do. These people have got to have more than food and jobs and a roof over their heads."

Riding back home in Bob's plush van, I silently evaluated the experience. *Only God can change people,* I thought. *MasterLife is a tool for God to change people, to give them discipline, to help them grow.* The realization was overwhelming and thrilling.

While I waited for the opportunity to get certified to teach MasterLife II, I drove to Beto II every Saturday for the two-hour weekly meeting of the MasterLife I group that was made up of half of the twenty-five volunteers. Mike Fleming led another group.

I was impressed with the way the studies helped the inmates understand and express what it meant to be a Christian. It was exciting to hear them recite the Disciple's Cross. Point by point, they drew a section of the cross and recorded summary statements, while explaining the basics of the Christian life.

Along with the prison ministry, I continued to drive back to Beautiful Gate every Sunday. Carol had joined Tabernacle Baptist in Ennis. She told the pastor and others about my involvement in the church in the ghetto and the prison ministry, but she didn't mention that I was an ex-con.

One Sunday night I decided to go to Tabernacle with Carol, instead of driving to Beautiful Gate. After the service, Pastor Moody and his wife invited us over for coffee. I decided that I would get my status out in the open up front. "I'm an ex-con," I told them, while drinking coffee in the living room. "I've been in San Quentin and Soledad and a few other places."

"Are you interested in pastoring a church part time?" Moody asked, without registering any shock whatever. I got the feeling they already knew about me.

"I would be open to that."

"We have a little church building across town from us. Other than an Alcoholics Anonymous group meeting in the kitchen once a week, nobody is using the building. I think some in our church would be

A Handle on Life

interested in going over there to help build a church. If you're interested, I'll present the idea to the deacons and the church."

"Yes, I'm interested."

"Why don't you come back Wednesday for prayer meeting, and we'll go over to see the building afterward?"

"OK. Sounds good to me."

On Wednesday after prayer meeting, four carloads went over to show me and Carol the building. The people talked like they were excited about the possibility of developing a church there. Before we left, Pastor Moody asked us to pray about the matter. Seated in the pews inside the little auditorium, one after another fervently asked God for direction. It was a precious moment.

That night me and Carol prayed that, if it was God's will, the church would ask us to serve there.

On September 1, I got word that the deacons wanted to talk to me. At the meeting, the deacon chairman got right to the point. "This will be a part-time undertaking. Now, we don't have any money for a salary, but. . . ."

"Let's stop the talk about money," I said decisively, interrupting him. "I didn't come here to talk about money. What I'm asking for is help and involvement."

During the meeting the group pledged their support and said they would ask the church to call me as pastor of the mission. At the next business meeting, the congregation voted unanimously to call me. Along with reaching out to the community, the church became a base of encouragement for the prison ministry. Moody and others in the mother church were very enthusiastic and affirming about what I was doing.

The first of October 1988, I went to the workshop to get certified to teach MasterLife. During the workshop, I talked to Avery Willis, who developed and wrote the MasterLife materials. When I told him about my plans for putting MasterLife into the prisons, he got excited and told me he would help. He said he didn't have any money, but he would help in other ways, such as writing letters.

Avery scheduled a meeting during the workshop to talk about getting MasterLife in the prisons. I called Bob Juliuson to come to the meeting. Everybody was excited and in agreement that they wanted to see something happen with MasterLife in the prison ministry. It was a time of great encouragement. The responsibility was left with me to move forward in organizing MasterLife groups in the prisons.

At the October meeting of the Exodus board, I presented the idea of taking MasterLife into the prisons under their sponsorship. "A lot of good ministries are carried out for inmates and ex-cons," I told them, "but there is a desperate need for this type of specific help. They need step-by-step guidance in developing Christian disciplines. Jobs and housing are vital, but they must have more than that to survive on the outside. These people must change their way of thinking and acting *before* they get out. Otherwise, they'll be back in the pen in no time."

I paused, took a deep breath, and looked from board member to board member. "I am sure this is the ministry God wants me to do," I said confidently.

"We know MasterLife is a very good discipleship program," one board member responded quickly. "I'm willing for you to spend *part* of your time on this kind of ministry." He gave measured emphasis to the word *part*.

"But we want the aftercare to continue," another added. "Jobs and housing are what Exodus is about." The others enthusiastically nodded in agreement.

"If you feel you can continue emphasizing these things," the chairman agreed, "we'll support you. I think it is the feeling of this group that we don't want you to neglect the aftercare. You've been doing a great job so far."

"I think I can do both," I agreed.

When I left the meeting I fully intended to do both the aftercare ministry of Exodus and MasterLife. Gradually, though, my major concentration gravitated toward preparing inmates to live daily both inside and outside the prison. MasterLife filled that bill as far as I was concerned.

As an Exodus board member and friend, Bob Juliuson kept me informed of the thinking of other board members. "They think you're spending too much time with MasterLife," he told me more than once in his quiet, nonthreatening manner.

"What they don't understand, Bob," I protested, "is that I've been working in aftercare for five years. I see how the ex-cons come and go. You get them a job and a place to stay. They last a few months and then move on. Aftercare alone simply does not work for the long haul. More is needed. They've got to have some discipline built into their lives."

"I know what you mean," he agreed, "but the majority of the board members don't feel that way. They want something they can measure right now. They can measure the number of ex-cons you place in jobs and how many you find housing for. I'm not saying they're right or wrong. I'm just saying that's how it is."

Even though I was amply warned, I decided to keep concentrating

A Handle on Life

on MasterLife. More and more inmates were getting involved. I was sure the good results would convince the Exodus board.

Bob continued to go with me to the prisons and was impressed by the results of the MasterLife program. Still, he kept warning. "They want you to concentrate on jobs and housing."

On Tuesday before Thanksgiving, me and Carol left for Memphis to spend Thanksgiving with her relatives. Feeling the pressure of the Exodus board, I gave Bob the phone number to contact me if anything developed that I needed to know about. About ten o'clock Friday morning, the call came. "Well," Bob began with an ominous tone in his voice. "The board got together Wednesday morning."

"Oh?" I questioned. "What happened?"

"They want your resignation, Don," he replied softly.

"Really?" I questioned sharply. "Don't they know how many inmates are getting involved in MasterLife?"

"Yes, they know," he said calmly. "But they want to support an aftercare ministry, not MasterLife."

"I have to be true to my calling."

"I know you feel strongly. And I can't blame you. But this is how it is. It's their money."

"Tell them they've got my resignation," I snapped.

"They've agreed to pay you through December, so you can find some other work or other funding."

"That's not far away," I sighed, the reality of the situation closing in on me.

I took a deep breath. "Bob," I said, "Are you still with me?"

"I'm ready to go back to the prisons as soon as you want to," he replied quickly.

"Brother, I appreciate you," I answered nervously.

When I got back home on Monday, a letter was in the mail confirming what Bob told me. I was officially fired! They wished me the best.

Bob had already started going to bat for me. He went to the major contributor for Exodus and got a commitment from him to pay my salary through February. I was tremendously relieved.

That night I renewed my vow to God not to quit a job until He told me to. I continued to go from prison to prison, forming MasterLife groups and enlisting free-world teachers.

Joe Mosley found out about my problem. He helped me arrange a meeting with Baptist leaders to let them know what was going on in the MasterLife prison ministry. I called Avery Willis and asked him to come to the meeting on January 19, 1989. Attending the meeting were a number of key leaders of denominational organizations. Mike Fleming from Beto II Prison and Chaplain Mike Green from Coffield Prison came to tell what was happening in the prisons with MasterLife. Gary Herron, Dallas Baptist Association Executive Director, and Joe Mosley verified that I was a good Christian leader. Everyone there was convinced we should go forward with the MasterLife ministry, but no one came forward with any money. Still, I was fortified by the encouragement.

By the end of March, me and Carol were down to our last few dollars. The rent was due, and we didn't have the money. Bob Juliuson went with me to talk to Pastor Moody.

"Why don't you call Bill Pinson at the Texas Baptist Convention?" Moody suggested. "If you can set up a meeting with him, I'll go with you."

I called Dr. Pinson, Executive Secretary of The Baptist General Convention of Texas, and asked if I could come and talk with him about the MasterLife prison ministry. He set a meeting time of 10 AM, Tuesday, March 21. He told me that he would have Joe Mosley sit in on the meeting. I suggested that it would also be good for Bob Juliuson and Pastor Moody to be included, along with Lewis Holman, a missions service volunteer who worked with me in the prison ministry.

This was not my first contact with Pinson. Several years before Bob Dixon asked me to visit a young man in the county jail. He told me that he was relaying a request from Pinson. I talked to the young man and tried to help him see what he needed to do to stay out of trouble when he got out. I felt good about the visit but never heard what happened to him.

As the six of us gathered around a table in Pinson's office, Pinson turned to me to say a personal word. "Don," he said, "I want to thank you for visiting with Tommy."

"How's he doing?" I asked.

"He's doing fine."

"Now, what can I do for you?" he asked.

I sat up straight in my chair and took a deep breath. "It's just like they say about Harry Truman," I began. "The buck stops here. It's a long way from San Quentin to your office. The MasterLife ministry is too important and too involved and too time-consuming to do part time. I feel I'm going to have to quit if I don't get help." I paused to look around the group, making eye contact from person to person. "I don't think God wants me to quit," I said decisively.

An eerie quiet descended on the meeting. Pinson patiently waited for someone to speak. "Don's been working hard in this ministry,"